Volunteering for a Cause

Volunteering for a Cause

GENDER, FAITH, AND CHARITY IN MEXICO
FROM THE REFORM TO THE REVOLUTION

Silvia Marina Arrom

University of New Mexico Press ❧ Albuquerque

© 2016 by the University of New Mexico Press
All rights reserved. Published 2016
Printed in the United States of America
21 20 19 18 17 16   1 2 3 4 5 6

Library of Congress Cataloging-in-Publication Data
Arrom, Silvia Marina, 1949– author.
Volunteering for a cause : gender, faith, and charity in Mexico from the Reform
to the revolution / Silvia Marina Arrom.
pages cm
Includes bibliographical references and index.
ISBN 978-0-8263-4188-4 (pbk. : alk. paper) —
ISBN 978-0-8263-5629-1 (electronic)
1. Women in church work—Catholic Church. 2. Women in church work—
Mexico—History—19th century. 3. Women in church work—Mexico—History—
20th century. 4. Society of St. Vincent de Paul—History—20th century. 5. Society of
St. Vincent de Paul—History—19th century. 6. Ladies of Charity of St. Vincent de
Paul—History—20th century. 7. Ladies of Charity of St. Vincent de Paul—History—
19th century. 8. Catholic Church—Mexico—History—19th century. 9. Catholic
Church—Mexico—History—20th century. 10. Catholic Church—Charities—
History—19th century. 11. Catholic Church—Charities—History—20th century.
I. Title.
BV4420.A77 2016
267'.44272—dc23
2015016440

Cover illustration courtesy of Fotosearch
Designed by Felicia Cedillos
Composed in Minion 10.25/14

To my grandmothers, Zoraida Boscowitz de Ravelo and
Marina González de Arrom, whose devotion to helping the
poor opened my eyes to a world that didn't exist in the history books.

CONTENTS

ILLUSTRATIONS

Tables

Figures

Maps

ACKNOWLEDGMENTS

In researching this book over fifteen years in three countries, I benefited from the extraordinary generosity of many colleagues, friends, and institutions. Financial support from the Jane's Chair in Latin American Studies at Brandeis University underwrote the costs of this project, including numerous trips to hunt for documents abroad. In Paris, Stéphan Joachim at the headquarters of the Société de Saint-Vincent de Paul and Father Paul Henzmann in the archives of the Lazarist Convent provided invaluable assistance as I began my research. In Mexico, Father Juan José Muñoz gave me a copy of the indispensable in-house history of the *familia vicentina* that was unavailable in Mexico outside the walls of the Iglesia de la Concepción. In Guadalajara Laura Benítez Barba helped me locate and copy the rich trove of documents in the archives of the Guadalajara Archdiocese and the Jalisco Public Library. I owe special thanks to Venecia Lara Caldera for sharing a cache of records she found in the Culiacán Cathedral that included two *Actas* (books of minutes) of the kind I had long been seeking. I am also grateful to the staffs of many archives and libraries who patiently aided me at every step of the way.

As I ventured into new (for me) subjects, time periods, and regions, I was fortunate to receive excellent suggestions from many knowledgeable scholars. My first debt is to Randy Hanson. In the process of advising his dissertation over twenty years ago, I learned from him that Mexican religious history was ripe for reassessment. As the book evolved, many colleagues read parts or all of the manuscript, commented on my presentations at seminars and conferences, answered questions, and shared documents that they discovered in their own research. I am particularly grateful to Ann Blum, Kristina Boylan, Beatriz Castro, William Christian, María Teresa Fernández Aceves, Susan Fitzpatrick-Behrens, María Gayón, Paul Jankowski, Catherine LeGrand, Clara Lida, María Dolores Lorenzo Río, Erika Pani, Macarena Ponce de León, Stafford Poole, Sol Serrano, Edward Udovic, Pamela Voekel, and Kirsten Weld. As the book neared completion, Margaret Chowning and Eddie Wright-Rios gave the full manuscript a close reading and offered many incisive comments. The book is much improved because of their wisdom.

I have been gratified by the early interest in this project. Portions of the book appeared in a different form as articles, and some were reprinted afterward: "Philanthropy and Its Roots: The Societies of St. Vincent de Paul in Mexico," in *ReVista: Harvard Review of Latin America* (Spring 2002): 57–59. "Catholic Philanthropy and Civil Society: The Lay Volunteers of St. Vincent de Paul in Nineteenth-Century Mexico," in Cynthia Sanborn and Felipe Portocarrero, eds., *Philanthropy and Social Change in Latin America* (Cambridge, MA: Harvard University, David Rockefeller Center for Latin American Studies, 2005), 31–62; reprinted in *Vincentian Heritage* 26/27, no. 2/1 (2007): 1–34; and as "Filantropía católica y sociedad civil: Los voluntarios mexicanos de San Vicente de Paul, 1845–1910," in *Sociedad y Economía*, no. 10 (April 2006): 69–97. "Mexican Laywomen Spearhead a Catholic Revival: The Ladies of Charity, 1863–1910," in Martin Austin Nesvig, ed., *Religious Culture in Modern Mexico* (Lanham, MD: Rowman and Littlefield, 2007), 50–77. "Las Señoras de la Caridad: Pioneras olvidadas de la asistencia social en México, 1863–1910," in *Historia Mexicana* 52, no. 2 (2007): 445–90; reprinted in Yolanda Eraso, ed., *Mujeres y asistencia social en Latinoamérica, siglos XIX y XX: Argentina, Colombia, México, Perú y Uruguay* (Córdoba, Argentina: Alción Editora, 2009), 57–94. "Filantropía católica en el siglo XIX: Las asociaciones de voluntarios de san Vicente de Paúl," in Jorge Villalobos Grzywobicz, ed., *Filantropía y acción solidaria en la historia de México* (Mexico City: Centro Mexicano para la Filantropía, 2010), 59–86. "La movilización de las mujeres católicas en Jalisco: Las Señoras de la Caridad, 1864–1913," in Susie Porter and María Teresa Fernández Aceves, eds., *Género en la encrucijada de la historia social y cultural* (Zamora, Michoacán: Colegio de

Michoacán/Centro de Investigaciones y Estudios Superiores en Antropología Social, forthcoming).

The final stage of book production has been a pleasure thanks to the expert editors at the University of New Mexico Press. Clark Whitehorn and Maya Allen-Gallegos deserve high praise for seeing the manuscript through to publication. I also owe special thanks to Anandaroop Roy for making the maps and to Mauro Renna for making the tables and graphs. My greatest debt is to my family. My husband David Oran, my son Daniel, and my daughter Christina have not only given me great joy but also left me alone to work in my study, offered technical help with computers and cameras when needed, and provided constant encouragement and support. Although my parents and grandparents are no longer with us, they too were part of the book project. The epilogue pays special tribute to their contributions.

Notes to Reader

1. All translations into English are the author's.

2. Monetary values are presented in Mexican pesos, with fractions rounded to the nearest peso.

3. The figures in the tables are underestimates because all conferences did not report each year. The records rarely specify how many failed to report to the central governing councils.

4. The *Memorias*, *Noticias*, and *Rapports* are cited by the year covered by the report rather than the publication date when these differ.

5. The year covered by the reports usually includes a few months of the previous year. The figures for the women's organization normally cover the fiscal year from July 1 of the previous year to June 30, while the men's cover the period from November 1 of the previous year through October 31.

Introduction

This work arose from a question that nagged at me as I completed my book *Containing the Poor: The Mexico City Poor House, 1774–1871*. After studying the limited—and often demeaning—assistance offered by public institutions, I wondered where else paupers could turn in times of crisis. The lucky ones could prevail on family, friends, or patrons. But what of the others who wanted to stay at home until they overcame temporary setbacks such as illness or unemployment? The secondary literature on Mexican welfare gives the impression that, because there was no system of "outdoor relief" (provided outside the walls of hospitals or asylums), their only alternative was to accept the "indoor relief" available within them. But I had learned from experience how dangerous it was to repeat the conventional wisdom without independently corroborating it. I knew that by the beginning of the twentieth century other areas of Latin America had a thriving system of domiciliary assistance delivered by organizations of Catholic women. Although they had not received scholarly attention when I began my research, I was aware of them because both of my Cuban grandmothers were members. So I suspected that there might have been equivalent groups in Mexico, at least by the late nineteenth century. I also recalled having read that the renowned scholar Joaquín García Icazbalceta served as president of the Mexican Society of Saint Vincent de Paul, an association of laymen who in Europe took aid to the needy in their houses. I therefore surmised that the Mexican branch might have provided similar services.

Thus began my quest to determine what options existed for people who wanted to avoid institutionalization. My journey took me not only to archives and rare book libraries throughout Mexico and the United States but also to Paris in search of documents that could shed light on the Mexican affiliate of the French lay group. The story I eventually pieced together was full of surprises. Although I found little information on the paupers I originally set out to study, I gradually discovered a dynamic philanthropic initiative that was hiding in plain sight, if largely absent from the historical record. What began as a history of the male Society of Saint Vincent de Paul soon turned into a gendered story when I found an even more vibrant organization of female volunteers, the Association of Ladies of Charity of Saint Vincent de Paul. This discovery permitted me to bring together my long-standing interests in the history of women, social welfare, and the poor. And it brought me closer to my long-departed grandmothers, whose passion for helping others inspired this book in many ways.

The men's society began on December 15, 1844, when ten idealistic gentlemen met in the Convent of San Francisco in Mexico City to pray for divine help in founding a Mexican branch of the French Société de Saint-Vincent de Paul. Thus did Dr. Manuel Andrade fulfill the dream he had nourished since studying medicine in Paris a decade earlier. It was there that he witnessed the birth of the Vincentian voluntary association dedicated to practicing Christian charity in the midst of troubled times. And it was there that he was inspired by the fervor of the Catholic revival that emerged as a response to the growth of urban poverty coupled with the secularization and anticlericalism that came in the wake of the French Revolution.

The organization born that cold day in the Mexican capital would take many turns its founding members could not have anticipated. Although the Sociedad de San Vicente de Paul was part of a transnational movement that united militant lay Catholics throughout the world, it developed several distinctively Mexican features. Established during a period of good relations between the church and the state, it was soon tested by persecution at the hands of Liberal reformers. Surviving the virulently anticlerical *Reforma* to make a quiet comeback, it also took on a gendered dimension. Although its female counterpart did not get off the ground in Mexico until 1863, the Asociación de Señoras de la Caridad de San Vicente de Paul quickly became the mainstay of the Vincentian lay movement as the Ladies of Charity eclipsed the male society with more members, more conferences (as the local chapters and the two lay groups were called), and far more people assisted each year. Together the zealous volunteers—men and, especially, women—created a national network with tens of thousands of members and supporters. Besides visiting the ailing poor in their dwellings, the two organizations offered educational, medical, and other welfare services to a clientele that numbered in the hundreds of thousands. Always spreading the faith as they worked to relieve suffering, the lay activists helped the church regain its influence and thus prepared the ground for the violent church-state confrontations of the revolutionary period. As they volunteered for their cause, they also expanded the roles of middle- and upper-class women in a socially acceptable—and completely nonthreatening—manner. After 1912 the conferences declined considerably, although they have continued to exist until the present.[1] Still, in their heyday on the eve of the Mexican Revolution, they constituted a formidable Catholic Armada.

It is surprising how little trace these organizations left in the history books. Even in their birthplace, France, there have been few studies of the Vincentian conferences since the volumes published to commemorate the centennial of the male society in 1933.[2] In Mexico the two Vincentian religious orders are well-known: the female order as the *Hermanas*, or sometimes *Hijas de la Caridad;* and the male order as the *Congregación de la Misión*, or *Padres Paúles*. Yet the two lay groups are barely remembered, and the women's association is often confused with the religious order that has a similar name.

The conferences are invisible in standard histories of modern Mexico that have privileged Liberal—and mostly masculine—actors. The dominant historical narrative, created by the winners of the bitter Reform Wars of 1857–1867, the Mexican Revolution of 1910, and the Cristero Rebellion of 1926–1929, cast Mexico's past in Manichean terms. The victorious Liberals and revolutionaries have been portrayed as the "good guys" who defeated the "evil" church and its Conservative allies. Catholic organizations "tainted" by their association with these "bad guys" have therefore been demonized or shunted into oblivion. The Vincentian conferences are also missing from most histories of the church, which have focused on its institutional development or the dramatic conflicts with the state without giving the loosely affiliated lay groups the recognition they deserve. Despite their central purpose of assisting the poor, they have been overlooked by historians of social welfare, whose research agenda has been shaped by the powerful discourse that claimed that public welfare supplanted the church and private philanthropists after the Reforma.

Broader intellectual fashions contributed to this neglect, even among scholars who distanced themselves from the liberal version of Mexican history. Historians during the past half century favored the lower classes over the elites, and if they mentioned charity at all, they dismissed it as a form of elite paternalism and social control. The focus on state formation also blinded scholars to the importance of nongovernmental organizations in building the social infrastructure. Moreover, because of the influence of modernization theory that correlates progress with secularization, religious groups were considered obstacles to modernization and remnants of an earlier age, destined to disappear and therefore unworthy of study. Finally, even though the Ladies of Charity was one of the largest female organizations of the nineteenth century with chapters covering the length and breadth of Mexico, it is invisible in histories of women that have largely focused on nuns for the colonial period or left-wing feminists, labor leaders, and revolutionaries for the modern era. Consequently, the Vincentian volunteers—mostly middle- and upper-class devout Catholics who worked with the dual goals of aiding the poor while also moralizing them and strengthening their faith— have been forgotten.

I am privileged to join a group of scholars who have been subjecting the master narrative of Mexican history to increasing scrutiny. Inspired by liberation theology, historians took a closer look at the church and discovered that a Catholic restoration occurred during the Porfiriato (1876–1911), when the government of Porfirio Díaz established a modus vivendi with the church. The Catholic social movements that flourished following Pope Leo XIII's Rerum Novarum encyclical of 1891 received particular attention.[3] Popular religion attracted serious investigation, with women emerging as prominent actors.[4] The militancy of Catholic women during the Mexican Revolution also became the subject of a burgeoning scholarship.[5] The interest in democratization led to studies of citizenship and civil society in the nineteenth century.[6] Revisionism even reached the study of Mexican conservatism,[7] and a few historians of social welfare noted the persistence of private philanthropy after the Reforma.[8] Some of these studies made passing references to the Vincentian conferences, and they recently became the focus of a dissertation on the development of the public health system in Jalisco, the Mexican state with the largest concentration of volunteers.[9]

My contribution is to provide the most systematic—and first book-length—study of these organizations in any country since the commemorative volumes that appeared in the first half of the twentieth century. It is also one of the few studies of any nineteenth-century lay association in Latin America. This reconstruction of the history of the Mexican conferences from the foundation of the first one in 1844 until the eve of their decline in 1913 not only illuminates a forgotten aspect of Mexican life but also challenges many deeply ingrained assumptions about its past.

Challenging the National Narrative

The story of the Vincentian lay groups questions the portrayal of the nineteenth century as the period when liberalism and secularization—usually conflated with modernity—prevailed over the dark forces of the past, represented by the Catholic Church and its allies. In the standard plot the battered church was crippled by its defeat in the Reforma as the victorious Liberals separated church and state; confiscated ecclesiastical properties; expelled religious orders; took control of birth, marriage, and death; and proclaimed the government's responsibility for providing education and poor relief. This book joins the growing scholarship that documents the Catholic recovery after the defeat; indeed, it suggests that by harnessing the energy of the laity the church began to recuperate much earlier than recent studies indicate. Long before the Pax Porfiriana, the Vincentian volunteers stepped in to supplement the depleted clergy, strengthen the faith, educate children, and care for the needy. Their success shows not only the persistence of faith in a supposedly secular world but also the important role of religion in forming the identity of the men and women who joined together to find a Catholic response to the challenges of the Liberal era. It also contradicts the widespread notion that a Conservative upper class confronted a Liberal middle class, for if most of the organizations' top leaders were well-to-do, they quickly incorporated middle- and lower-middle class individuals into their ranks.

This book likewise provides an important corrective to the predominant narrative of Mexican welfare history that posits the decline, if not disappearance, of religious welfare organizations in the Reforma period. Although the Liberals nationalized Catholic hospitals and asylums in 1861, the Vincentian lay associations—along with other private groups—created a parallel welfare system that easily held its own against public assistance. In addition to their home-visiting programs, the volunteers built a national infrastructure of schools, hospitals, orphanages, soup kitchens, vocational workshops, discount pharmacies, lending libraries, mutual savings funds, employment agencies, and other establishments to help the poor. While government services were concentrated in the capital and a few major cities, the conferences provided coverage in a much larger area that included provincial cities, small towns, and even some factories and haciendas. Moreover, as public institutions became more selective and increasingly focused on children, youth, the demented, and the sick, the conferences offered services to groups of paupers—such as single mothers, the working poor, and the unemployed—that were excluded from public assistance. The volunteers thus helped fill glaring gaps in the existing welfare system. While providing health care, education, and poor relief for the needy in their communities, they also worked to win hearts and minds for the church.

Vincentian charity should not be dismissed as retrograde. Despite many similarities with traditional Christian charity, it represented a new kind of practice and ideology. Although its leaders sided with Conservatives in the Reform Wars, the conferences shared in many modernizing tendencies. They consistently defended freedom of association, freedom of the press, and freedom of instruction. By organizing in voluntary associations similar to the Masonic lodges, scientific and mutual societies, and social clubs that flourished contemporaneously, they contributed to the formation of republican civil society. They governed themselves internally with democratic practices. They were part of highly structured and bureaucratized transnational networks so characteristic of nineteenth-century organizations. Their systematic procedures for training and deploying volunteers and for rationalizing the distribution of aid provided precedents for the professionalization of twentieth-century social work. Their clinics, hospitals, and pharmacies helped lay the foundation for a modern public health system. Their elementary schools and night classes fostered popular literacy. Moreover, they differed from traditional almsgivers because, instead of handing out aid indiscriminately, the volunteers investigated potential clients to make sure that they were truly needy, tried to modify their behavior and values, and took steps to prevent their future poverty by providing education, vocational training, tools, credit, and job placements.

In "going to the poor" (to use the language of liberation theology) the volunteers foreshadowed some aspects of Social Catholicism. Although these progressive movements are said to have stemmed from Pope Leo XIII's Rerum Novarum encyclical of 1891, this study suggests that we should look even further back to find their roots in the Vincentian lay movement founded in Paris in 1833 and reaching Mexico in the 1840s. Decades before Rerum Novarum, these charitable organizations pioneered a new kind of Catholic activism that focused on improving the lives of the impoverished masses. As they developed an extensive network of volunteers, supporters, and clients, the conferences expanded the reach of the church. Putting members of the upper and middle classes in contact with the misery of the Mexican poor, the conferences enhanced the volunteers' social awareness and spread the idea that laypeople had an important role to play in solving their community's problems. Indeed, just as the strength of Mexico's Catholic revival by the end of the nineteenth century built on the mobilization of the laity over many decades, the strength of Mexico's Social Catholic movement built on a half century of charitable activities by the Vincentian volunteers.

Another way the conferences promoted modernization was by mobilizing Mexican women. The emerging narrative of Mexican women's history makes the Revolution of 1910 the defining event that brought women out of the home and sparked their interest in public affairs. Yet these processes began under Catholic auspices as early as the 1860s. By recruiting middle- and upper-class women to defend the faith and assist the poor, the church gave them a base from which to move into the public sphere. Although the work of benevolence was justified as a natural extension of women's domestic roles, it was far more than that. It took them out of their comfortable homes and into the barrios and pueblos as well as the public prisons and hospitals that demanded their attention. It gave them new experiences such as running voluntary associations, administering welfare agencies, and disseminating Catholic doctrine to strangers. It enhanced the volunteers' expertise by providing opportunities for them to become leaders, raise and manage large sums of money, and engage in modern associational practices. In the process

of organizing to help the needy, the women thus expanded their own horizons and exercised power beyond the private sphere. Because the crisis of the
nineteenth-century church required an activist laity, the impetus for changes
in women's roles came from groups normally classified as "right wing," as
well as from the "left." Indeed, this study highlights the inadequacy of these
categories for understanding the history of Mexican Catholicism. This movement of devout volunteers also serves as a reminder that modernization does
not require a shift from religious to secular world views, as often posited, and
that Catholicism is not necessarily an obstacle to progress.

Because these groups attracted so many more women than men, it is
tempting to argue that Mexican piety and charity were feminized, as is often
argued for other parts of the world. Yet my research suggests that the Mexican story was much more complicated. Most studies of the feminization of
religion and charity only study the women's side. Existing research on the
Vincentian conferences has concentrated on either the men's or the women's
organization. By examining the male and female groups together, this study
reveals important gender differences. Yet they are not those posited by the
feminization thesis. While Liberal discourse certainly denigrated the church
by associating it with women, male piety flourished throughout Mexico.
Pious laymen in the late nineteenth century published Catholic periodicals
and founded devotional and mutual aid associations. In the early twentieth
century they formed confessional trade unions and attended national congresses to find Catholic solutions to the Social Question. In 1911 they proclaimed their religious fervor openly by founding a Catholic political party,
the National Catholic Party (Partido Católico Nacional, or PCN). If few men
joined the Vincentian conferences, it was because Mexican Catholics had
developed a kind of gender complementarity. Women specialized in the routine hands-on caregiving required of the volunteers, while men put their
efforts into other—often more public—kinds of activities to support the
Catholic reform project. Thus while women prevailed in some Catholic organizations, men prevailed in others. Although Vincentian charity was increasingly dominated by women, it is not even accurate to say that Mexican men
were not charitable. They simply practiced a male variant of charity that
included donating large sums of money for works of mercy, founding asylums and schools, and providing goods and services to support the female
volunteers from behind the scenes. Even those men who participated in the

conferences tended to engage in different sorts of activities than their female counterparts. Both men and women—equally devout—thus contributed to the Catholic restoration and to the provision of social assistance, albeit in different ways.

The reemergence of militant Catholicism—a surprise to those who believed that the Reforma had settled the church question for once and for all—highlights the political dimensions of charity. It also forces us to question the discursive construction of "politics" and the "public sphere" in the nineteenth century as exclusively male. At a time when the role of the church in society was a burning partisan issue, the faith-based Vincentian philanthropy was far from apolitical. Shaping public opinion as they worked to aid the needy, the volunteers disseminated their critique of secular liberalism, Protestantism, and socialism along with their vision of Catholic renewal. Their efforts to reinsert religion into popular education and public life defied the secularizing policies of Mexican governments. As the Mexican Revolution approached, the volunteers played the additional role of helping to create and maintain the networks that would form the constituency for the National Catholic Party. Indeed, this book's case study of Jalisco—the stronghold of the Vincentian conferences as well as of the PCN—suggests that it is difficult to explain the meteoric rise of the party in that state (and, later, the strength of the Cristero rebels in Jalisco's countryside) without understanding the extensive base built by lay activists over many decades as they established connections with the poor and spread their ideological message, one person at a time. Because of the prominence of the Ladies of Charity in the lay movement, women—and charity—must be included in any discussion of the late nineteenth-century Catholic revival as well as of the Catholic political movements of the revolutionary years.

Sources

The Vincentian lay groups are difficult to study. They have been rendered invisible not only by the selectivity of historical memory but also because they left a weak paper trail. Even though the conferences kept careful records, these were not regularly collected by either government or ecclesiastical entities. The volunteers' desire to maintain a low profile by shunning publicity hardly helps the historian's task. Indeed, their activities were almost never

covered by the contemporary press. Although the Paris headquarters of the
male society preserves some of the Mexican files, there is no comparable
repository for the early women's association.[10] I found few of the unpublished
records kept by local chapters, perhaps because their officers took them home
where they gathered dust and were eventually discarded. Most of the surviving documents are the published summary reports that circulated among
ecclesiastical officials and conference members.

The *Memorias*, *Noticias*, *Boletines*, *Rapports*, and *Informes* have many
limitations. For one thing, many issues have been lost. For another, as colla-
tions of reports from individual chapters, they are apparently lacking some
of the local information. Moreover, their statistics give a false sense of preci-
sion because the categories are not always comparable from year to year and
the numbers in the tables occasionally fail to add up due to transcription
errors. Because some chapters neglected to report to the central governing
councils, their tabulations also underestimate the scale of the Vincentian
enterprise. Most frustrating, for my purposes, is that the reports emphasize
the activities of the conferences rather than the people involved. The recipients of charity rarely appear and even the volunteers remain in the shadows.
The men's reports almost never identify their officers, let alone members.
Although I found some of their names in Paris for the early years and for
Mexico City in published lists from the beginning of the twentieth century,
the membership of the intervening years remains a mystery except for the
occasional necrological note that gives the names of deceased volunteers. The
Ladies of Charity's reports are somewhat better in this regard because they
sometimes list the full slate of conference officers. Although the title of
Señora or Señorita reveals their marital statuses, other information that
could be used to flesh out profiles of the organization's members (such as ages
or family relations) is not provided. Nor do the reports contain detailed
descriptions of the home visits or chapter meetings. And, despite diligently
searching, I have found very little biographical information on the women
or complementary sources such as letters or diaries that could shed light on
the perspectives of the volunteers.

Fortunately, there is much to be learned from the published reports. A
treasure trove of these documents in the archive of the Archdiocese of Guadalajara is particularly valuable.[11] Because it includes reports published by
the Guadalajara conferences as well as by the national governing councils,

this collection permitted me to undertake a regional case study. Several surviving books of minutes from Culiacán (Sinaloa) and Coyoacán (today part of the Federal District) allowed me to see how the local chapters functioned administratively. An in-house history of the "Vincentian family" written by two Paulist priests in 1993 helped round out the picture.[12] Although it mostly focuses on the two religious orders, the book contains valuable short chapters on the lay organizations based on some documents to which I did not have access.[13] Many other papers undoubtedly languish in parish churches and private archives waiting for some enterprising scholar to discover them.

After many years of chasing elusive documents, I have decided to end my quest. The history that I am offering is far from definitive and sure to be modified as others locate additional information. Yet it provides answers to the questions that kept me awake so many nights: yes, there was an organized system of home relief in Mexico as early as the mid-nineteenth century that gave many paupers an alternative to entering public institutions; and yes, like my Cuban grandmothers, battalions of Mexican laywomen devoted themselves to alleviating the poverty and suffering in their midst. So finally, despite my desire to keep looking for the many still-missing pieces of the puzzle, it is time to begin restoring the Vincentian volunteers to their rightful place in Mexican history.

Chapter Sequence

As I hope to show in the following pages, this history provides new insights into a number of subjects that are normally studied separately but benefit from being put in conversation with each other. The first two chapters provide a chronological study of the male conferences. Chapter 1 shows that the Catholic revival was already beginning by the 1840s, at least in Mexico City, and highlights the role of the laity in this process. Chapter 2 shows that, contrary to expectations, the Reforma did not interrupt the expansion of the lay movement. Indeed, the men's society reached its high point in the 1870s, and the men retreated only after they saw that the women's association was thriving. It also shows that, despite the heated rhetoric, the gulf between Liberals and Conservatives was not as deep as often posited, for most Liberal leaders valued the place of Catholic organizations in providing for social welfare. Chapter 3 traces the growing strength of the women's association from its foundation in 1863 until 1913 and analyzes the impact of the work of benevolence on women's roles. Because the Ladies of Charity quickly dwarfed the male society, this chapter reveals the degree to which the Catholic restoration—as well as the creation of a national infrastructure to provide social services—was based on the energy and labor of women. Chapter 4 compares the activities of the male and female volunteers and develops a critique of the feminization thesis. It shows how the project of Catholic renewal and social assistance was an effort conducted jointly by pious men and women working in often complementary ways. Chapter 5 provides a regional case study of both the male and female conferences in Jalisco and elaborates on the political implications of their charitable endeavors. The relative richness of the material for this state reveals the overlapping web of social and organizational networks that put the volunteers in the thick of a collective effort to improve society. Chapter 6 concludes by summarizing the major contributions of Vincentian charity and analyzing the distinctive approach that made it a vehicle of modernization as well as a precursor to Social Catholicism. Together they demonstrate the complicated relationship between gender, faith, and charity in Mexico from the Reform to the revolution.

1.

The First Decade

Preparing the Ground for Social Catholicism

THE SECOND VATICAN Council (1962–1965) that ushered in liberation theology is rightly considered a major turning point in Catholic history. In recent years, however, scholars have begun to identify its significant continuities with earlier progressive movements, particularly with those that emerged after Pope Leo XIII's Rerum Novarum encyclical of 1891.[1] In Mexico, Social Catholicism was flourishing by the turn of the twentieth century. Catholic trade unions and other workers' organizations proliferated, national congresses regularly brought together Catholics who sought solutions to the Social Question, and in 1911 a Catholic political party was created to pursue a Social Catholic agenda. Indeed, on the eve of the revolution, Mexico had what was arguably the strongest Social Catholic movement in Latin America.

Yet its roots in Mexico are much older than usually assumed, the culmination of a long process of building Catholic structures that is sometimes termed the Catholic Restoration. Until recently, few scholars were aware that a religious revival occurred after the supposedly definitive defeat of the church during the Reforma. Those who recognized its existence usually followed Father Mariano Cuevas in dating its beginning to 1876, when Porfirio Díaz came to power and proceeded to mend fences with the church.[2] A few scholars pushed the date back to 1867, immediately after the fall of the Second Empire brought the church to its knees.[3] There are several hints that it may have begun much earlier, however. Margaret Chowning identified three new pious associations founded in Michoacán in the 1840s, and David Gilbert posited that "the Mexican church was actually in a period of dynamic growth and renewal when the Liberal assault began."[4] He attributed the Catholic resurgence not only to the confirmation of the first republican bishops in 1831 and the resolution in 1851 of the dispute between the church and state over the right to appoint clerics (the *patronato*) but also to the increased fervor and activism of the Catholic laity who were inspired by the religious revival occurring throughout Europe.

The history of the Vincentian conferences in Mexico shows that this process was already underway in 1844 when the French lay movement reached Mexico City. Indeed, the founding members of the Sociedad de San Vicente de Paul were at the center of an effort to strengthen Catholicism while simultaneously working to improve public health, poor relief, and elementary education. The conferences were only one part of their multipronged strategy, which included founding two new religious orders and combating the spread of anticlerical ideals through a vibrant Catholic press.

The Vincentian lay movement had a strong social component from the outset. Half a century before Rerum Novarum, the Mexican volunteers were the Latin American pioneers of a new kind of lay activism with a social conscience that saw service to the poor and helpless as a form of manifesting their devotion. Although the Sociedad de San Vicente de Paul got off to a slow start, by the end of the first decade it had planted the seeds of a dynamic charitable initiative that would survive the onslaught of the Liberal Reforma and blossom during the Porfiriato. One of many Catholic organizations that contributed to the religious revival of the late nineteenth century, it stood out because of its early use of social programs to reinvigorate the faith. By mobilizing committed Catholics to work for the common good, building lay institutions dedicated to serving the needy, and expanding the influence of the church, it helped prepare the ground for the Social Catholicism of the 1890s.

The Foundational Story

The few available chronicles of the Mexican Society of Saint Vincent de Paul overlook these aspects of the lay movement because their authors had a very different set of concerns.[5] Written by Vincentian priests or society officers to commemorate the 50th anniversary in 1895, 100th anniversary in 1945, and impending 150th anniversary in 1995, these short "in-house" histories glorify the organization and highlight the role of its founders. By starting their stories in France, they privilege the French context. In addition, they minimize the differences between the Mexican and French branches of the organization and gloss over the problems of the first decade.

The chronicles written by priests usually begin in the seventeenth century with Father Vincent de Paul (1581–1660), creator of three of the four organizations that comprised the Vincentian family. His first foundation, in 1617, was the organization of laywomen known as the Dames de la Charité. He then founded two religious orders in quick succession, the male Congrégation de la Mission in 1625 and the female Filles de la Charité in 1634. For his patronage of charitable works he was canonized in 1737. Focusing on the role of Saint Vincent, these histories emphasize the timelessness of Vincentian charity and neglect its eighteenth-century decline and nineteenth-century renewal and transformation.

When in 1945 Father Ramiro Camacho wrote the centennial history of the Vincentian organizations in Mexico, he instead chose to open his story in Paris in 1793. His tale began with the "delirium of nightmares enveloping that period of the French Revolution known as The Terror." The first page recounted the "horrible" nights of July 12 and13, when a crazed mob sacked the Lazarist Convent, headquarters of the Vincentian organizations, chopped the head off a statue of Saint Vincent de Paul, and paraded it on a pike through the streets of Paris. The second page bemoaned the woes that followed: the confiscation of ecclesiastical property, the assassination of Paulist priests, and the near death of Saint Vincent's "marvelous" works of "charity, drowning in a pool of blood." For Father Camacho, the persecution and survival of the French church was the logical starting point because it mirrored the experience he had just lived through in Mexico: attacks on the church at the hands of revolutionary caudillos, especially after 1913, and an all-out war between the church and revolutionary state from 1926 to 1929 that poisoned church-state relations until 1940, when the new president, Ávila Camacho, signaled the end of the conflict with the simple declaration "*Soy creyente*; I am a believer."

Earlier histories did not set their narratives in the context of defending the church from hostile forces because the situation when the conferences reached Mexico was far less embattled. Most chronicles simply begin in Paris with the birth of the men's organization in 1833. On April 23 the twenty-year-old university student Frédéric Ozanam (1813–1853), along with several other youths under the guidance of Catholic journalist Emmanuel Bailly, founded the Conférence de la Charité as a way to combat the decline of Catholicism in postrevolutionary France. As they looked at the society around them, Ozanam and his fellow students identified a host of problems—from immorality, materialism, individualism, and alienation to class conflict—that they blamed on the separation of the church from public life and the subsequent loss of faith. They were also deeply troubled by the growing poverty that accompanied nineteenth-century industrialization and urbanization. The solutions proposed by utopian socialists like Saint-Simon further threatened the centrality of religion. The pious young men therefore resolved to use Christian charity to defend Catholicism while addressing the needs of the urban poor. Their method was to meet weekly in their small groups, pray together to strengthen their own devotion, and then go to the abodes of ailing paupers, taking them corporal as well as spiritual aid. The volunteers hoped that establishing direct, face-to-face connections with the needy would help restore social harmony while simultaneously working to achieve the salvation of both the clients and the volunteers. Although the home visits would remain the principal activity of the conferences, they quickly took on additional projects that went beyond simple charity, such as distributing religious texts, providing children with a Christian formation, "patronizing" apprentices by giving them both a practical and religious education, and establishing night schools, mutual savings funds, and job placement services for the unemployed.[6]

The first conference founded in 1833 was the germ of the lay movement that would become the international Société de Saint-Vincent de Paul. This fourth member of the Vincentian family differed from the other three in that, rather than being directed by Paulist priests, it was nominally independent from the church and run exclusively by its lay leaders. It was a sign of the lay activism that would characterize the nineteenth century as the spread of liberalism created a more self-consciously Catholic laity eager to champion their religion as well as to help solve the social problems of their communities. The new model of militant Catholicism found many adherents throughout the world where the church was under attack and poverty was deepening.

Even when the foundational narratives moved to Mexico in 1844, they emphasized the French connection. Dr. Manuel Andrade y Pastor (1809–1848) had witnessed the birth of the men's conferences while studying medicine in Paris from May 1833 to June 1836 (fig. 1.1). After returning to his homeland, he worked tirelessly to establish branches of the four Vincentian organizations in Mexico. His efforts began to bear fruit in 1844, when the first Sisters of Charity arrived and the first male chapter met. The next year the Sociedad de San Vicente de Paul was formally aggregated by the French association, making 1845 the founding date later recognized by the Mexican society. The Paulist priests also received permission to operate in Mexico in 1845, and a few years later they proceeded to found the Ladies of Charity's conferences.

There could be other ways of telling the story. For example, instead of focusing exclusively on the three male protagonists (Saint Vincent, Ozanam, and Andrade), one could highlight the role of women in creating these organizations. In France it was apparently Marguerite de Silly and Geneviève Fayet who encouraged Father Vincent de Paul to found the Dames de la Charité in the first place,[7] and it was Sister Rosalie Rendu (a Fille de la Charité) who gave Ozanam the idea of creating laymens' conferences modeled on the centuries-old women's organization; indeed, according to her nineteenth-century biographer, she was the "soul" of the male conferences.[8] The initiative for refounding the Dames de la Charité in 1840 also came from a laywoman, the Vicomtesse Le Vavasseur.[9] In Mexico the ex-*condesa* Ana Gómez de la Cortina, who funded the establishment of the Sisters of Charity

Figure 1.1 Portrait of Dr. Manuel Andrade y Pastor (1809–1848), founder of the Mexican Society of Saint Vincent de Paul. From collection of the Sociedad San Vicente de Paul de México.

and then took the habit herself, deserves to share the credit with Andrade for that foundation.[10] Reinserting female agency helps explain why the Mexican conferences would so quickly become feminized in the 1860s. A close look at the society's early history shows that the male volunteers were in fact collaborating with women from the start.

An alternative narrative would also emphasize the distinctiveness of the Mexican society. Its early foundation date put Mexico at the forefront of the Vincentian lay movement and helps explain some of the differences between the Mexican and French branches. The first conference in Mexico City was established on December 15, 1844—only twelve years after the Parisian Conférence de la Charité. The Mexican sociedad was thus born before the French société was fully institutionalized. It preceded its official recognition by the Vatican, which came in two papal briefs of January 10 and August 12, 1845, that granted indulgences to its volunteers and benefactors; and it preceded the publication in 1847 of an instruction manual for forming new conferences.[11] Although the organization would eventually expand to cover the entire world, in 1845 it had barely spread beyond French borders. Mexico was the sixth country where it took root after Belgium, England, Ireland, Italy, and Scotland, and it was home to the first branch in the Americas, closely followed by the United States and Canada.[12] The other Latin American associations came later, beginning with Puerto Rico in 1853.[13]

The singularity of the Mexican society also reflects its adaptation to local needs and conditions. Unlike many foreign branches of the Society of Saint Vincent de Paul founded by missionary priests intent on exporting Catholic organizations from France, Mexico's conferences came as a result of local lay initiative. Given Dr. Andrade's active role in promoting it, Mexico's cannot be considered an external imposition. Yet his efforts to establish the Vincentian organizations did not only stem from similarities between Mexico and France. Although France provided the inspiration, Andrade had his own plans for his home country.

A Modest Beginning, 1845–1855

The history of the sociedad's first decade can be told as a celebratory tale of steady membership growth and regional expansion that replicated the progress of the French société on Mexican soil. The new organization began with great confidence. After its formal affiliation with the French société in 1845, it founded new conferences every year from 1846 through 1854—except 1847, apparently because of the chaos created by several changes of government and the war with the United States. In 1848 the society began to branch out from its core in Mexico City by adding a chapter in Puebla and another in San Miguel de Allende. After 1850 most of its expansion was outside of the capital, especially in the central states of Mexico, Guanajuato, Puebla, Michoacán, and Jalisco. By 1855 the society had 32 chapters with 567 active volunteers as well as 33 "honorary" members who gave the organization significant support but did not participate in its activities. That year its volunteers visited 256 "adopted" families and engaged in a variety of projects to assist the needy. They spent 20,084 pesos on their good works. And they had a network of benefactors who donated food, clothes, and medicines that are not included in this sum.[14]

Yet a less triumphal tale lurks beneath the surface. The few sources available for the first decade suggest that the society suffered from leadership problems after the death of its founder in 1848. Home visiting did not come easily to the Mexican volunteers. The conferences apparently attracted few young men. Many of the early initiatives did not follow French precedents. Moreover, the society's initial expansion could not compare with that of the French organization, which by its tenth year (1843) had 4,561 active members—eight times more than the Mexicans had mobilized in the same time span.[15]

If we shift the focal point from France to Mexico, however, a moderate success story emerges. By paying close attention to local circumstances and placing the volunteers' charitable works in the context of their other activities, we can see how the early Vincentian conferences were an effective response to the problems and possibilities that Mexican Catholics confronted in the decade prior to the Reforma.

The first issue that concerned the founders was the decline of the once-powerful colonial church. The Bourbon regime had already taken a number of steps to impose royal power over the institution. The most dramatic came in 1767, with the expulsion of the Jesuit order and the confiscation of its property, and in 1804, with the nationalization of assets belonging to *capellanías* (chantries) and *obras pías* (pious funds). Less sweeping measures like the secularization of the parishes (which were transferred from the regular to the secular clergy) and attempts to limit clerical legal privileges and regulate *cofradías* (confraternities) also reduced the scope of ecclesiastical control. On the eve of Mexican independence in 1821 the Spanish crown suppressed the hospitaler orders that had provided nursing care in some of the colony's hospitals.

Although the new nation established Roman Catholicism as its official religion, the church faced additional threats during the early republic.[16] While the government negotiated the right to appoint clerics with the Vatican, the number of priests dwindled and by 1829 not a single bishop remained. The pope began to address this problem by confirming six bishops in 1831, but the Vatican did not officially recognize Mexico's independence until 1836, and the patronage question was not resolved until 1851. In addition, some Mexican politicians contemplated several measures to restrict the church. The Masonic lodges that dominated political life in the 1820s had an anticlerical reform program partly influenced by the radical priest José María Luis Mora, whose criticisms of the laxity of the Mexican church and proposals for disentailing its property would become the basis of the Liberal Reforma. The first attempt to implement these ideas came in 1833 with a short-lived liberal experiment that included abolishing mandatory tithes, secularizing the California missions and nationalizing their property, and closing the ecclesiastically controlled University of Mexico. Although the government quickly fell because of the public outcry, concerned Catholics were well aware of the anticlerical threats nipping at their heels. Moreover, the church faced the long-standing problem that, despite being nominally Catholic, much of the population—especially in the lower classes—practiced an unorthodox version of folk Catholicism and had little contact with the institutional church.

The next two decades were a period of relative calm. While anticlerical storm clouds hovered on the horizon, successive governments supported the Catholic church and offered their wholehearted backing to the Vincentian project. Thus, when the first Sisters of Charity arrived from Spain in November 1844—accompanied on their entrance into Mexico City by Dr. Andrade himself—they were not only warmly greeted by jubilant crowds lining the streets of the capital but were also received in the National Palace by President Antonio López de Santa Anna.[17] The next year, when the new laymen's society submitted its *bases* for government approval, the "deeply Catholic" president, José Joaquín Herrera (so devout that when hostile forces occupied Rome in 1848 he offered the Pope asylum in Mexico[18]), granted it almost immediately, on February 8, 1845.[19] This close relationship with the state distinguished the early Mexican society from its French counterpart and helps explain some of their different emphases. Until the liberal tempest finally arrived in 1855, the Mexican laymen took on welfare responsibilities in partnership with the federal and municipal governments. They also worked hand in hand with the church, an open collaboration that was still possible in Mexico because Catholics had yet to experience the kind of persecution that led the French volunteers to maintain a prudent distance from the beleaguered institution.

Another difference was that the Social Question that motivated the French laymen was far less pressing in Mexico. There was, to be sure, no lack of indigence. Still, by the 1840s the late eighteenth-century fear of the poor, heightened by the flood of desperate country people flocking to Mexico City, had abated along with that migration. Independence had not unleashed massive uprisings or class conflict. The riots in Guanajuato in 1810 and Mexico City in 1828—although sufficiently worrisome to sour some Mexicans' commitment to democracy—were tame in comparison with the great riots of the seventeenth century.[20] They also paled in comparison with the upheavals of the French Revolution. As Mora explained in commenting on the Parián riot of 1828, the French populace was far more "ferocious and barbaric" than the good-natured Mexican poor.[21] Well-to-do Mexicans were certainly embarrassed by the poverty and perceived backwardness of their popular classes, whom they hoped to transform through moral, civic, and religious education. They worried that the indigent were vectors of disease in a country battered by recurrent epidemics, such as the devastating cholera epidemic in 1833. Nonetheless, control of the poor was not being contested by Liberals, as it would be during the Reforma, let alone by Protestants, spiritists, positivists, anarcho-syndicalists, or socialists, as during the Porfiriato. Consequently, Mexican Catholics were not yet competing with the openly hostile forces that animated their French counterparts. It was therefore less important for the Mexican volunteers to establish personal contacts with the needy through home visitations. Indeed, the creation of new conferences to serve the poor was not their highest priority.

Mexico in the 1840s had other critical problems that the Vincentian

TABLE 1.1. Founding Members, First Conference of the Society of Saint Vincent de
Paul, 1844

Laymen	Priests
Manuel Andrade (vice president)*	Joaquín Fernández de Madrid (president)
Joaquín Velázquez de la Cadena (secretary)*	Manuel Pinzón (pro secretary)*
Manuel Canseco (treasurer)*	Agustín María Moreno (majordomo)*
Manuel Arias	Francisco López Cancelada*
Domingo de la Fuente*	Antonio Cruz*
Pedro Rojas y Pérez	Esteban Muriel*
Juan Santelices	Ramón Sanz*

* Indicates presence at the first meeting on December 15, 1844.
Source: Sociedad, *Acta,* 8–9.

gentlemen wanted to help solve. Independence was a disappointment for
Mexican elites as the glorious future they anticipated degenerated into political instability and economic recession. The country's hospitals and asylums
were in disarray because of the expulsion of the hospitaler orders and the
decrease in institutional endowments during the independence wars. Despite
the epidemics that highlighted the need to improve public health and sanita-
tion, weak and financially strapped governments failed to enact necessary
reforms. Although the issuance of comprehensive sanitary regulations in
1840 and the creation of the Consejo de Salubridad (Board of Health) in 1841
signaled the government's desire to address these issues, its limited resources
meant that it welcomed private sector help in delivering social services.[22] It
was at this juncture that the Society of Saint Vincent de Paul was founded.

Some of the early Mexican organization's emphasis reflects Dr. Andrade's
personal preferences. Like Ozanam, he wanted to strengthen the faith in an
increasingly secular world. A committed Catholic with a special devotion to
Saint Vincent, he named his youngest son—who would become a Paulist
priest—Vicente de Paul.[23] From 1845 to 1847 Dr. Andrade was the coeditor,
along with several Paulist priests, of *El Católico,* one of the first Catholic
newspapers in Mexico. He and his brother, José María Andrade, the well-
known publisher and fellow society member (though it is unclear whether he

was active or honorary), promoted the publication of works on Saint Vincent as well as the reprinting of religious texts from Europe.[24] Dr. Andrade was thus actively engaged in a collective effort to shape public opinion through the Catholic press.

As a physician, he had another vision as well. As director of the Hospital de Jesús and professor of the medical school responsible for introducing new surgical techniques to Mexico, he was deeply concerned with improving public health. Impressed by the nursing services the Sisters of Charity provided in France, he saw an opportunity to renew Mexico's struggling hospitals. Andrade therefore began by petitioning the Mexican government on November 22, 1842, to authorize the foundation of that religious congregation in Mexico. Only after the first sisters arrived two years later did he turn his attention to establishing the conferences for laymen and bringing the order of Vincentian priests to Mexico—partly to provide guidance for the sisters as they were awarded contracts to run various hospitals and asylums. Thus, one of the first acts of the new chapter that met on December 15, 1844, was to immediately petition the government to allow the Paulist Fathers to come to Mexico.[25]

The inauguration of the first Mexican conference already signaled its divergence from the French model. Whereas the French society was only loosely affiliated with the church, the Mexican society had a close relationship with the church—so much so that although the French organization insisted that only laymen could join, half of the fourteen men who formed the first Mexican chapter were priests.[26] Indeed, because of absences, they represented six of the ten who attended the first meeting (table 1.1). The role of the clerics was not just honorary. The bishop of Tenagra, Joaquín Fernández de Madrid, served as the new society's president and signed much of the early correspondence. He along with two other priests constituted half of the six officers on its first governing board. The prior of the Convent of Santo Domingo, Francisco López Cancelada, was one of three members who drafted the first bylaws. And the founders worked closely with the archbishop of Mexico, Manuel Posada y Garduño; indeed, they sought—and received—his approval before they contacted the society's French headquarters.[27] The archbishop immediately entrusted the fledgling organization with the Iglesia del Espíritu Santo that had been abandoned since the suppression of the hospitaler orders. In return, the society promised to maintain it and thus obtained a meeting place and office space in the church.[28] This close cooperation shows the degree to which the volunteers considered themselves partners with the church in reinvigorating the faith and fulfilling the Christian obligation to care for the needy.

One of the new organization's first acts—even before applying for affiliation with the international body—was to take over the management of the Hospital del Divino Salvador for Demented Women, which had been foundering since the expulsion of the Jesuit order that previously directed it.[29] Apparently relieved to be rid of this responsibility, the city council on February 21, 1845, "gave" the asylum—including its *rentas* (income)—to the society. It named as the director conference member Joaquín Velázquez de la Cadena, who offered his services without charge.[30] The society set up a commission composed of seven of its members to administer the institution and appointed a women's committee to work directly with the female inmates until the Sisters of Charity arrived.[31] Although most Vincentian sources erased the memory of the female board, it is evident that from the start the volunteers established a division of labor where the men supervised and the women provided hands-on services.[32]

Only after assuming control of the asylum did the Mexican society reach out to the French headquarters. Recognition from the parent organization did not come as quickly as from the Mexican church and state, however. Although the Mexicans submitted their application for aggregation to Paris on February 28, 1845, the Conseil Général of the Société de Saint-Vincent de Paul only granted it on September 15.[33] The French council blamed the delay on the slow mail between Mexico City and Paris—and, indeed, it took nearly four months for their letter to reach the Mexican capital.[34] Yet the affiliation was also complicated by a series of issues that are only obliquely referred to in the correspondence.

Desiring to preserve consistency across all its branches, the French General Council was apparently dismayed by the first constitution that Andrade sent to Paris along with his application. Dismissing it as highly idiosyncratic, the société only approved the affiliation of the Mexican society after it agreed to adopt the French bylaws.[35] The original Mexican *reglamento* reveals the Mexicans' initial priorities. It listed five goals for the new sociedad: promoting Christian charity, spreading the Catholic faith, stimulating the love of God and of one's neighbor, fostering the cult of Saint Vincent de Paul, and forming conferences of Saint Vincent de Paul. It did not even mention visiting the poor, the central mission of the French organization.

Indeed, it is clear that during the first few years the Mexican volunteers did not "go to the poor" as did their French counterparts, and they appear to have been considerably older than the students who joined the early Parisian conferences. The letter of aggregation, signed by the société's vice president, Frédéric Ozanam, and its secretary general, Luis de Baudicourt, reminded the new Mexican branch that the two main goals of the organization were "the sanctification of Catholic youth" through works of charity and, especially, "the visitation of the poor in their houses." Although they allowed that "you will know best what is suited to the customs of Mexican Catholics," they encouraged the Mexicans to "incorporate in your ranks a large number of young laymen who need to be supported, instructed, and animated . . . and to dedicate them to visiting the poor."[36] They also admonished the new branch to have its chapters meet more often—weekly or at the very least biweekly—since these regular gatherings where the volunteers prayed, reflected, and planned their charitable works were essential not only to the edification of the society's members but also to developing a "spirit of fraternity" among them.[37]

On January 11, 1846, soon after receiving the letter of aggregation from Paris, the Mexican sociedad met and agreed to translate and print some four thousand copies of the French société's rules—an indication of the large membership it envisioned.[38] It also began to adopt the form of the French organization. The original conference became a governing council supervising three new chapters that were founded in Mexico City during the spring and fall of 1846. Two years later, when the society expanded to the provinces, it put in place the centralized hierarchical system used by the French organization, with the capital's Superior Council overseeing what were called Particular Councils for major cities with multiple chapters. Decades later it added Central Councils, an intermediate level of regional governing bodies.[39]

Yet the tensions were not entirely resolved. A letter to Paris of March 2, 1846, which thanked the French society for approving the Mexican affiliation, explained that "we have been forced to replace some of your customs with others that are more in harmony with our political institutions, our habits, the nature of our country, and the education, needs, virtues, and vices of our poor."[40] Correspondence with the French headquarters referred

to differences concerning "home visits, the patronage of youth of the opposite sex, various issues relating to indulgences, the aggregation of Conferences and the institution of Councils, and the money of San Pedro," but did
not provide details.[41] A letter from the Conseil Général on February 6,
1849, clarified that one source of friction stemmed from the Mexicans'
desire for too much independence. Scolding them for founding new conferences without permission, the French General Council recognized them
nonetheless.[42] In 1850, when the Mexican Superior Council requested the
power to aggregate future chapters on its own—which would have put it on
a par with the French General Council—the petition was immediately
denied.[43] Yet these tensions were usually swept under the rug, with the
Mexicans insisting that whenever disagreements arose they "always submitted to the decisions of the General Council . . . with filial tenderness
toward the head of the Society."[44]

Despite their polite protestations, the differences remained. Available
information on the volunteers' activities in 1846 and 1847 hints at the Mexicans' distinct priorities. For example, in 1847 the sociedad printed twelve
thousand copies of Father Ripalda's *Catecismo* for free distribution as a reading primer in elementary schools.[45] This endeavor reflects its desire to not
only promote literacy but also to strengthen the role of Catholicism in public
education. It also bolstered the government's educational agenda because
Ripalda's *Catechism* was one of the principal textbooks used to educate Mexican children in the middle of the nineteenth century: in 1853 and 1854 Presidents Manuel María de Lombardini and Antonio López de Santa Anna
decreed that the *Catechism* should be an obligatory text in all public
schools.[46] This initiative thus demonstrates how the early volunteers worked
in concert with the state to achieve shared goals.[47]

From the start the society participated in emergency relief efforts. These
began as early as April 1845, when a strong earthquake damaged the chapel
of the Señor de Santa Teresa in the Mexican capital. The volunteers immediately raised money for its repair.[48] They expanded their assistance into the
international arena in 1847 by sending a thousand francs to the Paris headquarters to help victims of the Irish famine. This substantial donation at a
time when the new conferences were struggling and their country was in the
midst of war with the United States shows the extent to which the Mexicans
identified as part of a transnational relief organization. In fact, such global

Vincentian aid efforts predated those of the International Red Cross, which was not established until 1863.

The society was also active in meeting recurrent health emergencies in the Mexican capital. When Mexico City was occupied by US troops during the Mexican-American War, with particularly bloody fighting on September 12 and 13, 1847, the society's members assisted wounded soldiers from both armies. Indeed, Dr. Andrade was reportedly shot in the face by a stray bullet while ministering to soldiers in the Hospital de San Andrés.[49] A few months later the volunteers helped tend victims of the typhoid epidemic that came in the wake of the war and on June 8, 1848, took the life of the society's thirty-eight-year-old founder.[50] During the terrible cholera epidemic of 1850, which claimed 9,619 lives in Mexico City alone, sixteen society members joined the Junta's coordinating relief efforts, with two volunteers serving alongside other leading citizens in each of Mexico City's eight wards.[51] By inviting the Vincentian gentlemen to serve, the city council recognized their expertise in public health and crisis management. In accepting, and thus openly inserting themselves into, the public sphere, the Mexicans did not merely imitate the French model.

The Mexican volunteers' preference for such high-profile initiatives contrasted with the work of the early French conferences. Shunning publicity, the French volunteers quietly delivered parish-level services, mostly hidden inside the homes of their clients. In contrast, many of the Mexican projects were citywide and often responded to requests from the government for help in providing public services.[52] Symbolizing their attenuated relationship to local parishes, the Mexican chapters rarely followed the French custom of taking parish names and instead preferred to adopt the name of their patron saint, San Vicente de Paul, or of popular devotions such as the Purísima Concepción, Santísima Trinidad, Señora de Guadalupe, and Sagrado Corazón de Jesús.[53] These naming practices not only highlight the Mexican society's distinctiveness but also reveal the devotions that the volunteers wanted to promote as part of their efforts to strengthen religious observance.

By 1848 the Mexican society was ready to begin home visiting in earnest. In November the Superior Council informed the Conseil Général of the death of its founder, Dr. Manuel Andrade, and of his replacement by interim vice president Pedro Rojas. It reported on the creation of three new chapters in Mexico City and the first two outside the capital. And it assured the parent organization that the conferences were complying with the French bylaws by meeting weekly and adopting the *obra* (special project) of visiting the poor.[54]

Reflecting its new resolve, the society published a second annotated Spanish-language edition of the French rules that outlined the organization's procedures for these visits.[55] First, the conferences assigned visitors to investigate the applicants and verify whether they were truly needy. The members then discussed each potential client in their weekly session and, if they voted to "adopt" the ailing pauper, determined the type and amount of aid to offer. After dividing "their poor" among themselves, the volunteers normally visited their charges once a week—and more often when a client's illness was acute. The visitors tended to the family's material needs by providing food, clothes, bed linens, and other necessities as well as, occasionally, money to pay the rent. Sometimes they delivered these goods in person, at other times they issued *vales*, or vouchers, for their clients to obtain the goods directly from a central repository or from contributing merchants. In addition, the visitors arranged for doctors, medicines, and legal aid when needed. They helped place children in school or find jobs for the adults. They also tended to the family's spiritual needs by praying with its members, encouraging them to attend Mass and other religious functions, and making sure that they knew the Christian doctrine and that the children were baptized and took first communion. The volunteers were supposed to offer advice and comfort with "humility," "patience," and "prudence." These activities were to be meticulously recorded in the conference registers, summarized once a year, and sent on to the Superior Council in Mexico City so that it could tabulate the results and disseminate them in an annual report to its members and contributors as well as to the French headquarters.

It is unclear when these plans took effect because the society evidently hit some snags in the next few years. It sent reports to Paris in 1848 but not in 1849 or 1850 because of "certain difficulties" referred to (but not elaborated on) in a letter of October 4, 1851.[56] These apparently began soon after Dr. Andrade's death in June 1848 because the new Superior Council president Luis Gonzaga Cuevas, a well-known statesman, was too busy to give the society the attention it deserved—not surprising, since he served as minister of foreign relations during 1848–1849.[57] Because of these responsibilities Gonzaga Cuevas resigned from his leadership of the organization after eleven months, in November 1849—one of only two nineteenth-century presidents who did not serve lifelong terms (see appendix 1).[58] Even after Teófilo Marín replaced him, it was some years before the Mexican governing body ran smoothly: the first printed report only appeared in 1857, and the formal aggregation of new conferences (which required that applications be submitted to Paris) often took several years. Although most local chapters continued to function despite the problems in the central office, at least one Mexico City chapter is mentioned in the 1857 report as having suspended its activities.[59]

Statistics available for 1855 indicate that by then home visiting was underway. It does not seem to have come easily, however. This practice was apparently so unfamiliar to Mexican laymen that the Superior Council acknowledged that the habit of "visiting poor families to ignite the love of our impoverished brethren" had to be taught in conference meetings where new members could "learn the spirit of the society."[60] In 1855 the rate of home visitation was relatively low: the 567 active volunteers that year visited 256 families, an average of 0.45 families per member.[61] In contrast, in France each volunteer on average visited at least two families, and many more in some chapters.[62]

Commitment to other popular French initiatives was also tentative. For example, the obra of San Juan Francisco de Regis, which the French conferences adopted in the 1840s to marry couples that were living in consensual unions, was instituted in Mexico in 1846 but dropped soon thereafter.[63] Following the French model, a few Mexican conferences "patronized" students. Yet instead of teaching them themselves, as did some of the early French volunteers, the Mexicans simply paid the cost of educating a few highly promising youths.[64] We know about this initiative only because two of the students they had supported "since childhood," a girl and a boy, chose to take religious vows in 1857.[65] The patronage of the girl was in and of itself unusual because the French bylaws prohibited the men from helping young members of the opposite sex. Yet the sponsorship of youth must have been quite limited, because the first comprehensive statistics, available for 1856, list only 8 orphans, 4 students, and 4 apprentices as "patronized."[66] In contrast, the French organization in 1846 alone reported visiting 17,300 families, patronizing 8,000 students and 2,500 apprentices, and regularizing 800 illegitimate unions.[67]

While the emblematic French obras lagged, the Mexican volunteers concentrated on other welfare projects. A society member continued to direct the Hospital del Divino Salvador, with the day-to-day management delegated to a hired administrator, six Sisters of Charity, one doctor, one chaplain, and six servants.[68] At least one Mexico City chapter, the conference of Señor San José, turned its attention to instructing children by establishing an elementary school for both sexes and paying a full-time teacher to staff it.[69] Following the age-old custom of the hospitaler orders and certain confraternities, the volunteers went into public hospitals to visit the sick and dying, offer them solace, pray with them, teach them Christian doctrine, and arrange for the last rites and proper Catholic burials.[70] We only know about this activity from the 1856 report that referred to the long-standing obra of visiting the poor in the hospitals of San Andrés and San Pablo, both run by the Sisters of Charity, with whom the men worked closely. The scale of the hospital ministry was extensive: in 1856 the volunteers visited 9,202 patients.[71] In contrast, although institutional visits were not unheard of in the French conferences, especially in the provinces, they were apparently quite rare in the nineteenth century.[72]

Differences in national practices are also hinted at in the footnotes to the early Mexican editions of the bylaws.[73] Where the original French version of 1835 described the members as young men, the Mexicans—who still apparently attracted few youths to their conferences—clarified that after a few years the French organization had begun admitting men of all ages. Where the French prohibited the men from visiting families that included young women and girls, the Mexicans added a note encouraging the visitors to work in pairs to avoid scandalous appearances that might arise from the contact of an unaccompanied man with the women in his adopted family. They also admonished their members to avoid any collaboration with women's charitable societies, an indication that they must have been doing so. Finally, the list of services was annotated to include arranging for a Catholic burial when a client died and designating a few members to accompany the body to its final resting place.

The distinctiveness of the Mexican activities is confirmed by discrepancies between the French and Mexican reports. When the French society became more bureaucratized in the 1850s and began furnishing printed forms to its branches, it did not include the categories of "sick and dying assisted," "cadavers buried," or "patients visited." The Mexicans had to add these categories by hand (see fig. 1.2).[74] In contrast, the Mexican conferences

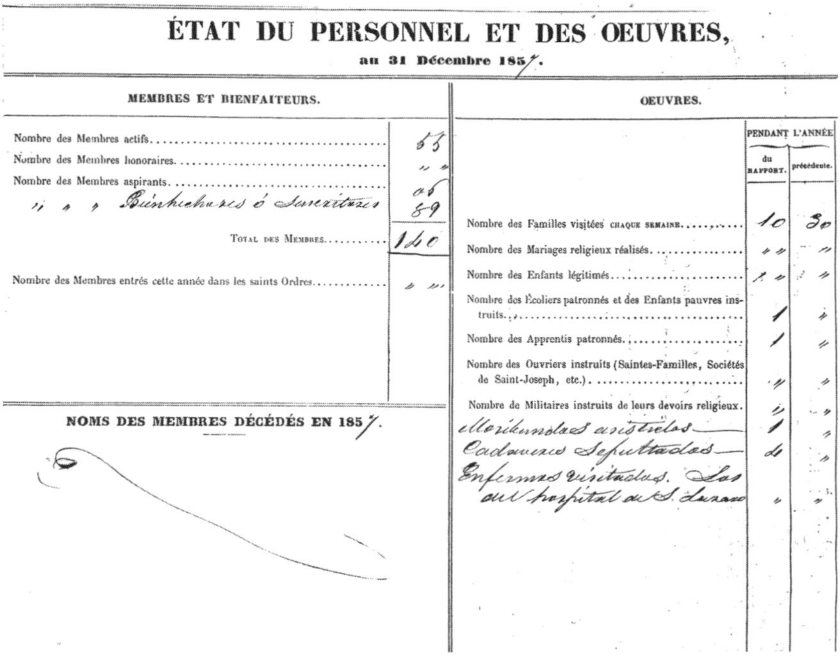

Figure 1.2. Activities of a Mexico City conference reported on the French société's form, with distinctively Mexican practices added by hand. "Tableau Statistique de la Conférence de l'Anunciación de N.a S.a de Encarnación," 1857. In ASSVP, CC114, Mexique.

could not report significant activity in four of the categories appearing on the French forms: "religious marriages arranged," "children legitimized," "workers instructed," and "soldiers instructed." By the 1860s, when the Mexican society was printing its own forms, it included the all-important categories of "sick and dying assisted," "cadavers buried," and "patients visited" (as well as a new category of "prisoners instructed") but dropped the category of "soldiers instructed" altogether.[75] Thus, the Mexican society was far from a carbon copy of the French organization.

A final difference was its continuing close relationship with the church. Following directives from the French headquarters, the Mexican society took pains to maintain the outward appearance of independence from the church. Beginning in 1849 the Superior Council presidents were always laymen, with the bishops and archbishops who protected the organization relegated to "honorary" rather than "effective" positions.[76] Yet priests remained as members throughout the 1850s. The 1857 report referred to the bishop of Tenagra as *nuestro consocio* (fellow member) as well as "honorary President of the Society."[77] And priests still served as individual chapter officers, as did two of the three vice presidents of the conference of Nuestra Señora de Guadalupe, Feliciano Arango and Juan Flores, and the vice president of the conference of El Santo Niño de Jesús, Pedro Rangel. These were not just continuities from an earlier time: the new Mexico City conference of El Sagrado Corazón de Jesús, founded in 1857, listed three clerics, including its president and vice president, among its seventeen members.[78] By then this practice violated the French regulations, because in 1850 the French Conseil had established the policy that priests were only to serve as "spiritual directors," not members or officers of the organization.[79]

The Mexicans' choices made perfect sense in the local context. They reflected opportunities to cooperate with the church and the state at a time when relations between them were still cordial. The volunteers' perception of how best to address their country's needs with a small number of members also dictated their emphasis, for it was extremely time-consuming to work one on one with individual paupers. Notions about the appropriate roles for elite men undoubtedly shaped the gentlemen's activities too, for even though the French bylaws specified that each volunteer should personally attend the needy,[80] Mexican men apparently found managing institutions and citywide projects at a high level to be more appealing than providing personal service. Whenever possible, it seems, they relied on the Sisters of Charity or hired employees to perform the daily work of caregiving and teaching children.[81] In addition, the volunteers' favorite activities embodied deeply entrenched charitable traditions, such as the visiting of hospital patients that had been practiced by some confraternities and religious orders in the colonial period. In contrast, home visiting was a new experience in a country that lacked a history of organized outdoor relief, though it was slowly taking root in the Mexican conferences.

Another reason for the discrepancies is that much of the group's energies were going into other projects. As liberal storm clouds became increasingly threatening, the volunteers' highest priority was to combat anticlericalism through political activity and shaping public opinion. Although we know very little about most of the early society members, several names emerge as part of a group that was deeply involved in the Catholic press. The first was Manuel Andrade, who coedited *El Católico* until 1847. The next year the *Voz de la Religión* appeared (1848–1853). One of its editors was Tomás Gardida, who is listed in an 1858 document as an active society volunteer.[82] Manuel Diez de Bonilla, society vice president in 1857, edited *El Universal* (1848–1855), the conservative and pro-Catholic newspaper founded by Lucas Alamán.[83] Dr. Andrade's brother and fellow society collaborator, José María Andrade, not only published the militant *La Cruz* from 1855 to 1858 but also printed numerous works in defense of religion through his publishing house, the Imprenta de J. M. Andrade y F. Escalante. After the Conservative Party was founded in 1849, Andrade published its political platform as well. His salon was a regular meeting place for many of Mexico's best-known conservatives, including society member Joaquín García Icazbalceta.[84] Luis Gonzaga Cuevas, the society's president in 1849, elaborated a conservative position through his *Porvenir de México*, published in four volumes between 1851 and 1859.[85] Teófilo Marín, an active member since at least 1849 when he became secretary of the Superior Council, was also heavily engaged in the conservative cause.[86] Thus, when liberal and conservative positions congealed after the traumatic defeat in the Mexican-American War, some of the best-known volunteers chose to align with the conservatives. Their participation in the Vincentian conferences was only one part of a much broader project of lay activism to support their church and faith.

Conclusion

The Mexican Society of Saint Vincent de Paul was part of a transnational movement that united militant Catholics throughout the world.[87] The volunteers participated in the larger Vincentian community in many ways. In establishing the first American branch of the French organization, they contributed to the global circulation of ideas about new ways that the laity could serve their religion and communities. They helped found the two Vincentian orders in Mexico and then welcomed the nuns and priests when they arrived from France and Spain. They spread French devotions such as the veneration of Saint Vincent de Paul and the Sacred Heart of Jesus. They distributed the French society's publications and shared information about other nations' activities in their *Boletín*. They corresponded with their fellow society members in other countries; indeed, the 1895 history praised the Mexican Superior Council for founding the Guatemalan organization in 1885 and "maintaining affectionate relations" with the councils in London, Dublin, Spain, Nice, New York, New Orleans, Guatemala, and El Salvador.[88] In addition, the Mexicans sent relief funds through a far-flung Vincentian network—and this was not a one-way street: in 1889, for example, the conferences in France and Costa Rica sent money to aid the victims of massive flooding in León, Guanajuato.[89] The Mexicans occasionally contributed to foreign projects such as in 1868 the foundation of a Catholic orphanage in London to combat Protestantism.[90] They regularly donated to help celebrate important Catholic milestones, such as the twenty-fifth anniversary of Pope Pius IX in 1871–1872.[91] By the early twentieth century, a few Mexican chapters were sending delegates to Rome to attend the meetings of the international association of the conferences of Saint Vincent de Paul.[92] Some individual members also visited the society's headquarters in Paris, where they were "received with great cordiality."[93]

While firmly embedded in these transnational networks, however, the Mexican society did not merely imitate foreign trends. The first generation of Vincentian volunteers spent more effort consoling the institutionalized sick and dying than providing domiciliary relief, regularizing marriages, or finding children to patronize—the favorite works of the French organization. Instead of going out to work with poor people in their homes and neighborhoods, the Mexicans preferred to meet the needy when they came into the schools and hospitals that they administered and protected. The gentlemen were evidently more comfortable leading institutions, fundraising and handling large sums of money, and sitting on boards as well as conducting short visits to hospital patients than in developing relationships with individual paupers through prolonged face-to-face contact. The early Mexican society thus initiated activities that reflected local needs and traditions as well as its members' identity as experts in managing social welfare projects. They also took advantage of their excellent connections with the government to take on highly visible projects in open partnership with the state.

The Mexicans were not alone in their idiosyncrasies. A recent study of the Vincentian conferences in Chile, where the organization was established in 1854, also notes the low incidence of home visitation during the early years. Another parallel with Mexico was the strength of the Chileans' alliance with the church; indeed it was apparently stronger in Chile, where—unlike in Mexico—the initiative to found the conferences was clerical.[94] And it was not just Latin America where churchmen played a leading role: Ozanam prohibited ecclesiastics from serving as chapter presidents in 1850 after learning that it was standard practice in Germany.[95]

Yet it is misleading to see the Mexican society as an "inferior" version of the French organization. By their standards, the Mexican conferences should be judged a success. It is true that they can hardly be described as thriving, for even the laudatory Vincentian chronicles occasionally mentioned their decadence by the end of the first decade.[96] The Mexican volunteers could nonetheless take pride in having established an organization that would persist until the present day. As they branched out from the capital city, they helped initiate a Catholic revival in central Mexico. After ten years they had a presence in seven states as well as the Federal District. Their strength was in Mexico City, with twelve chapters, and Guanajuato, with eight. They also had several chapters in the states of Mexico (two), Michoacán (three), Puebla (two), and Jalisco (two), and single conferences in Querétaro, Hidalgo, and Oaxaca. The society was one of the first private organizations to operate on a national scale, part of the expansion of voluntary associations in the 1840s. Indeed, with six hundred active and honorary members in 1855, it had a larger membership and lasted longer than many of the early Mexican civic groups that included Masonic lodges, social clubs, and scientific and literary societies.[97] And it worked with a large budget for the time, spending 20,084 pesos in 1855—though much of this sum probably represented the income of the endowment that supported the Hospital del Divino Salvador.

Despite being relatively few in number, the Mexican conferences attracted a core of enthusiastic volunteers. The surviving lists of Superior Council officers show that many of them made lifelong commitments to the society. For example, founding member Manuel Canseco served as treasurer of the Superior Council for nineteen years, from December 1844 until his death in 1863. Teófilo Marín served at least eighteen years, since he was already listed as secretary of the Superior Council in 1849 and then served as its president from May 1850 until his death in 1867. Antonio Vértiz, who succeeded him as interim president in 1868, already appeared in a Superior Council list twelve years earlier. Colonel Pedro Pablo Iturria appeared in the same 1856 list and again, thirteen years later, in a notation about the

members who had died in 1869. Several men who likely joined the conferences during the society's early years, since they were already listed as officers in 1857, participated for many decades. José María Rodríguez
Villanueva, who served as Superior Council president from 1868 until his
death in 1886, volunteered for at least thirty years, and two did so for close
to forty years: Joaquín García Icazbalceta, the treasurer of Mexico City's
Conferencia de Monserrate by 1857 and Superior Council president from
1886 until his death in 1894; and Jesús Urquiaga, the Superior Council pro
secretary by 1857 and its secretary from at least 1868 until 1895, when he
signed the organization's fiftieth-anniversary history (appendix 1).[98]

The fragmentary available information provides glimpses of a social network of pious gentlemen tied to the Catholic press and Conservative Party
and collaborating with priests on a regular basis. Although we know very
little about the rank-and-file members during the first decade, most of the
society's leaders were quite well-to-do. They listed professions such as merchant, lawyer, doctor, military officer, city councilman, and proprietor. One
member of the founding conference was a *relojero*, a highly skilled clockmaker.[99] As they met together in their local chapters week after week, year
after year, they solidified the ties among themselves. They also began to build
a clientele among the lower classes. They were thus gradually establishing
new patterns of Catholic lay associationism as well as expanding the popular
base for the church.

While coming together to contribute to the public good, the volunteers
created the building blocks of civil society. With an average of eighteen
members in 1855, each conference was deliberately kept small enough to
facilitate the all-important fellowship of its members. The neighborhood-
level cells were tied into a complex national and international structure that
was independent from the Mexican state. In major cities the presidents of
each individual conference met regularly in the Particular Council, and all
Mexican members—whether active or honorary—were invited to attend the
society's annual assembly, where they forged ties that went beyond their local
community. Although the Vincentian organization was still quite small by
the end of its first decade, its eventual growth and longevity belies the view
so widespread in the older social science literature that, unlike the Americans observed by Alexis de Tocqueville, Latin Americans were not "joiners."
By tracing the formation of nineteenth-century civil society in secular

associations, scholars have simply ignored a large segment of the groups they joined.[100]

By organizing to help the less fortunate, the conferences also challenge one of the persistent stereotypes about Latin America: that because of its weak "civic culture,"[101] the "haves" do very little to help the "have nots." This idea, presented in many different forms over the past half century, has been accepted by contemporary social reformers who assert that civil society and philanthropy are new to Latin America. On the contrary, the Sociedad de San Vicente de Paul reveals that as early as the 1840s, Mexicans were developing a tradition of joining civic organizations, giving money and resources to help alleviate suffering, and volunteering their time to serve others beyond their family and social group. Their efforts demonstrate the importance of including religious initiatives in the history of modern philanthropy. They also show that Rerum Novarum did not initiate the mobilization of the laity for Catholic social projects.

Moreover, although the early society's charitable works were limited in scope, they helped fill gaps in the Mexican welfare system at midcentury, when public asylums and hospitals were faltering and organized home-relief programs nonexistent. They also contributed to improving popular education at a time when public schooling was sorely deficient. The Mexican government, both federal and municipal, delegated important responsibilities to the volunteers—evidence that the state was still happy to cooperate with private welfare institutions, including those that made no effort to hide their religious mission and church connections.

This favorable situation began to change after March 1854 with the promulgation of the Plan de Ayutla that ushered in anticlerical reforms and civil war. Yet, despite its modest beginning, the organization created by the early volunteers not only proved solid enough to withstand the attacks that came during the Liberal Reforma but was also poised to spring into action when the conflict between church and state made the Mexican environment more like the French, where the militant lay movement originated. In facing the challenges of the next two decades, the Mexicans drew strength both from their deep faith and from the knowledge that they were part of a larger transnational community of like-minded Catholic activists.[102]

2.

The Male Volunteers Face the Liberal Reforma

THE MASTER NARRATIVE of Mexican history posits that the Liberal Reforma of 1855 to 1876 dealt the Catholic Church and its allies a crippling blow, the most devastating suffered by any country in Latin America. Part of this tale is certainly true: the two decades of Liberal reforms and Conservative resistance that encompassed a bloody civil war and foreign intervention were ruinous for the church. The victorious Liberals ended the church's monopoly on faith; confiscated its properties; extinguished its regular orders; removed it from control of birth, marriage, and death; and attempted to substitute it as the provider of education and poor relief. By forbidding public religious ceremonies, silencing church bells, and prohibiting priests from wearing clerical garb in public, the Reform Laws even sought to banish the ever-present religious sights and sounds from everyday life. Yet the experience of the Society of Saint Vincent de Paul suggests that the Catholic defeat was not as complete as both liberal and conservative histories posit.[1] Contrary to what might be expected, the organization was strengthened during the Reforma. Indeed, the male society reached its highest membership in 1875, a year before Porfirio Díaz entered the presidency and began to mend fences with the church.

The chronicle of progressive secularization accompanied by a marginalization of the church ignores the process of laicization whereby—long before the Pax Porfiriana—committed lay people stepped in to defend the institution, supplement the depleted clergy, catechize the young, and help the poor.

Despite choosing the losing side in the Reform Wars, the Vincentian conferences were only briefly weakened. As the volunteers rallied to the Catholic cause, they were certainly drawn into the maelstrom. They had to navigate a hostile political climate and occasionally faced direct threats. Yet the men's society not only recovered but thrived in the face of anticlerical policies, and the flourishing women's association dates to this period. Although part of their expansion came during the Second Empire (1863–1867) when Conservatives briefly regained power and the conferences enjoyed the protection of Emperor Maximilian and Empress Charlotte, much of it came during the Restored Republic that followed—not only under the moderate Liberal president Benito Juárez (1867–1872) but also under the vehemently anticlerical president Sebastián Lerdo de Tejada (1872–1876). While the lay groups grew, they were also transformed. The post-Reform organization was different from the one that Dr. Andrade founded thirty years earlier because its close relationship with the municipal and federal governments was definitively sundered. And the feminization of the conferences provides crucial insight into the Catholic revival of the late nineteenth century.

The First Phase of the Reforma: 1855–1863

Although the Vincentian conferences eventually suffered persecution at the hands of "exalted" Liberals, especially after these took the Mexican capital in 1861, they were not directly affected during the initial phase of the Reforma. The Revolution of Ayutla, which began as a coup that toppled the government of President Santa Anna in August 1855, took a few years to escalate into a full-fledged assault on the Catholic Church. The first volleys in what would become a bitter conflict were relatively tame: the Ley Juárez (1855) restricted clerical exemptions from civil jurisdiction, and the Ley Lerdo (1856) mandated that the church sell its extensive lands and buildings unrelated to religious purposes. A new constitution promulgated the next year went a step further, expanding these provisions and disestablishing the Catholic church—a huge reversal for an institution that had for centuries been a partner in ruling Mexico. Yet it did not immediately go into effect. The Constitution of 1857 unleashed three years of civil war as Conservatives refused to accept the "heretical" charter and began negotiating with Napoleon III to install a Catholic monarch in Mexico.

The outbreak of the Three Years' War in the fall of 1857 put a damper on the activities of some of the Vincentian volunteers. By late 1857 there was open fighting between Liberal and Conservative armies. On February 22, 1858, the society's president, Teófilo Marín, informed the Paris headquarters that combat around the capital had crippled some of its obras.[2] It may also have aggravated the perennial problem of provincial chapters that failed to report to the Superior Council in Mexico City. Yet the disruptions were fleeting, as the Conservatives gained the upper hand in central Mexico and the Liberals fled to set up a separate government in Veracruz. Indeed, the society prospered during the three years that Conservatives controlled Mexico City, from January 1858 until December 1860, as pious Mexicans, faced with the threat to their beloved church, redoubled their efforts on its behalf.

For the Society of Saint Vincent de Paul, the period from 1856 to 1860 was one of institutional consolidation. The Superior Council was reenergized, with President Teófilo Marín at the helm and a new secretary, José María López Monroy, replacing the departing one, whose "multiple commitments" had prevented him from giving the organization the attention it deserved.[3] For the first time, it sent comprehensive statistics to Paris in 1856 and 1857. Also for the first time, it printed the minutes of its general assembly, held in the Archiepiscopal Palace in Mexico City on April 26, 1857. These *actas* reported that the central office had reestablished communication with provincial chapters and was working to revive a few that had declined during the past few years. In 1857 the Paris headquarters of the société received stacks of requests for the formal aggregation of new Mexican chapters.[4] In another sign of organizational health, in August 1857 the Superior Council began printing a Spanish-language edition of the French society's *Bulletin*, and later issues of the *Boletín* would occasionally incorporate Mexican news as well.[5] In 1858 it published an annotated version of the French bylaws to serve as a guide for the Mexican volunteers.[6]

The society's renewal during the first four years of the Reforma is evident in its conference foundations and membership. These dipped in 1855 to 1856, when no new chapters were founded and membership apparently dropped from 567 active volunteers to 192—though some of the decrease may simply reflect loss of contact with far-flung chapters (table 2.1). The decline was soon reversed, with eight new chapters established in 1857 and another ten in the next three years. Since only two of these were in Mexico City, the expansion occurred primarily in the provinces, especially in the states of Michoacán with seven chapters and Guanajuato with five (table 2.2). Provincial growth was sufficient to warrant two more Particular Councils to oversee local conferences: in addition to the one created in Toluca (state of Mexico) in 1851, new ones arose in León (Guanajuato) in 1857 and Zamora (Michoacán) in 1860. A fourth Particular Council was established in Mexico City in 1858, separating the supervision of the capital's conferences from the overburdened Superior Council, which oversaw the entire republic (table 2.3).

The membership mirrored the expansion of the conferences. The active volunteers increased to a reported 275 in 1857—probably more, since three chapters did not submit reports. Another five men had become honorary members who provided significant support to the society without participating in its daily activities, and 331 had signed on as subscribers who pledged regular sums of money to support its good works—a category that would be lumped together with honorary members in most future statistics. The membership continued to grow in 1858. The number of active volunteers doubled to 558 in thirty chapters. Finally attracting the next generation, the society had recruited 164 youths over the age of twelve as "aspiring members" training to become full-fledged participants in the conferences when they turned eighteen.[7] These numbers remained approximately steady in the next two years. Moreover, the early statistics separately listed a few "corresponding members" who had moved to cities where there were no chapters such as, in 1856, the military officer Francisco Palafox, who was posted to Veracruz, and Juan Nepomuceno Pereda, who served as plenipotentiary minister in Guatemala.[8]

As the society grew, its social class base expanded. Although gentlemen from Mexico's leading families continued to dominate the Superior Council (appendix 1), by 1857 several conferences that applied to Paris for aggregation listed members who were *empleados, dependientes, preceptores, filarmónicos,* and occasionally *artesanos.*[9] The benefactors included not only doctors and lawyers who provided their services free but also pharmacists, bakers, and shopkeepers who contributed goods. Thus the organization was reaching beyond a small elite to draw from the middle and lower-middle classes.

The increasing strength of the Vincentian lay movement is also evident in the numerous activities listed in available reports.[10] Table 2.4 summarizes many of the society's charitable works. The volunteers more than doubled their home visits between 1856 and 1860. In addition to providing food, clothes, bed linens, candles, charcoal, and sometimes rent for their adopted

TABLE 2.1 Membership of the Society of Saint Vincent de Paul, 1855–1908

	Active	Honorary	Aspiring
1855	567	33	
1856	192	225	12
1857	275	331	22
1858	558		164
1859	516	527	43
1865	791	347	
1868	1,094	342	26
1869	1,412	507	309
1870	1,922	666	233
1871	1,665	763	244
1875	2,824	640	
1881	1,317	787	
1885	1,647	236	
1887	1,538	440	
1894	1,536	432	
1896	1,672	633	
1900	1,433		
1908	1,613	78	142

Note: Aspiring members were between twelve and eighteen years old. Honorary members provided significant support but did not participate in the activities of the conference. Although the early statistics distinguished them from subscribers who contributed regular sums of money and corresponding members who had moved away, I have combined them with honorary members in all years for comparability.

Sources: "Etat du Personnel el des oeuvres . . ." (1856, 1857, 1894), ASSVP, CC113, Mexique; Sociedad, Reseña, 47; Sociedad, Acta, 17; Sociedad, Noticia (1868–1870); Sociedad, Memoria (1871); Sociedad, Boletín (February 1859; February 1860; May 1883, 148; May 1887, 142; July 1897, 215; November 1900, 317); Sociedad Guadalajara, Boletín (July 1909), 152.

families, they gave their clients cigarettes, at the time considered a necessity (in 1856 one Mexico City conference alone distributed 126 *cajillas de cigarros*). They patronized students and prepared children for their first communion. They continued going into public hospitals to work with the sick and dying; indeed, the conference of Nuestra Señora de Guadalupe in Mexico

TABLE 2.2 Conference Foundations of the Society of Saint Vincent de Paul by Region, 1845–1895[*]

	1845–54	1855–64	1865–74	1875–84	1885–95[*]	Exists 1895
Mexico City	12	3	2	1	3	16
Guanajuato	8	6	10	2	3	11
Michoacán	3	8	6	3	1	9
Mexico	2	4	4	3	1	6
Querétaro	1	2	2	0	3	4
Puebla	2	2	10	1	0	9
Jalisco	2	6	5	7	27	34
Hidalgo	1	0	3	0	0	0
Oaxaca	1	0	1	0	0	1
Veracruz		1	3	8	1	11
Nuevo León		1	0	0	0	0
S. Luis Potosí		3	0	1	2	
Yucatán		6	5	6	6	
Guerrero		1	1	0	0	
Zacatecas		1	0	3	3	
Durango		1	0	0	0	
Morelos		2	1	0	0	
Tlaxcala		1	1	1	2	
Campeche			0	1	0	
Tamaulipas			1	0	0	
Aguascalientes				4	4	
Colima				3	3	
All	32	32	62	34	58	121

Note: Not including governing councils. Of the 218 conference foundations, 97 (45%) had folded by September 1895. Although some state boundaries shifted during the nineteenth century, I follow the state identification in the 1895 report.

[*]Statistics go through September 1895. Only one conference was founded in 1895, in Ixtlán, Michoacán, in April.

Source: Sociedad, Reseña, 50–60.

TABLE 2.3. Development of Governing Structure, Society of Saint Vincent de Paul, 1844–1901

Consejo Particular	Consejo Superior	Consejo Central
Mexico City 1846–49*	Mexico City 1850*	
Toluca 1851		
León 1857		
Mexico City 1858		
Zamora 1860		
Morelia 1864		
Guadalajara 1864		
Puebla 1868		
Mérida 1874		
Orizaba 1884		
San Luis Potosí 1888		
Querétaro 1888		
		Guadalajara 1889
		Mérida 1895
Aguascalientes*		
Colima, 1901		Tabasco, 1901

Note: Particular Councils supervised conferences in one city; Central Councils supervised an entire region. The first Consejo Particular in Mexico City was replaced by the Consejo Provincial in 1849, which was in turn replaced by the Consejo Superior in 1850.
* The Particular Council of Aguascalientes was added at some point between 1897 and 1902.
Sources: Sociedad, Reseña (50–57); Sociedad, Boletín (July 1897, 214; January 1903, 18); for 1901 and 1911, De Dios, Historia de la familia vicentina, 2:630, 634.

City proudly reported among its accomplishments in 1856 that it had arranged for the confirmation of most of the patients in the hospitals of San Andrés and San Pablo. Following the age-old practice of some confraternities, the society initiated a new prison ministry that gradually overshadowed the visiting of hospital patients. Perhaps because the Sisters of Charity had taken over the management of so many hospitals by the 1850s,[11] the men increasingly turned their attention to offering prisoners consolation, religious instruction, and legal aid—as well as clothes, blankets, and special meals on religious holidays. As the hospital ministry declined from visiting 9,202 patients in 1856 to 647 in 1860, the prison ministry grew from working with 58 prisoners to 2,460. The volunteers also began visiting the Mexico City and Morelia poorhouses to offer the inmates catechism lessons, and when the owners permitted, they did the same with the *operarios* in bakeries who toiled as forced laborers.[12]

In addition to providing services to the needy in their homes and in public institutions, the volunteers created their own establishments to serve a wider public. In Mexico City, for example, the conference of Nuestra Señora de la Luz opened a primary school. Several chapters founded night schools to provide free Catholic instruction to workers. With the help of a generous

TABLE 2.4. Activities of the Society of Saint Vincent de Paul, 1856–1908

	1856	1860	1868	1871	1887	1896	1908
Families visited	213	520	433	669	783	1160	727
Marriages	0	9	50	79	95	90	35
Children legitimized	0	7	3	23	195		13
Baptisms					11		20
First communions	140	126			45		226
Students patronized / children taught	301	183	1,164	1,233	1,707	2,053	1,379
Apprentices patronized	4	0	112	55	83	60	36
Workers/prisoners instructed[*]	58	2,460	1,072	1,457		1,375	909
Patients visited / dying assisted[†]	9,202	647	93	143	349	1071	172
Cadavers buried	2	29	106	119	294	284	226
Income (pesos)			17,157	30,995			70,247
Expenditures (")		30,509	15,481	28,738	38,802	48,800	69,717

[*] The category is listed as "prisoners visited" in 1856 and 1860, "prisoners/sick" in 1868, "workers/ prisoners/sick" in 1871, "prisoners/artisans" in 1908.
[†] Category is "sick/moribund" in 1860, "dying assisted" in 1868–1908.
Sources: "Tableau Statistique," 1856, ASSVP, CC113, Mexique; "Cuadro Estadístico," 1860, ASSVP, Conseil Superior du Mexique, 1845–1920; Sociedad, *Noticia* (1868); Sociedad, *Memoria* (1871); Sociedad, *Boletín* (May 1887, 142; July 1897, 215); Sociedad Guadalajara, *Boletín* (July 1909), 152.

member who spent 913 pesos from his own pocket (a substantial sum at a time when the top administrator of the Mexico City Poor House only earned 1,000 pesos a year and the best-paid schoolteacher earned 330).[13] The conference of Nuestra Señora de los Dolores on November 1, 1858, opened a *cocina económica*, or soup kitchen, which served hot meals to two hundred paupers a day. In 1859 two other conferences in the capital planned to sponsor similar soup kitchens.[14] In 1858 the society also opened a library to lend religious as well as morally uplifting works to its members and client families.[15] The Morelia (Michoacán) chapters had by 1859 established two *talleres* (workshops) to give young artisans religious education along with vocational training in carpentry and shoemaking. And they were in the process of founding two chapters composed entirely of artisans as well as a temperance association, La Templanza, that sought to combat excessive drinking among the city's workers.[16] The society was therefore reaching out beyond the sick and destitute to work with new groups of people that included artisans and workers.

Other conferences reported a host of additional projects to reinvigorate Catholicism. These included working with soldiers in a new *obra de los militares* and distributing rosaries, religious medals, missals, and breviaries. Ever mindful of the need to fortify the volunteers' own faith, the Superior Council in November 1857 initiated the *obra de los retiros*—daylong retreats where the society's members and benefactors could renew their commitment to serving the poor—while earning at least eighty days of indulgences to reduce the time their souls spent in Purgatory (see fig. 2.1). The volunteers often brought the men in their adopted families to join them in attending these spiritual exercises, activities that reflect the volunteers' continued efforts to promote more orthodox religious observance in Mexico.[17]

The society was placed on the defensive in 1859 as Liberal armies closed in on the capital. From their outpost in Veracruz, Liberals issued the most radical attack yet on the church in a series of decrees known as the Reform Laws. The July 1859 decree outlawing confraternities hit close to home by raising doubts about the legality of the conferences; the confusion was compounded by the volunteers' habit of referring to themselves not only as *miembros* and *socios* of the organization, but also as *hermanos* and *cófrades*—terms used for members of religious orders and confraternities.[18] Other measures did not directly affect the conferences but threatened their church and faith, particularly the nationalization of ecclesiastical property, the complete

REGLAMENTO DE LOS RETIROS ESPIRITUALES

PARA LOS SOCIOS DE LAS CONFERENCIAS

DE SAN VICENTE DE PAUL.

Art. 1º Se establecen cuatro retiros espirituales, con el nombre de Ordinarios, correspondientes á las asambleas generales; y servirán para prepararse á celebrar dignamente la Inmaculada Concepcion de la Virgen María; la entrada de la Cuaresma; el Domingo del Buen Pastor y la festividad de Nuestro Santo Patron San Vicente de Paul.

Art. 2º Ademas de los cuatro retiros establecidos en el capitulo anterior, habrá otros con el nombre de Estraordinarios, que se celebrarán mensualmente ó cuando la comision directiva lo juzgue por conveniente, de acuerdo con el Señor Presidente del Consejo.

Art. 3º Aunque estos retiros se establecen esclusivamente para los socios activos de las conferencias, podrán ser admitidos los socios bienhechores, honorarios y corresponsales de las mismas.

Art. 4º Los retiros tendrán lugar en el Convento de los PP. de la Mision, cuyos Sacerdotes serán los directores.

Art. 5º El fondo para los gastos de alimentos y cera, se compondrá del valor de los boletos que se espendan.

Art. 6º El retiro se anunciará por medio de avisos que se dirigirán al Consejo y á las conferencias, á fin de que se lean en las dos sesiones que tengan dichos cuerpos anteriores al dia que espira el plazo señalado para la venta de boletos

Art. 7º Los boletos se venden desde el dia que se anuncia el retiro, hasta el juéves anterior al Domingo que deba verificarse. Pasado dicho dia no se venden boletos ni se devuelve el importe de los ya vendidos.

Art. 8º El precio de los boletos es el de seis reales, y se espenderán precisamente por un socio en el lugar que se anuncie oportunamente, cuidando la comision de que reuna las circunstancias convenientes al objeto. Los boletos solo servirán para el dia que en ellos esté marcado.

Art. 9º Comenzando la distribucion á las ocho en punto de la mañana. los socios acudirán un cuarto de hora antes, presentando el boleto respectivo al hermano portero, á fin de que se les indiquen los aposentos que deban ocupar y se impongan de la distribucion del dia, la que se fijará impresa en dichos aposentos y en la puerta de la Capilla.

DISTRIBUCION DEL DIA.

A las ocho, misa rezada y comunion para los que vayan preparados.

A las ocho y tres cuartos, chocolate.

A las nueve, plática.

A las nueve y media, oracion.

A las diez, descanso.

A las diez y cuarto, conferencia sobre un punto práctico de doctrina cristiana.

A las once y cuarto, lectura.

A las once y media, esposicion de la Sagrada Escritura.

A las doce, Exámen y comida.

A las doce y media, recreacion.

A la una y media, descanso.

A las dos y media, rosario.

A las tres, lectura.

A las tres y media, oracion.

A las cuatro, chocolate.

A las cuatro y cuarto, descanso.

A las cuatro y media, plática.

A las cinco, esposicion del Santisimo Sacramento, Visita, Estacion, Trisagio, Letanías cantadas, bendicion y reserva.

El Illmo. Sr. Dr. D. Lázaro de la Garza y Ballesteros, dignísimo arzobispo de México, por su decreto de 4 de Diciembre de 1857, se dignó conceder 80 dias de Indulgencia á cada socio, por cada vez que concurra á estos retiros.

El Exmo. é Illmo. Sr. D. Luis Clementi, arzobispo de Damasco y Delegado Apostolico, por su decreto de 5 del mismo mes y año, concedió 100 dias de Indulgencia (pudiendo aplicarse por las almas del Purgatorio) á los fieles de Cristo que forman la Sociedad de San Vicente de Paul, cuantas veces practiquen estos ejercicios.

Igualmente el Illmo. Sr. D. Joaquin Fernandez de Madrid, obispo de Tenagra, se dignó conceder 40 dias de Indulgencia por cada acto de los que practiquen los socios en los retiros, segun consta en su decreto de 8 del citado mes y año.

COMISION DIRECTIVA NOMBRADA POR EL CONSEJO.

PRESIDENTE.

PRESBITERO, D. ANDRES DAVIS BRADBURN.

COLEGA.
D. ANTONIO VERTIZ.

COLEGA.
D. JESUS URQUIAGA.

Figure 2.1. Announcement of the new program of spiritual exercises for Society of Saint Vincent de Paul members, established in November of 1857. "Reglamento de los retiros espirituales para los socios de las conferencias de San Vicente de Paul." In ASSVP, CC113, Mexique.

separation of church and state, the suppression of monastic orders, the prohibition of public religious ceremonies, and in December 1860 the establishment of freedom of religion.

To be sure, these decrees were only implemented when the Liberals returned to power, which occurred at the national level in January 1861. Yet the process began earlier in some states. For example, in December 1858 the government of Michoacán forced the Paulist Fathers from their convents in Pátzcuaro and Morelia. Many fled to the nearby safety of the order's seminary in León, but their haven was short-lived as the Vincentian priests were forced to flee León in August 1860 when Liberals took the state of Guanajuato as well.[19] A few lay volunteers were also pulled into the fray. Members of the Toluca conferences sheltered, fed, and clothed penurious priests after their exclaustration.[20] In Morelia, when Liberal soldiers evicted the priests from the Compañía church on December 29, 1858, they tried to arrest the members of a conference that happened to be meeting in one of its rooms; the men were released only after a heated discussion.[21] In September 1860 the Mexican society informed Paris headquarters that "the Civil War has forced the dissolution of some of the provincial chapters and obstructed the progress of others."[22] Years later it reported that the Morelia conferences had been barred from meeting or from entering public hospitals and prisons, and that those in León, Toluca, Tenancingo, Tianquistengo, and Calimaya were totally "uprooted by the whirlwind."[23]

Still, in the fall of 1860 the Superior Council insisted that the Mexico City conferences were doing well. They held their annual assembly that year, published three issues of the quarterly *Boletín*, and printed the *Practical Guide* to orient the volunteers.[24] Although the Council had apparently lost contact with many provincial chapters, it had good news about the capital. The number of active members had risen to 307, from 291 the previous year,[25] and Mexico City's twelve conferences had initiated several new projects. One was the creation of Sunday schools where the pupils received free breakfast, uniforms, and books along with doctrinal instruction. Another was a special *obra de los emigrados* to help "the multitude of refugees who, fleeing the revolutionary troops, take refuge in the Capital, abandoning their homes and properties . . . and daily arriving famished to a place where they have no friends or relatives." The volunteers provided food and lodging to as many as possible, placed the children in *escuelas de beneficencia*, and sought to find

employment for the artisans and domestic servants. In addition, they distributed 5,451 religious books and calendars.[26] Thus, when confronted with a
humanitarian crisis, the men intensified their volunteer efforts.

The "political hurricane"—as the Superior Council officers put it in a letter
to Paris—hit the Mexico City conferences when the Liberals reoccupied the
capital in January 1861.[27] The society rode out the storm by insisting that it
was simply a secular charitable association, totally apolitical and independent from the church. These principles were clearly spelled out in the French
organization's literature that the Mexican society regularly translated and
published. Only the year before, the *Practical Guide* reiterated that the conferences were "entirely laical" and "never engaged in politics under any pre-
text."[28] In case there was any doubt about their relationship to the church,
however, the Superior Council instructed individual chapters to remove the
names of priests from their membership lists—even if the priest was the
original founder—in order to maintain the appearance of independence and
to differentiate the conferences from the prohibited confraternities.[29] By
lying low the society was spared the kind of persecution visited upon its
counterparts in France and Spain, which were outlawed in 1861 and 1868 during those countries' fiercely anticlerical movements.[30]

The Mexican society nonetheless suffered because of its ties to the church
and to the Conservative Party. For if the conferences lay low, members of its
governing body did not. Several Superior Council officers were prominent
Conservative politicians. Foremost among them was President Teófilo Marín,
who in 1859 served as minister of development in the Conservative government and who later served in the Assembly of Notables that arranged to establish the Second Empire under Maximilian. Other conference members who
participated in the Conservative government of 1858–1860 or served the foreign emperor from 1863 to 1867 included Joaquín Velázquez de la Cadena (the
society's founding secretary), Luis Gonzaga Cuevas (its former president),
Juan B. Alamán, Juan Barquera, Manuel Diez de Bonilla, Joaquín García
Icazbalceta, José María Iturbe, Joaquín Mier y Terán, Juan Nepomuceno de
Pereda, José María Rodríguez Villanueva, Antonio Vértiz, and José María
Andrade (brother of the society's founder and publisher of much of its literature).[31] Rather than being conservative ideologues, some of these men may
have been practical politicians who collaborated with the Empire in the hopes
that a monarchy would bring the stability and prosperity that had eluded

Mexico since independence.[32] Yet others made no bones about their antipathy to the Liberals. The Superior Council officers sprinkled their correspondence to Paris with vivid denunciations of the Liberal triumph, which "here, as in other parts of the world" represented "impiety and . . . the anarchic ideas that have caused so much ruin and spilling of tears."[33]

The society feared for its life in the winter of 1861 when Superior Council president Teófilo Marín and vice president Manuel Diez de Bonilla—along with several members of provincial conferences—were imprisoned by the Liberals for their role in the Conservative opposition. The Superior Council named two additional vice presidents just in case: Manuel Urquiaga and José María Rodríguez Villanueva. The men watched as the Liberals confiscated ecclesiastical property, occupied and looted churches and convents, and sent the archbishop and bishops into exile or hiding. They worried about the future of the Vincentian family when the government suppressed monastic orders and removed hospitals and welfare establishments from ecclesiastical control. As the church fell into disarray and the society's leaders remained imprisoned, the Superior Council ordered individual chapters to continue their charitable endeavors but to stop meeting to avoid being charged with conspiracy.[34]

By the spring of 1861 the "political hurricane" seemed to have blown over. In a May 5 decree Francisco Zarco, President Juárez's minister of foreign and internal affairs (*ministro de relaciones y gobernación*), cleared up the doubts about the society's legality and offered it his protection. Some Liberals had apparently interpreted the decrees of February 2 and 28, 1861, which nationalized the remaining ecclesiastical welfare institutions and created a central office to administer Mexico City's eleven hospitals, asylums, and prisons, as prohibiting Catholic charity organizations altogether. But Zarco insisted that it had never been the government's intent to extinguish private associations that assisted the poor. Reviewing the society's bylaws, he found nothing that contradicted the Reform Laws. On the contrary, he concluded that the conferences were "modern" (that is, not like the old confraternities), apolitical, and—although of Catholic origin—totally compatible with religious freedom because they helped the needy without distinguishing between those of different religions. He therefore encouraged the "charitable association" to "persevere in its good works." He gave its members explicit permission to meet openly, taking advantage of the freedom of association guaranteed by the Liberal government, and to visit public prisons, hospitals, and asylums as well as to engage in other philanthropic endeavors. Praising the services that the society "with the most laudable zeal provides to the needy classes," Zarco celebrated "the existence of citizens who, solely motivated by the desire for public good, dedicate themselves to alleviating misery, illuminating intelligence, and fostering virtue in the midst of troubled times."[35]

Thus recognizing the important contributions of the Society of Saint Vincent de Paul, some leading Liberals were willing to allow it to continue its benevolent activities. Indeed, after the government sent a commission to inspect the Hospital del Divino Salvador that the volunteers had managed since 1845, it was so impressed that it left the institution under the society's care and offered it the management of two more asylums: the Hospital de San Hipólito for demented men and the Hospital Nacional de San Lázaro for lepers.[36] Despite the official separation of church and state, the government thus continued to cooperate with the Vincentian conferences—an indication that the gulf between Liberals and Conservatives was not as wide as often assumed.

Yet the calm was only the eye of the storm. The Liberals were divided, and the more anticlerical *exaltados* soon got the upper hand. In an October 1861 letter to the Paris headquarters, the Superior Council vice president, Manuel Urquiaga, lamented that the conferences had stopped meeting, their good works and the *Boletín* were "paralyzed," and "our situation is so anguished that we doubt for our very existence." The radicals in control of Mexico City's government, who "did not trust us and desired our extermination," removed the newly acquired Hospital de San Hipólito from the society's hands and prevented it from taking control of San Lázaro—though it retained the Hospital del Divino Salvador, at least for the time being. Declaring a state of siege in the Mexican capital, its governor prohibited the reunions of the conferences and "clearly manifested his hostility, and even insisted that our Society was illegal."[37]

The society weathered the tempest, though it was visibly diminished during the three years of Liberal rule. By Christmas 1861 Teófilo Marín was back from prison and again sending reports to Paris, signing as president of the Superior Council. In February 1862 he applied for the aggregation of new chapters in Zamora, where "the destructive hand of the revolution respected our conferences." And in April 1863 he assured the French headquarters that the Mexican volunteers were continuing their works of mercy: "In addition to the succor and visiting of the poor, the education of children and other obras, we endeavor to propagate the cult and achieve the sanctification through religious acts of both our conference members and the paupers we aid."[38] The society nonetheless stopped many of its routine activities, such as holding the annual general assembly, publishing the *Boletín*, or compiling comprehensive statistics.

The Vincentian orders also survived this period, despite being the target of Liberal ire. After Congress decreed the exclaustration of the Paulist Fathers on October 22, 1861, many of them continued to work as secular priests, although often apparently underground and without the financial resources the order had previously enjoyed.[39] The Sisters of Charity was spared during this phase of the Reforma by the ever-practical President Juárez, who desired to preserve the smooth functioning of the hospitals and welfare institutions run by "these charitable women."[40] Because of their "important services to the helpless and afflicted," on February 18, 1861, Juárez decreed that the sisters could continue staffing the newly secularized hospitals and asylums. In order to avoid any conflict with the Liberal goal of separating church and state, on May 5, 1861, he clarified that they did so as a "purely civil society" without any "recognized religious character."[41] The Sisters of Charity also received semiofficial support from the Junta de Beneficencia, composed of the wives of leading Liberals (including the spouses of President Juárez, Governor Baz, and Minister Zarco): even while the "exalted" faction was ascendant, the Junta in October 1861 donated a thousand pesos to the organization for its Hospital de Sangre in Mexico City, and in May 1862 the Junta requested that it establish a similar emergency field hospital for war victims in Puebla.[42] When Juárez outlawed nunneries on February 26, 1863, he exempted the Sisters of Charity because of its "devotion to serving humanity."[43] The exemption could also be justified on the grounds that it was an active rather than contemplative order, and because its members were not cloistered and renewed their vows annually, their practices were more compatible with individual liberty than the enclosure and permanent vows of women in other female religious orders. Yet these sisters nonetheless experienced several tense incidents; the most serious, in February 1861, ended with the French government's offering them its protection and the Visitadora Sor Agustina Inza refusing to submit to Mexican authority.[44]

This act of defiance made the sisters many enemies, and rumors of their pending suppression persisted until becoming a reality a decade later. Thus the two religious congregations with which the lay volunteers cooperated, and in whose churches they often met, were severely compromised. Although the men's society enjoyed a respite from Liberal hostility during the Second Empire, it was never again as secure as during its first decade.

The Second Empire, 1863–1867

The return of the Conservatives to Mexico City in June 1863 brought the Sociedad de San Vicente de Paul immediate relief. The conferences again functioned openly under the governments of the Regency (June 1863–June 1864) and then of Emperor Maximilian, who ruled Mexico from July 1864 until his defeat and execution in June 1867. On July 19, 1863, feast day of Saint Vincent—and only one month after the Liberals fled the Mexican capital—the society held its first general assembly in three years and celebrated the glorious "second epoch" that awaited. Yet the Mexico City chapters stagnated during the next four years. In contrast, the Second Empire was a time of rebuilding and expansion in other areas of the Mexican republic.

When the society met in July 1863, its members expected a return to business as usual. They reported on their dismal experiences during the past few years. They named a new treasurer of the Superior Council, Juan B. Alamán, to replace the deceased Manuel Canseco, a founding member of the organization who had kept its books since 1845. In a sign of how safe they felt with the full force of the French supporting the new government, they named as honorary president of the Superior Council the priest Manuel Moreno y Jove, a well-known Liberal opponent who had penned the *Exposición del Cabildo Metropolitano de México contra la tolerancia de cultos* in 1856.[45] Thus the society no longer attempted to maintain its distance from the church or to hide which side it had chosen in the civil war.

By 1864 the organization seemed well on the road to recovery. It resumed publication of the *Boletín* in November. In 1865 it formally adopted the thriving prison ministry as a special obra and translated the French society's manual for forming new chapters, for the first time complete with a printed Spanish-language form for submitting statistics to the Superior Council in

Mexico City. In 1866 it published a Catholic almanac for distribution among its members and clients. Although no new conferences were established in 1863, a flurry of foundations followed after the bishops of Querétaro and Oaxaca and the archbishop of Guadalajara—all of whom occupied honorary positions in the society—encouraged the *obra de las conferencias* in their respective dioceses.[46] By 1865 the national membership had ascended to 791 active volunteers and 347 honorary members, a category that now included subscribers. Indeed, the Second Empire witnessed the highest annual rate of chapter formation in the society's history.[47]

Even as Liberals intensified the war against Conservatives, conference foundations proceeded at a steady pace, with eleven created in 1864, nine each in 1865 and 1866, and the last one in January 1867, a month before Maximilian fled to Querétaro. The thirty new chapters approximately doubled the size of the organization (table 2.2). Some were founded by laymen, such as the chapter in Orizaba (Veracruz) established by a "long-time member" in 1864. Others were founded by Vincentian priests, as in Tulancingo (Hidalgo) and Coatepec de las Harinas (Guerrero) in 1865.[48] The majority were in the central states of Jalisco (eight), Puebla (six), Michoacán (two) Guanajuato (three), and San Luis Potosí (two). Indeed, the growth in the city of Guadalajara (Jalisco) was impressive enough to warrant the creation of the society's fifth Particular Council in 1864. The organization also spread into areas of Mexico where it had never before had a presence: not only in Veracruz to the east and Guerrero to the south, but to the far north where a branch sprang up in Monterrey (Nuevo León) in January 1865.

These examples show that the society was establishing a foothold in small towns as well as in major cities. In addition, some conferences were reaching beyond their urban neighborhoods to undertake rural ministries. For example, the Conferencia del Sagrado Corazón in León founded several small schools among the indigenous residents of nearby haciendas and rancherias; the chapter president reported with pride how the ragged children in white pajamas and sandals—so poor they are "nearly naked and wearing only a few strips of leather on their feet"—were making rapid progress in learning the Christian doctrine.[49]

The society also continued expanding its social class base. Thus in 1865 a group of master artisans created a new conference in Mexico City dedicated to instructing their apprentices and providing work for impoverished journeymen. Its twenty members included carpenters, shoemakers, silversmiths, and a painter, blacksmith, tinsmith, and upholsterer.[50]

The new chapters prospered despite the increased warfare. In the Bahío region of central Mexico—where particularly violent fighting was accompanied by famine and epidemics of typhus, dysentery, and small pox—the volunteers organized emergency services to help the refugees who streamed into the cities seeking food, medical care, and safety. In Morelia, where the only hospital was dedicated to treating military casualties, the four Vincentian conferences divided the city among themselves into quadrants where they took charge of aiding the hungry and sick. By November 1864 they had spent over 4,000 pesos providing spiritual and corporal aid to 500 sick paupers, burying the 100 who died, and then providing corn and *metates* for making tortillas to feed the orphans left behind. In Guadalajara "the generalized misery caused by the war and concurrent harvest failures" moved many "pious persons" to join the city's seven chapters. With membership growing to 252 active volunteers, the Guadalajara conferences inaugurated several new institutions to attend the needy: a cocina económica staffed by the Sisters of Charity, a pharmaceutical dispensary (*botica*) to supply medicines to the poor, and a laundry and sewing workshop to provide work for impoverished women. (The latter provoked a reprimand from the Superior Council because the bylaws prohibited the male conferences from patronizing youths of the opposite sex.)[51] Society members also served on Guadalajara's Junta de Caridad that coordinated the relief efforts.[52]

Yet Mexico City did not share in these trends. In December 1864 the *Boletín* bemoaned the "despondence and tepidity of the conferences of the capital, so different from the vibrant activity of the chapters in the provinces. In Morelia, Guadalajara, and other areas the dispersed volunteers make great efforts to meet and reorganize, while in the capital, which should be like the heart that communicates energy to distant points, the spirit decreases, activities flag, ties are loosened, and perhaps a complete dissolution is near."[53] Individual chapter meetings were poorly attended, the obra of the religious retreats had ended with the expulsion of the Paulist Fathers from their convent, and the *obra de los militares* failed to take hold because of the instability in the army. The society held its annual assembly in 1864 and 1865 but not in 1866 or 1867. Again, as in other times of crisis, the publication of the *Boletín* was suspended; the last issue appeared in May 1865.[54]

The society's decline in Mexico City reflects its members' many competing preoccupations. Because they were located in the seat of imperial power, the capital's volunteers had numerous opportunities to be involved with the new government. Some of them were called upon to help improve the system of public welfare. Thus in July 1863 the government of the Regency commissioned Joaquín García Icazbalceta, the wealthy landowner and scholar who had been a member of Mexico City's conference of Nuestra Señora de Monserrate since at least 1857, to investigate the state of the capital's prisons and welfare establishments. He presented his beautifully bound report to Emperor Maximilian on July 18, 1864, shortly after the archduke's entrance into Mexico City. The foreword was written by fellow society member José María Andrade. And a large part of it was based on the investigation of another Vincentian volunteer, Tomás Gardida, president of the Conferencia de la Santísima Trinidad and founder of the society's lending library in 1858. In his position as alderman in the imperial City Council, Gardida reported extensively on the condition of the Mexico City Poor House and arranged for the Sisters of Charity to run that asylum in October 1863. We know about García Icazbalceta's *Informe sobre los establecimientos de beneficencia y corrección de esta Capital* because it was published posthumously half a century later and became an indispensible source for historians of social welfare, and his connection with Gardida emerged from my study of the Poor House.[55] These examples reveal a network of Vincentian volunteers who, working in concert with the Paulist Fathers and Sisters of Charity, collaborated with the imperial government as experts in dealing with disease and poverty. In addition, a few society members continued to supervise the Hospital del Divino Salvador, although the day-to-day administration was in the hands of the Sisters of Charity.

Other men were, however, distracted from their charitable activities by political developments. Many of them were busy serving the government of Maximilian, and after a short honeymoon, protecting it from the aggressive assault waged by Liberals against the foreign emperor. As the struggle intensified, they evidently neglected the work of the conferences. Indeed, Superior Council president Teófilo Marín was so closely allied with the Empire that he had to flee into exile when it was defeated in July 1867; he died in Havana of yellow fever four months later.[56] No wonder, since he remained at the head of the organization throughout these trying times, that it floundered at its center. No wonder as well that when the Liberals regained power during the Restored Republic, the conferences of Saint Vincent de Paul remained suspect.

The Restored Republic, 1867–1876

Finally emerging as the winners, the triumphant Liberals resumed their anti-clerical reform project. The first two years of the Restored Republic unleashed a new set of attacks on the conferences. On July 1, 1867—immediately after returning to Mexico City—the government wrested control of the Hospital del Divino Salvador from the society's hands, finally banishing it from the asylum it had managed for twenty-two years. In the state of Jalisco, on July 3, 1868, the legislature outlawed the association, and in León authorities closed at least one of the society's elementary schools. Yet the organization accepted the new restrictions and quickly bounced back. The Superior Council promptly turned the women's mental asylum over to the municipality, according to Vincentian sources, in excellent shape and with more than 4,000 pesos in its coffers.[57] The Guadalajara branch temporarily changed its name to Sociedad de Misericordia and submitted a new set of bylaws to state officials in order to continue functioning in a different guise until the ban was lifted the following year.[58] The Liberals, for their part, having established the principle that public welfare institutions should be secular, left the volunteers alone to continue their private charitable activities. Indeed, after nine years of Liberal rule the society would be larger—and in many ways stronger—than it had been at the end of the Second Empire.

The organization's health during Juárez's last presidency (July 1867–July 1872) is perhaps not surprising, given his pragmatism; in his desire to reestablish peace after the divisive civil war, Juárez was reluctant to enforce many Reform Laws or to take reprisals against his Conservative enemies. During his term, the society founded thirty-one new conferences, and membership more than doubled from the 791 active volunteers of 1865 to 1,655 in 1871 (table 2.1).[59] They were backed by more supporters than ever before. The rise in the number of aspiring members—to an average of 262 each year from 1869 through 1871—shows that the society continued to recruit a new generation. The Mexico City chapters recovered from their "decadence," with active membership rising from 134 in 1868 to 275 in 1869 and then holding approximately steady until 1871 (fig. 2.2). The organization's expansion was even more robust in the provinces (table 2.2), particularly in central Mexico, which in 1868 added its seventh Particular Council, in Puebla (table 2.3). In addition, the first branches were founded in the states of Yucatán, Zacatecas, Durango, Morelos, and Tlaxcala. The society now counted a few rural conferences,[60] and it continued to incorporate members from the lower-middle classes: in 1870, for example, a new chapter in Puebla was composed entirely of bakers, and several chapters in Toluca and Tulancingo were composed mostly of artisans.[61]

As in other periods of institutional health, the Superior Council produced regular reports. This time, instead of the *Boletín*, it published the *Noticia* annually from 1869 to 1871 and the *Memoria* in 1872 (fig. 2.3). Despite year-to-year fluctuations, their statistics show an overall expansion of most activities since the 1850s (table 2.4). Fundraising and expenditures registered a steady increase from 1868 to 1871. The home visits to needy families rose to 712 in 1870. The number of dying assisted and cadavers buried also rose substantially. So did the number of "apprentices patronized" and, especially, "students patronized/children taught." The society apparently attempted to revive the obra of arranging religious marriages and legitimizing children, although there was a steep drop in these activities after the peak year of 1869. Still, only

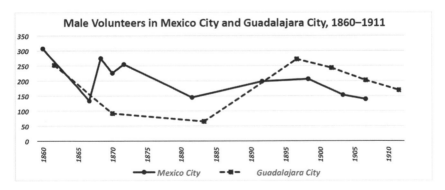

Figure 2.2. Based on statistics in De Dios, *Historia de la familia vicentina*, 1:535–36; Sociedad, *Noticia* (1867–1870), Sociedad, *Memoria* (1871), Sociedad, *Boletín* (April 1893, 102–10; April 1898, 100; May 1901, 144; August 1902, 179–82; February 1909, 34–46; March 1909, 69); and Sociedad Guadalajara, *Boletín* (December 1911, 200–203).

prison visiting had decreased since the 1850s, although it is difficult to quantify because the new report forms combined the category of "workers/ prisoners instructed." It is significant that the volunteers continued visiting hospitals and prisons at all (unclear from the statistics, but confirmed in the texts[62]), for it shows that the Vincentian conferences did not completely withdraw from public institutions despite losing control of the Hospital del Divino Salvador. The reports also refer to other activities that are not listed in the statistics, such as sponsoring Catholic elementary schools and Sunday schools, and organizing group spiritual exercises and visits to venerate the host of the Santísimo Sacramento in local churches. Some of these events were quite large: at one retreat in 1871 some 1,300 people allegedly partook of the Eucharist, a sign of the continued strengthening of the Catholic revival.[63]

The society's expansion appears to have slowed under the more radical President Sebastián Lerdo de Tejada. Ruling as interim and then as elected president from the time Juárez died in July 1872 until he was ousted by a coup in November 1876, Lerdo incorporated the Reform Laws into the constitution

Cuadro Sinóptico de la Sociedad de S. Vicente de Paul en la República Mexicana, EL AÑO 1869.

CONSEJOS Y CONFERENCIAS.	Miembros activos.	Miembros de honor.	Miembros honorarios.	Miembros aspirantes.	Familias socorridas.	Matrimonios realizados.	Hijos legitimados.	Enfermos socorridos.	Aprendices patrocinados.	Obreros y presos instruidos.	Moribundos asistidos.	Cadáveres sepultados.	INGRESOS.	EGRESOS.
Consejo Superior de la República	15	1	0	0	0	0	0	0	0	0	0	0	$ 212	197
Idem particular de México	275	1	13	19	192	6	6	140	72	40	0	0	10108	9282
Idem idem de Toluca	61	0	6	3	30	0	0	12	6	0	0	0	795	662
Idem idem de Leon	308	0	158	51	53	4	1	94	5	1278	43	51	738	730
Idem idem de Zamora	223	0	16	72	76	327	705	111	17	90	176	30	1170	1017
Idem idem de Guadalajara	73	0	34	11	35	0	0	2	0	800	0	0	867	853
Idem idem de Puebla	176	0	39	23	105	2	1	544	0	1	14	18	3493	3593
Conferencia de la villa de la Encarnacion	34	4	42	6	21	3	0	22	3	0	0	0	86	834
Idem de Jalapa	31	0	3	7	16	3	0	58	2	0	0	0	418	359
Idem de San Juan del Rio	23	0	0	0	36	0	0	0	0	0	0	0	468	439
Idem de Tulancingo	12	0	36	0	4	0	0	0	2	0	0	0	210	209
Idem de Tianguistenco	29	0	46	9	4	2	1	0	0	0	0	0	133	133
Idem de Irapuato	12	0	0	4	2	0	0	0	93	179	0	0	112	112
Idem de Orizava	24	0	6	0	8	0	0	6	0	0	0	0	685	684
Idem de Texcoco	19	0	9	5	12	0	0	0	0	0	0	0	309	320
Idem de Cotija	60	0	2	78	27	0	0	16	0	0	0	0	2301	1300
Idem de Mérida	37	3	88	21	30	1	0	79	0	0	0	0	2004	1834
TOTALES	1412	9	498	309	651	348	714	1084	200	1888	233	99	$ 24104	22058

BALANCE.

INGRESOS......... $ 24,104
EGRESOS.......... ,, 22,058
DIFERENCIA ...... $ 2,046

Figure 2.3. Chart summarizing the membership and activities of the Society of Saint Vincent de Paul, 1869. Sociedad, *Noticia* (1869), "Cuadro Sinóptico." In Rapports Nationaux, 1869–1952, ASSVP, Mexique.

and enacted enabling legislation to put them into effect. Notable among these was the Ley Orgánica of December 14, 1874, which, as part of a list of anti-clerical measures, prohibited religious instruction in public institutions, banned religious acts outside of churches, and suppressed the order of the Sisters of Charity.[64] As in other difficult times, the society stopped publishing its reports and may not have held its annual assembly in 1873. Another hint of trouble in 1874 is that the Particular Council of León cited its concern about the "decay of its conferences" when promoting a special set of spiritual exercises for its members.[65]

Yet the situation could not have been that bad, because the society continued growing. It founded new conferences every year of Lerdo's presidency, for a total of twenty-one foundations. Indeed, the rate of chapter formation was only slightly lower than under his predecessor: five per year compared with some six per year under President Juárez. In 1872 the society was solvent enough to contribute 1,750 francs to the celebrations of Pope Pius IX's twenty-fifth jubilee. In 1874 it created a Particular Council in Mérida (Yucatán), where in only six years the city had developed sufficient strength (with five chapters) to support the society's eighth municipal governing body and the only one outside of central Mexico.[66] The organization was thus broadening as well as deepening its national presence. It was also continuing to become more socially heterogeneous: an application for the aggregation of a new conference in Mexico City's Barrio de los Angeles in 1874 included not only artisans but also some farmworkers listed as *agricultores*, *jornaleros*, and *labradores*,[67] and conferences were established on two haciendas—perhaps for the first time—in the state of Guanajuato in 1873 and 1874.[68]

By April 1875 the *Boletín* (now in its "third epoch") had resumed publication with a long report on the general assembly held in December 1874. The society characterized 1875, when it consecrated itself to the Sacred Heart of Jesus, as a year of notable expansion.[69] It was also a year of sadness and anger for pious Mexicans because in January the members of the Sisters of Charity were expelled from their houses. As they made their way into exile, thronged on their route by tearful crowds and sparking riots in some areas, the sisters were accompanied by José María Andrade, who explained that "since my brother brought them, I will lead them away."[70] The suppression of this member of the Vincentian family was particularly galling. If anything, however, this "sacrilege" boosted the volunteers' resolve to continue their work. With 2,824 active members in 1875, the society's membership reached a peak that would never again be equaled (table 2.1). Although its fundraising and expenditures had declined somewhat since 1871, it spent a respectable 23,793 pesos on good works—far more than during the prosperous Second Empire—and assisted more needy families (714) than in any previous year for which statistics are available (table 2.4). The Restored Republic was thus the high point in the society's history.

The Porfiriato, 1876–1911

The Porfiriato should have been the heyday of the Society of Saint Vincent de Paul in Mexico. It was an auspicious time for Catholic organizations because, although President Porfirio Díaz left the anticlerical Reform Laws on the books, he implemented few of them. During the Pax Porfiriana that characterized his long reign, the number of priests increased; some religious orders returned; and parochial schools, pious associations, religious trade unions, and other Catholic organizations multiplied throughout Mexico.[71] The recuperation of the church was particularly notable after Díaz assumed his second term in 1884. It was also an auspicious time for private philanthropy. Contrary to the Liberal propaganda about how public assistance supplanted private and religious charity after 1861, the Porfirian years were in fact halcyon days for both. Recognizing its limitations, the government openly welcomed the contributions of the private sector. Philanthropy blossomed as benevolent associations founded hospitals, asylums, and schools to supplement the meager resources of the government.[72] Contradicting these trends, however, the male conferences stagnated in the late nineteenth century and first decade of the twentieth.

The first years of the Porfiriato were particularly difficult. The number of active volunteers slid from the peak of 2,824 in 1875 to only 1,317 six years later, a 54 percent decline (table 2.1). The society's leaders were painfully aware of the organization's problems. In 1877 the Superior Council president, José María Rodríguez Villanueva, lamented that "unfortunately the Mexican conferences, in past years so prosperous, today . . . have decayed considerably to the point that we fear for their existence, due to the notable and gradual diminution of the membership."[73]

The situation improved when a new visitor of the Congregación de la

Misión arrived in 1882. Under the leadership of Father Félix Mariscal, the pace of new conference foundations picked up, rising from two in 1882 to four in 1883 to nine in 1884. The state of Veracruz provided particularly fertile ground: with nine conferences established between 1876 and 1884, it warranted a Particular Council to govern the chapters in the city of Orizaba by 1884. National reports from 1885 and 1887 showed substantial increases in the number of volunteers, money spent, and charitable activities. The elementary schools were a favorite obra, with the records listing 1,707 "students patronized/children taught" in 1887—a figure that would rise to 2,053 in 1896 (table 2.4).

Yet the society was never again as robust as during the Restored Republic. The number of volunteers fluctuated between 1,433 and 1,672 for the next two decades. The "scarcity of socios," the poor attendance at conference sessions, and the dearth of young male volunteers became recurring refrains.[74] Although the organization managed to publish the *Boletín* regularly, it mostly reprinted the French society's *Bulletin*. When Mexican news was included, it was largely from Mexico City—an indication that the Superior Council had lost contact with many chapters outside the capital.[75]

The problems did not stem from lack of leadership. From 1886 to 1894 the society was led by Joaquín García Icazbalceta, longtime member, who devoted himself energetically to reinvigorating the organization (fig. 2.4). During his nine-year presidency, the Superior Council produced a flurry of documentation. Fifty-six conferences were established and sent their applications for aggregation to the French headquarters. In 1888 the society added two more Particular Councils for the cities of San Luis Potosí and Querétaro. Reflecting its growing presence in the states of Jalisco and Yucatán, the society created its first Central Councils—the governing bodies that oversaw a wide region beyond one city—in Guadalajara in 1889 and Mérida in 1895 (table 2.3). Several chapters adopted new projects during this period, such as the *obra del aguinaldo* that gave Christmas presents to impoverished children and the *cajas de ahorros*, mutual savings funds that promoted saving for future needs.[76] The Particular Council of Mexico City also recommitted itself to catechizing, training, and placing artisans and servants by formally adopting the *patronato de los aprendices* in 1889.[77]

García Icazbalceta nonetheless failed to halt the society's decline. Clearly frustrated with the limited results of his efforts, in 1891 he deplored the weak commitment of many members who joined the conferences only to abandon

Figure 2.4. Posthumous portrait of Joaquín García Icazbalceta (1825–1894), Society of Saint Vincent de Paul member and Superior Council president. According to his son, García Icazbalceta was too modest to have allowed himself to be portrayed wearing these medals during his lifetime. Oil painting by Santiago Rebull, reproduced in García Pimentel y Elguero, *Don Joaquín García Icazbalceta*. Reprinted courtesy of the Library of Congress.

them soon thereafter, or who remained on the books but did not participate regularly. He was particularly troubled by the "deplorable" situation of some chapters that, even with money in their coffers, could not adopt new families because they lacked enough volunteers to visit them.[78] When he died in November 1894, the society had fewer active members—despite the new chapter foundations—than when he started: only 1,536 compared with 1,647 in 1885 (table 2.1). By September 1895 only 121 chapters remained of the 218 that had been founded during the past half century (table 2.2). As many conferences disappeared, the society lost its presence in the northern states of Hidalgo, Durango, Tamaulipas, and Nuevo León, as well as in the southern states of Morelos, Guerrero, and Campeche (see map 1).

Ecclesiastical officials made valiant efforts to stem the tide. Although priests were not supposed to found the nominally secular men's conferences, they sometimes did.[79] More often, they simply tried to provide

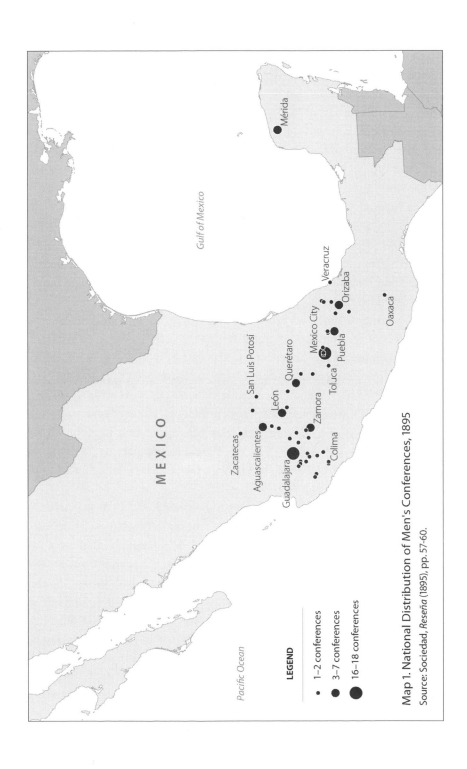

Map 1. National Distribution of Men's Conferences, 1895

Source: Sociedad, *Reseña* (1895), pp. 57–60.

encouragement and support. In Yucatán, for example, Bishop Cresencio Carrillo y Ancona in 1886 fostered the formation of the "indispensable" Vincentian conferences that worked to remedy "the most general, urgent, and peremptory needs of each city, town, and hamlet," especially in remote places where there was a shortage of priests.[80] In 1896, when Mexico's top ecclesiastical hierarchy met in the Fifth Provincial Council, they likewise issued an appeal for the clergy to promote the conferences and for the faithful to join.[81]

The Superior Council was able to report a few bright spots at the turn of the century. So many new conferences—forty-two—were founded in the southeastern state of Tabasco that in 1901 a Central Council was established to govern them.[82] Growth in Aguascalientes and Colima was sufficient to warrant new Particular Councils in those cities (table 2.3).[83] Yucatán's conferences were also thriving. Mérida's volunteers supported a large number of schools, with the elementary schools enrolling five hundred children and the night schools for apprentices enrolling four hundred adults. The *obra de instrucción religiosa* was flourishing in the state of Jalisco, where in Guadalajara City over a thousand children were catechized and organized to participate in monthly retreats. The chapter in the Atemajac textile factory on the outskirts of the city obtained many conversions among the workers and brought back into the fold one man who had not set foot in a church for twenty years. And in Mexico City the religious exercises and *obra de la Adoración del Santísimo* were thriving, thereby "maintaining the spirit of piety alive among the members of the Conferences."[84]

The respite was brief, however. Table 2.4 shows a significant drop in most of the volunteers' good works by 1908. Although the budget continued to increase, it may largely be because the sum is not corrected for the high inflation of the period. The dearth of documents for the first decade of the twentieth century further suggests that the organization was floundering. In Mexico City and Guadalajara—the two cities with the best available statistics—the membership plummeted. In Mexico City the retrenchment was fairly steady, with the number of active volunteers falling from 255 in 1871 to 206 in 1898 and 139 in 1908. In the city of Guadalajara, where membership grew substantially in the 1890s, the contraction came in the next decade, with the number of active members dropping from 272 in 1897 to 169 in 1911 (fig. 2.2).[85] These declines were partially counterbalanced by the expansion of conferences in other areas. Yet, nationwide, the organization not only failed to keep up with the dramatic population growth of the period but ended the Porfiriato with far fewer members than during the Restored Republic.

Conclusion

At first glance, the decline of the Society of Saint Vincent de Paul in the late nineteenth century fits the standard historical narrative about the weakening of Catholic organizations after the Liberal Reforma. Upon closer inspection, however, it contradicts key aspects of that story. The society's progress between 1855 and 1876—precisely during the Reform Wars and the Restored Republic—challenges the conventional wisdom, and its contraction during the Pax Porfiriana, just as other philanthropic and religious associations blossomed, begs explanation.

The male society and its sister organization that is the subject of the next chapter were only two of the many lay groups that emerged during the supposedly dark period of the Reforma. Numerous devotional associations also flourished, such as the old Congregaciones Marianas that were resurrected in 1871 and the newer Vela Perpetua, founded in Michoacán in 1840, which gained an increasing national presence during the 1860s and '70s.[86] The Sociedad Católica de México and its female counterpart (which overlapped with the Vincentian conferences by founding Catholic schools and teaching the catechism to children, prisoners, and hospital patients) experienced a remarkable expansion after being established in December 1868 and February 1869, respectively.[87] These lay organizations that operated semi-independently of the church, and thus "under the radar"—both of Liberals and of historians—followed a different trajectory from the official institution: they grew while it shriveled.

The lay groups represented a response by both the church and the laity to contemporary circumstances. The ecclesiastical hierarchy reached out to the faithful after a series of setbacks such as the prohibition of confraternities in 1859, the establishment of freedom of religion in 1860, the nationalization of the remaining ecclesiastical welfare institutions in 1861, the suppression of conventual orders in 1859 to 1861 (male) and 1863 (female), and the defeat of the Empire in 1867 that left the institution in the unenviable position of having functioned as the "enemy within."

The Pastoral Instruction issued by the archbishops of Mexico, Michoacán, and Guadalajara on March 19, 1875, in reaction to the crippling Organic Law of December 1874, reveals the degree to which the church relied on the laity during these troubled times.[88] The archbishops explicitly recommended that parish priests "multiply the conferences" of Saint Vincent de Paul in cities and towns throughout Mexico to help it provide religious education and poor relief. As an incentive for lay people to support these worthy "charitable associations," the instruction offered eighty days of indulgence for joining or contributing. Since eighty more days were granted for each act of mercy as well as for attending the general assemblies, these spiritual benefits could quickly accumulate. Recognizing the potentially dangerous political climate, the archbishops sought to reassure the timid that it was safe to volunteer by explaining, "No law . . . prohibits you from participating in such a grand obra and, on the contrary, the Constitution of the Republic formally recognizes the right of all Mexicans to associate for any honest and licit purpose. Why not, then, make use of this liberty to favor the poor of Jesus Christ?" Moreover, as set forth in their bylaws, the conferences "are entirely secular with respect to their organization and administration" because clerics "do not interfere with their funding or activities" and "only exercise the functions they perform for all the faithful, namely exhorting and advising them to keep the spirit of faith alive." Finally, the archbishops insisted that the organizations' publications "cannot offend any public functionary" because, instead of producing publically disseminated periodicals, they "only print occasional reports concerning the Conferences themselves, for the edification and stimulation of their members." The Vincentian lay groups were thus a central part of the ecclesiastical strategy to recover from the new restrictions.

As devout men rose to defend their church and faith, they breathed new life into the lay movement. The organization had its ups and downs during the chaotic years of the Reforma, Second Empire, and Restored Republic, with 1859–1861 and 1868 being the most difficult and 1863–1866 the easiest. Yet the general trend was unmistakably upward. By 1876 the society was larger and more broadly national in scope than it had been in 1855. During these two decades, it quintupled its membership from 567 active volunteers to 2,824. It founded 105 new conferences, fully half (54) during the Restored Republic alone. The available documents do not specify how long each conference lasted, and some evidently folded during periods of crisis. The society's overall expansion is nonetheless evident, not only in the statistics on membership figures and chapter foundations, but also in the number of ailing families, hospital patients, and prisoners aided, students and workers instructed, money raised and spent, geographical coverage, and new governing councils established.

Its vigor during the time period when Catholic organizations supposedly suffered mortal blows is also evident in the variety of people who supported it. The society may have begun with a small circle of Catholic activists in Mexico City, but it had branched out considerably since the 1840s. To be sure, the conferences were almost always located in cities and towns. Even there the society's membership did not include the urban poor who were its clients, since it only admitted individuals who were in a position to give aid to others rather than to need aid themselves.[89] It also largely excluded Indians, who, according to the fiftieth-anniversary review, "make up two thirds of our population" but are "incapable of participating in this sort of activity" because of their residence in rural areas. (Nonetheless, in Jalisco Don Inocencio Yxlahuac, "an elderly Indian with lots of money," served as second vice president of the Cocula chapter in 1892.[90]) Yet the *Reseña del Quincuagenario de la Sociedad* was not entirely wrong when it boasted that in urban areas the society's members and benefactors "represented all the social classes from the magistrate to the humble artisan."[91] It included not only gentlemen from the old elite families but also professionals, businessmen, shopkeepers, artisans, and occasionally manual laborers. In Guadalajara, factory owners and merchants were prominent from the start.[92] The society's appeal to men from many walks of life shows the continuing strength of Catholicism in post-Reforma Mexico—even among the new industrial and commercial classes. Its growing base in the lower-middle and middle classes also challenges the view that the split between Liberals and Conservatives followed the lines of social class, for Catholic militants (as well as Liberals) could be found in every social group.[93]

The society was particularly strong outside of Mexico City. With branches scattered in twelve states by 1875, it had expanded its national presence (table 2.2). There were certainly some regions where the society barely penetrated, such as the rural areas, and others where it remained weak, as in the far north and the deep south. Its core was in the central states of Mexico,

Guanajuato, Michoacán, Jalisco, and Puebla, where seven of the eight Particular Councils were located. Indeed, two-thirds of the conferences founded between 1856 and 1876 were in those five states alone, adding to the presence that the society had already developed there during its first decade.

In his study of the Catholic restoration of the late nineteenth century, Manuel Ceballos Ramírez noted its strength in the central region of Mexico that extended from Puebla to Zacatecas.[94] The history of the Society of Saint Vincent de Paul shows that the construction of Catholic structures in this area had begun long before, when the organization spread from Mexico City to San Miguel de Allende and Puebla in 1848, and that the foundation continued to be built throughout the Reforma and Restored Republic. By the 1860s the society born in the Mexican capital had been upstaged by the provinces. Although the Superior Council was so capital-centric that it designated the provincial chapters *foráneas* (literally, "foreign"), the stagnation of the Mexico City conferences shows that the organization's center of gravity had shifted to central Mexico. In the 1870s Yucatán also became a major growth pole for the society, as did Veracruz in the 1880s and Tabasco in the 1890s. This expansion in the peripheral regions shows that the religious resurgence was not restricted to the well-known Catholic heartland.[95] These contradictory regional trends serve as a reminder of the dangers of writing the history of Mexico on the basis of the capital city. They also suggest that the Catholic revival did not proceed evenly throughout the country.

The new geographical makeup was not the only feature that distinguished the post-Reforma society from the fledgling organization of the first decade. Because of the rupture of church and state, it had been forced to abandon some of its public functions. Responding to the loss of Catholic influence in public schools and institutions, the volunteers increasingly concentrated on shaping the values of future generations by founding their own schools as well as providing doctrinal and moral instruction for young workers and children. They still visited public hospitals and prisons, though at a lower rate than in earlier years. After 1867, however, the society no longer participated as an active partner with the local government by advising on welfare initiatives or managing the Hospital del Divino Salvador. It no longer organized highly visible relief efforts, as it did from 1860 to 1864 when warfare, famine, and epidemics caused widespread suffering. The volunteers had thus lost the prominent public role they played in earlier decades. Consequently, they focused their efforts on the characteristic religious and charitable activities of the Vincentian conferences, which flourished during the Restored Republic as never before. Moreover, some of the projects that they took up in the new climate, such as training and educating artisans, pointed them more in the direction of Social Catholicism with its emphasis on improving the lives of workers.

Yet the years between 1867 and 1876 were the society's swan song. After thriving during the difficult period of the Liberal Reforma, the male conferences stagnated during the Porfiriato. Although their geographic coverage expanded into a few new areas, many of the old chapters disappeared or lost members. As the twentieth century opened, the organization barely held its own—and indeed ended the first decade with fewer members than when the Porfiriato began. This pattern is perplexing because it coincided with the government's rapprochement with the church that would make life easier for the volunteers. It also ran counter to the continued growth of other Catholic voluntary associations as well as of private philanthropic groups during the late nineteenth century.

It was not that the demand for Vincentian charity had lessened. On the contrary, the condition of the Mexican poor deteriorated despite the Porfirian economic boom. Although new industries brought phenomenal wealth for some, the benefits did not trickle down to the masses. The population exploded without concomitant job creation, and the expansion of commercial agriculture caused many villagers to lose their lands. Flocking to the cities, desperate country people faced unemployment and punishing inflation of basic food prices. Traditional almsgiving was insufficient to meet these needs, and—despite the government's self-serving rhetoric about providing for the poor—the Porfirian state decreased its provision of welfare at the very time that indigence was growing.[96] Public services were extremely limited even in Mexico City, the nation's crown jewel with numerous beneficence institutions supervised by a central welfare bureau (the Junta de Beneficencia). In 1879, for example, the capital's nine hospitals and public asylums barely served 12,721 people—a very small number in comparison with the city's approximately 250,000 residents, a large portion of whom lived in dire poverty.[97] In subsequent decades, municipal spending on social assistance declined while the capital's population increased to some 470,000 by 1910.[98] The educational system was similarly wanting.

Despite the government's desire to provide universal elementary education, in 1882 only one-fourth of Mexico City's school-age children attended public or private schools.[99] The situation was much worse outside the capital, leaving an open field of action for the conferences in provincial cities and towns where the government had a much weaker presence.[100]

The need to bolster Catholicism was also urgent. By the late nineteenth century the Mexican church was openly competing with Protestants and spiritists.[101] Church fathers considered Freemasonry and the materialistic positivist philosophy as additional threats to their religion. According to the Vincentian analysis, social problems were increasing because of the weakening of Catholic values since the Liberals separated church and state, instituted civil marriage, and "threw God out of the public schools."[102] The growing gap between rich and poor, recurring peasant uprisings, and the spread of socialist and anarchist ideologies raised the specter of class conflict that Catholic reformers so abhorred.

The ills of the modern world likewise demanded the moralizing influence of the volunteers. At their general assemblies, ecclesiastical dignitaries exhorted society members to increase their efforts to combat the "egoism, indifference, and impious press" of the day."[103] They decried the "terrible . . . cancer of modern society, which is luxury in all its forms, and the . . . insatiable thirst for pleasure and diversion" that "separates us from the path of true virtue." They lamented the corruption of Mexico's "simple and pure" country people drawn to the cities where they were exposed to vice, especially in the "*cantinas* and *billares*, true temples of sensuality."[104] As the archdeacon of the Guadalajara Cathedral melodramatically warned in 1895, "The conferences of which you are members not only have a religious goal, but also one that is eminently social and, I might add, extremely patriotic. Yes, because . . . you work to resolve the tremendous problems of our times, which are already agitating the old continent, especially the choice between peace and good harmony or the war without mercy between proletarian and patron, capital and worker, poor and rich, property and communism, between chaos and nothingness or the existence of an orderly society, threatened as never before with dissolution and death."[105] These alarmist warnings nonetheless failed to energize the male organization, even though the Vincentian method of establishing personal bonds with the ailing poor was more relevant than ever.

In their diminished state, the male conferences were unable to meet the challenges facing their communities. As the 1896 *Boletín* reported with chagrin, in Mexico City the society had to turn paupers away because "the sixteen conferences that today exist, are absolutely insufficient to attend to the multiple needs of the numerous destitute inhabitants of the capital, augmented by families from all over the Republic . . . who come to us, taking advantage of the railroads that are uniting the circumference with the center of the Nation, to the point that the needy population has nearly doubled in the past few years, causing sadness for the conferences which are unable to extend assistance to the many families who request it and who remain indefinitely inscribed on our lists of those waiting to be adopted."[106] In subsequent years—even as Mexico's poverty grew—the organization's leaders lamented the shrinking number and growing apathy of the volunteers, the penury of the chapters, and their resulting inability to provide for "the necessities of our poor brethren, which increase each day."[107]

To be sure, a small core of faithful male volunteers continued working to defend Catholicism while providing social services. Yet the Porfirian Society of Saint Vincent de Paul was a pale shadow of its former self. What had happened was that the momentum of the lay movement had passed to the Ladies of Charity, which quickly eclipsed the men's organization with more members, more chapters, and far more people assisted each year. As Mexican women took up the banner of Vincentian charity, pious men increasingly left the work of caring for the needy to their wives, sisters, mothers, and daughters. It was consequently the women's association that follows the expansive trend of Catholic lay organizations in the late nineteenth century. Taken together, the experiences of the male and female conferences demonstrate the successful survival—indeed growth—of Catholic institutions despite the Liberal Reforma. They also show that the Catholic restoration of the late nineteenth century cannot be understood without paying close attention to what Mexican women were doing.

3.

The Mobilization of Women

IN THE LATE nineteenth century thousands of pious laywomen moved quietly through Mexican cities and towns carrying out works of mercy. Leaving their comfortable neighborhoods, the volunteers entered the homes of the ailing poor bearing baskets of food and clothing. They cared for the sick; offered solace to the dying; assisted the elderly, blind, and orphaned; taught catechism to destitute children; and arranged for baptisms, first communions, and marriages. They went into public prisons, hospitals, and factories to help—and proselytize—the inmates, patients, and workers. They organized community celebrations of religious holidays. They took to the streets to solicit charitable contributions. They founded their own institutions, especially schools and clinics. They substituted for the nuns who were expelled during the Reforma and assisted the beleaguered priests who remained.

The Association of Ladies of Charity of Saint Vincent de Paul was one of the great success stories of Porfirian Mexico. Yet, though a familiar sight to its contemporaries, the organization left an even fainter trace in the historical record than the much smaller male branch of the Vincentian lay movement—so faint, in fact, that my initial attempt to reconstruct their history led me to list an incorrect founding date in my book on the Mexico City Poor House, for I mistakenly believed that the women's group was established at the behest of Empress Charlotte during the Second Empire—when it was in fact founded by Paulist priests and predated her arrival in Mexico.[1]

The story I finally pieced together is in many ways surprising. The Asociación de Señoras de la Caridad de San Vicente de Paul was one of the largest women's organizations in nineteenth-century Mexico, with local chapters throughout the republic.[2] In the process of helping the poor, the Ladies did a few things rarely associated with charity, such as expanding the boundaries of women's traditional roles and contributing both to the development of the welfare system and to a religious reform movement that had political implications. While providing important social services in the period before nursing, teaching, and social work became professionalized, they also served as missionaries. By involving themselves in the daily lives of the masses, they helped the church regain its influence. Until recently, however, even the historians who recognize the existence of a Catholic restoration in late nineteenth-century Mexico have missed its gendered dimension.[3] The women's conferences show that much of the energy and labor for the religious renewal came from women. They also suggest that, if the seeds of Social Catholicism were planted by the men's society beginning in 1844, they were increasingly nurtured by women after 1863.

The Ladies of Charity forces us to revise the traditional narrative of Mexican women's history that makes the Revolution of 1910 the defining event that mobilized women, brought them out of the home, and sparked their interest in public affairs. Histories of nineteenth-century women often start by quoting an old Spanish proverb: "Man in the street, woman at home." Although scholars recognize that this dictum did not apply to the lower-class women who worked for a living, they have clung to the notion that upper- and middle-class women's lives revolved exclusively around family, home, and church. The rare portrayal of women engaging in charity, such as an 1871 painting by Manuel Ocaranza (fig. 3.1), shows a mother directing her child to place a coin in the alms box inside a temple—an extremely tame version of what Mexican women's charitable work encompassed. It was also a far cry from the postrevolutionary view of Porfirian "aristocrats" as degenerate, self-centered, and useless—or, at best, as social Darwinists who turned their backs on the poor. On the contrary, many of them were socially committed volunteers whose horizons and impact reached far beyond the domestic sphere or the protected precinct of the church.

Foundation and Growth of the Ladies of Charity, 1863–1911

The Mexican Association of the Ladies of Charity was a branch of the international Dames de la Charité headquartered in Paris. The French group was

Figure 3.1. A stereotypi-
cal view of women's char-
ity. The alms box reads,
"For the orphans, by the
love of God." Oil painting
(*Charity*) by Manuel
Ocaranza, 1871, in the
Museo Nacional de Arte,
Mexico City. Reproduc-
tion authorized by the
Instituto Nacional de Bel-
las Artes y Literatura,
2014.

the second incarnation of the Confréries des Dames de la Charité, the first
organization founded by Father Vincent de Paul in the seventeenth century.
The original Ladies of Charity consisted of groups of laywomen who cared for
sick and infirm paupers in their parishes. Lasting until the French Revolution,
this voluntary association was refounded in 1840 as part of the nineteenth-
century revival of the Vincentian organizations.[4]

The rebirth of the Dames de la Charité was inspired by the creation of the
male Society of Saint Vincent de Paul in 1833, which was itself modeled after
the earlier laywomen's organization. The new Ladies of Charity copied much
of the society's bylaws and performed similar works of mercy. It also adopted
a simplified version of its organizational structure that omitted the Particular Councils for individual cities and instead had only regional Central
Councils reporting to national Superior Councils that reported to the Paris

headquarters in the Lazarist Convent that housed the Paulist priests who directed the women's association.[5] The French Dames even applied for affiliation with the male society, but the group was rebuffed by its General Council on the grounds that the statutes only allowed men to join. In practice, however, the nineteenth-century Ladies were its female counterparts. Although the women had closer institutional ties with the church than the men, both voluntary associations were affiliated with the order of Vincentian priests and initially worked in partnership with the Sisters of Charity, who referred needy families to the volunteers.[6]

It was in its second incarnation that the Ladies of Charity reached Mexico. The organization was apparently established more than once, because the early conferences failed to survive the initial chaotic stage of the Reforma. The association's first chapter was founded in Puebla in 1848 (at the same time as the first male chapter), and the first Mexican edition of the French Dames de la Charité's bylaws was published there that year to familiarize the volunteers with the Vincentian approach.[7] Scattered chapters followed in León, Huichapán, Nopala, Guanajuato, and Toluca. Yet at some point during the Reform Wars these provincial conferences disappeared. Although the male society weathered the difficulties of those years by insisting that it was an apolitical welfare organization independent from the church that supported the Conservative cause, the women's conferences could not similarly claim to be autonomous. Unlike the men's group, the Ladies of Charity was not only founded and directed by the Congregación de la Misión, but its individual chapters were organized around local parishes and supervised by the parish priest. Since the female conferences were widely known as cofradías, they would have been particularly hard hit by the law outlawing confraternities in 1859 as well as by the disruptions caused when the Paulist Fathers were expelled from their convents in 1861.

The Ladies of Charity reappeared only after the Conservatives ousted Liberal president Benito Juárez in July 1863. Reestablished in Mexico City the following month, the association later recognized August 2, 1863, as its birth date.[8] According to the in-house history written by "a priest in the Church of San Lázaro" around 1901, the association began when Vincentian father Francisco Muñoz de la Cruz convened "various principal ladies of the capital's Christian and cultured society" in the Central House of the Sisters of Charity (see table 3.1). Future bishop of León José María Diez de Sollano

TABLE 3.1. Founding Officers, First Conference of the Ladies of Charity, 1863

President: Ana Furlong de Guerra	Purveyor: Prudencia Polo
Vice President: Angela de Paredes	Guardarropa: Luz Cárcoba de Morales
Treasurer: Vicenta Montes de Oca	Librarian: Adelaida Castillo y Pacheco

Source: Asociación, Memoria (1902), 6.

presided over that first meeting where, after praying and hearing "an animated exhortation about charity, . . . all the ladies present . . . agreed to erect the obra of the sick poor in the capital's Sagrario parish, under the name of the Asociación de las Señoras de la Caridad."[9]

The women's conferences immediately prospered. The minutes of the first general assembly—held in the Casa Matriz of the Sisters of Charity on the feast day of Saint Vincent in July 1864—reported impressive growth. In one year the association had expanded from one chapter in the Sagrario parish with twenty-three active members to twenty-one chapters with 566.[10] Within that first year the organization had already spread beyond its original base in the capital, which had grown to twelve chapters, to establish another nine in central Mexico: four in nearby Toluca and one each in Puebla, Guanajuato, Zimacantepec, Tenancingo, and Santiago Tianquistengo. A Superior Council had been created in Mexico City to govern the emerging national network of local conferences. In addition the group had obtained the backing of 839 honorary members, a term used interchangeably with subscribing members who pledged a monthly donation— and that did not include the many men who supported their work by providing free goods as well as medical, legal, and accounting services. Collections had increased from a modest 9 pesos and 25 cents in alms when the plate was passed at the first meeting to 10,004 pesos a year later.[11]

The Ladies of Charity continued its dramatic expansion throughout the Second Empire. In 1865 it published its first Memoria, which included statistics for the first two years (fig. 3.2). By 1866 it had quadrupled in size to eighty-seven conferences with 2,251 active and 5,226 honorary members. These included six chapters composed of niñas training to become full-fledged members when they turned eighteen.[12] The association's operating

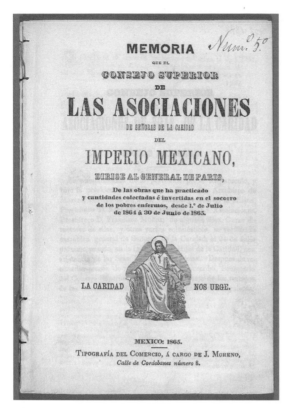

Figure 3.2. Title page of the annual report of the Association of Ladies of Charity, 1865. Asociación, *Memoria* (1865). In Typ. 73–1372, Houghton Library, Harvard University. Reprinted courtesy of the Houghton Library, Harvard University.

budget was 39,900 pesos. It had added Central Councils, the second tier of regional governing bodies, in Guadalajara, Tenancingo, Toluca, Orizaba, Puebla, and Morelia. Although primarily an urban organization, it had moved beyond major cities to found chapters in small towns and even on two rural haciendas. Indeed, the Hacienda de San José Tecualoya (state of Mexico) was so remote that, because its members lived scattered in several rancherias that lacked a church bell, they convened their conference sessions by setting off a rocket.[13]

This early success reflects the auspicious climate when the organization was founded. The church, once again feeling safe under the Regency and Second Empire, offered the Ladies protection at the highest level. Their annual meetings were attended by ecclesiastical dignitaries as well as by the Vincentian priests who continued to direct the association. The first general assembly was presided over by the archbishop of Michoacán, Clemente de Jesús Munguía, newly returned from exile. The archbishop of Mexico, Pelagio Antonio de Labastida, also newly returned from exile, "took the Association under his paternal wing and devoted himself with his great affection and charity to sustaining, favoring, and propagating it." Following the example of Pope Pius IX, he signed the diplomas and patents that the organization distributed to its members, obtained permission for the volunteers to place collection boxes in churches, and lost no opportunity to encourage the formation of new chapters.[14]

The association also received protection from the imperial regime, as part of its effort to ameliorate the poverty that the foreign rulers found so shocking upon their arrival in Mexico.[15] Hoping to remake the Mexican welfare system in the French image, in 1865 Empress Charlotte's new General Council of Beneficence commissioned the translation and publication of three pamphlets describing the Parisian model they wanted to emulate. The Ladies of Charity was to be at its core, collaborating with the Junta de Beneficencia in each municipal ward to distribute home relief to the needy.[16] Although the Second Empire was cut short before it could implement this plan, the Mexican Ladies of Charity enjoyed the financial support of the imperial government while it lasted. Empress Charlotte and Mariscal Elías Forey pledged regular sums to support the organization, and in 1865 Emperor Maximilian contributed 2,000 pesos as a one-time donation. In addition, the association received funding from the government-run lottery known as the Lotería de la Divina Providencia; during four months in 1866 alone, this income amounted to 1,700 pesos.[17] In a further sign of his appreciation for the Ladies' charitable endeavors, the emperor bestowed the Cross of San Carlos on Nicolasa Luna de Corcuera, the president of Guadalajara's thriving Central Council.[18]

The women benefited from the support of their male counterparts as well. Shared surnames such as Montes de Oca, Icasa, Dosamantes, and Terán suggest some overlap with the male conferences (compare appendixes 1 and 2). Longtime society member Antonio Vértiz served as the first secretary of the Ladies of Charity's Superior Council, and Pedro Ebromar served as its treasurer.[19] Because we lack comprehensive membership lists for the men's society, it is unclear whether Ebromar was also a society member. What is evident is that the female conferences received considerable aid from many well-placed men. The 1901 history singled out the distinguished politician

Mariano Riva Palacio for his generous monetary contribution. In addition, four medical doctors (brothers Francisco and Lázaro Ortega, Francisco Cordero, and Antonio Velaroy) immediately signed on to provide their services gratis to the association's clients, and the pharmacist Máximo Río de la Loza donated medicines out of "compassion for the poor." Many other physicians, phlebotomists, pharmacists, lawyers, businessmen, industrialists, employees, and "men of letters and professions" collaborated with their good works. Some donated money, others medicines, clothes, food, charcoal, or parcels of land for their buildings. Still others contributed with their labor, such as the *procuradores* (attorneys) who represented the Ladies in court and helped them collect donated goods, the tailors who sewed clothes for the indigent, and those who "in a thousand other ingenious and always charitable ways helped the *señoras socias*."[20]

Given its close ties to the Empire, one might have expected the Ladies of Charity to stop expanding when Maximilian was defeated in 1867. Yet the opposite occurred because it had widespread and nonpartisan support at many levels of Mexican society. Indeed, the early benefactor Mariano Riva Palacio (1803–1880), known as a committed republican who refused to cooperate with the imperial regime, nonetheless donated to the association despite its connections with Maximilian and Charlotte.[21] To be sure, it skipped its 1867 general assembly, which would have been held just as the government was changing hands in Mexico City. Yet meeting again in July 1868, the association reported that despite the "terrible catastrophes" of the war that restored the Liberals to power, it was continuing its ascendance. Its national presence was extensive enough to warrant twelve Central Councils to oversee the chapters in the provinces—twice the number of just two years earlier.[22]

Table 3.2 shows that the association flourished during the Restored Republic. At the end of Juárez's presidency in 1872, there were 127 female conferences with 2,877 active volunteers and 6,688 honorary members. Despite losing the imperial government's subsidies—which were never restored by subsequent governments, as far as I have been able to determine[23]—the Ladies collected 72,933 pesos that year. The organization continued expanding under the more radical President Lerdo de Tejada, and by 1875 it counted 4,022 active and 10,166 honorary members in some 300 chapters and spent 94,874 pesos on good works, not including the value of in-kind donations.[24] Their steady growth after the Liberal victory contradicts the view that the Reforma weakened Catholic organizations and follows the trend exhibited by the male conferences, for which the years 1867 to 1875 were also a time of progress.

TABLE 3.2. Membership of the Ladies of Charity, 1864–1911

	Active	Honorary
1864	566	839
1865	997	1,863
1866	2,251	5,226
1872	2,877	6,688
1875	4,022	10,166
1878	3,003	5,709
1885	1,485	3,344
1886	3,511	5,113
1888	7,344	10,601
1891	5,977	8,449
1892	6,123	10,061
1895	9,885	12,777
1896	11,264	18,550
1898	15,850	20,938
1900	15,237	23,007
1901	14,933	21,047
1902	15,010	20,772
1903	13,083	20,105
1904	14,208	18,525
1905	16,067	20,910
1907	17,921	28,991
1908	18,180	23,343
1909	20,188	23,018
1910	18,034	24,338
1911	21,184	22,879

Sources: De Dios, Historia de la familia vicentina, 1:545, 550 (for 1864 and 1868); ibid., 2:641–46 (for 1885–1891, 1907, 1910); Asociación, Memoria (1865–1911). The 1902 Memoria contains statistics for 1872 and 1875.

Although the Ladies of Charity then fell on hard times, these were not directly correlated with political developments. On the contrary, they occurred after Porfirio Díaz came to power and reached a modus vivendi with the church. The expulsion of the Sisters of Charity in 1875 may have caused some disruptions because the volunteers had worked so closely with that religious congregation. Yet the example of Guadalajara suggests that these troubles were temporary: although the two female chapters in the Analco parish stopped functioning when the sisters departed, they had been reestablished within the year.[25]

The real problem was apparently the declining health of the association's founder and director, Father Múñoz, who succumbed to his death on September 13, 1877, after directing the Ladies of Charity for fourteen years and traveling throughout Mexico to expand the network of conferences.[26] By 1878 the number of volunteers had dropped by a quarter and the number of chapters by two-thirds. The association nonetheless kept its broad geographical network. Despite losing contact with the Central Council in Puebla as well as with fifteen chapters in the state of Jalisco, the Superior Council received reports from twelve Central Councils and one hundred chapters (table 3.3). It still retained a presence in northern cities such as Zacatecas, Aguascalientes, Monterrey, Durango, and Saltillo, in southeastern ones such as Jalapa and Orizaba, and in Huamantla in the southern state of Tlaxcala.[27] Although the organization thus remained vigorous in 1878, the next few years saw further decline. Notwithstanding the efforts of several Vincentian priests (including Vicente de Paul Andrade, son of the men's society's founder[28]), the membership of the women's association bottomed out in 1885 with only 1,435 volunteers (table 3.2).

The conferences recovered their momentum with the arrival of two new energetic directors. The 1901 history of the association attributes its recovery to Father Félix Mariscal, visitor of the Congregación de la Misión and director of the women's conferences from 1882 to 1890, while the 1993 history of the Vincentian family attributes it to Father Ildefonso Moral González, who served in these positions from December 1891 until his death in 1907.[29] Both clerics deserve some credit. By 1886 the Ladies of Charity had turned the corner, with 3,511 active members in 276 chapters, and by 1888 the number of volunteers had again doubled. The association's recovery was thus well underway before the arrival of Father Moral—as well as before the promulgation of the Rerum Novarum encyclical that coincided with the beginning of his term as director. Then, under Father Moral's stewardship, the Ladies of Charity took off like wildfire.

The remarkable expansion of the Ladies of Charity in the last two decades of the Porfiriato contrasts with the experience of the male society, which

TABLE 3.3. Conference Foundations of the Ladies of Charity by Region, 1865–1911

Central Council	1865	1878	1895	1902	1911
Mexico (D.F./state)	625	191	522	399	510
Toluca (state Mexico)	131	306	266	305	426
Guadalajara (Jalisco)	136	329	4,341	4,783	5,250
Tenancingo (state Mexico)	105	60			
San Luis Potosi (SLP)		128	895	586	378
Morelia (Michoacán)		581	434	843	2,327
Monterrey (Nuevo León)		251	174	670	255
Orizaba (Veracruz)		198	153		
Jalapa (Veracruz)		57		190	
Jojutla (Morelos)		137			
Chilapa (Guerrero)		46		195	
Huamantla (Tlaxcala)		43			
Veracruz (Veracruz)			128		106
Zamora (Michoacán)			545	1,644	1,082
Iguala/Cuernavaca (Morelos)			59	114	69
Oaxaca (Oaxaca)			14	137	222
Teziutlán (Puebla)			70	568	416
Tabasco (Tabasco)			35	17	8
Zacatecas (Zacatecas)			104	301	854
Guanajuato (Guanajuato)			294		54
León (Guanajuato)			280	633	349
Coahuila (Coahuila)			91		
Chihuahua (Chihuahua)			60	68	225
Durango (Durango)			14	75	303
Aguascalientes (Aguascalientes)			23	131	1,894
Querétaro (Querétaro)			73	32	11
Culiacán/Sinaloa (Sinaloa)			380	338	253
Mérida/Yucatán (Yucatán)			920	45	1,093
Colima (Colima)				911	4,613
Saltillo (Coahuila)				628	91
Tamaulipas (Tamaulipas)				137	
Tepic (Nayarit)				1,216	
Tulancingo (Hidalgo)				44	

Table 3.3 continued

Central Council	1865	1878	1895	1902	1911
Ciudad Victoria (Tamaulipas)					69
Huajaán (Oaxaca)					156
Campeche (Campeche)					113
Chiapas (Chiapas)					20
Sonora (Sonora)					25
Single conferences*		676			12
Total socias activas	*997*	*3,003*	*9,885*†	*15,010*	*21,184*
Consejos reporting	*4*	*12*	*23*	*26*	*31*‡

Note: The table lists the number of active members in conferences reporting to the national association, and the listing follows names in original documents. Some council names and boundaries changed over time. For example, Tenancingo (which in 1865 oversaw the conferences in Tenancingo, Malinalco, Tecualoya, and Coatepec) later became part of the Toluca Central Council. The area governed by the Guadalajara Central Council was notably reduced when new dioceses were carved out if its jurisdiction in Colima (1881) and Tepic (1891). New council names are indicated by a slash.

* In 1878 twenty-three conferences were not yet part of a Central Council; in 1911 there was one.

† Council statistics add up to 9,875. I kept the printed total of 9,885 because I do not know whether the mistake was in the reporting of the total or of an individual conference.

‡ The totals include figures for only twenty-eight Central Councils because the 1911 report specified that three had failed to report.

Sources: Asociación, *Memoria* (1865, 1878, 1895, 1902, 1911).

stagnated during that period. Table 3.2 shows that, annual fluctuations notwithstanding, overall membership in the female association rose sharply. By 1895 there were 9,875 volunteers supported by 12,777 honorary members in some 400 chapters. With an additional 19,000 niñas in training, the organization was laying a solid foundation for future growth.[30] In 1900 there were 15,237 volunteers and 23,007 honorary members. In June 1911, apparently unaffected by the six months of fighting that had toppled Porfirio Díaz the previous month, the conferences reported that their active membership had reached a historic high of 21,184 volunteers. The association had enlarged its geographical coverage as well (table 3.3). With thirty-one Central Councils, it had attained a presence in most of Mexico's states.[31] It had thereby constructed an extensive national infrastructure for the delivery of Catholic

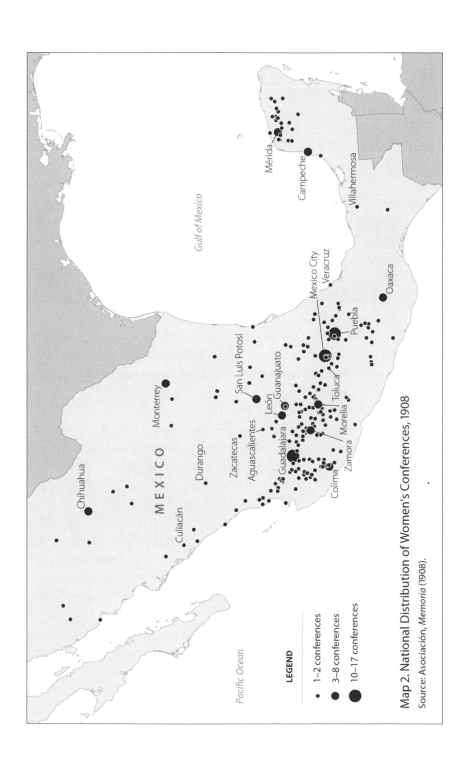

LEGEND

· 1–2 conferences

● 3–8 conferences

● 10–17 conferences

Map 2. National Distribution of Women's Conferences, 1908

Source: Asociación, *Memoria* (1908).

Pacific Ocean

Gulf of Mexico

M E X I C O

Chihuahua

Culiacán

Durango

Zacatecas

Aguascalientes

Monterrey

San Luis Potosí

León

Guanajuato

Guadalajara

Colima

Zamora

Morelia

Toluca

Mexico City

Veracruz

Puebla

Oaxaca

Mérida

Campeche

Villahermosa

social services that included remote areas distant from the capital and from
major urban centers.

Mission and Activities

The activities of the Ladies of Charity expanded over time as well. The association's original mission, as defined in the *Reglamento* it adopted in 1863,
was fairly narrow: to "visit the sick poor, provide them with spiritual and
corporal relief, console them, and exhort them to take advantage of their illness to resign themselves to God's will."[32] The corporal aid included bringing
the patients medicines, food, clothes and bed linens; paying their rent; washing them; "sweeping the room, making the bed and such"; and arranging for
doctors and phlebotomists to provide medical care. The spiritual relief was
achieved by praying with their clients, making sure they confessed, and preparing them to receive the last rites when the end was near.

Yet the agenda was in fact much broader. First, the women were to help
remedy the widespread poverty and suffering intensified by years of warfare.
As the secretary general of the association, Francisco G. del Valle, explained
at its first general assembly in 1864, "In a country such as ours that has been
torn by over fifty years of civil war, . . . private individuals should be more
solicitous of the poor."[33] Second, they were to help the church reinvigorate
Mexican Catholicism. The bylaws envisioned the volunteers as intrusive visitors who became intimately involved in the life of the entire client's family.
They were to see that all members of the household understood their Christian obligations, that they attended mass on Sundays and feast days, that the
parents were married, and that the children were baptized, knew how to
pray, and took first communion. In addition to their evangelizing efforts, the
volunteers were supposed to foster Catholic values by dispensing moral
advice and even insisting, for example, that boys and girls sleep in separate
beds to avoid impropriety. The 1864 bylaws added the task of ensuring that
the children attended school.[34] Moreover, the women's guidance of their
"adopted" families did not end when the patient was cured: during Lent they
were to visit all the people they had helped to exhort them to confess and
receive Holy Communion. The volunteers were to prepare themselves for
these good works by meeting in their small groups regularly—usually once
a week—to pray and plan their activities. They were also encouraged to

participate in spiritual exercises—usually once a month—to strengthen their faith and love for the poor, and to celebrate the Feast Day of their patron Saint Vincent on July 19.

In its first year the Ladies of Charity hit the ground running. By July 1864 the association reported that the 321 volunteers in Mexico City's twelve conferences served 2,240 sick and dying paupers by caring for them personally and "going to visit them at all hours." They arranged proper Catholic burials for the 156 who died and cared for their surviving children afterward. They gave out 45,678 "ordinary" food rations, consisting of rice, beans, peas, corn, chocolate, bread, and charcoal, as well as 3,000 "extraordinary" rations for special feast days, consisting of milk, chicken, soup, desserts, and wine. They distributed 6,820 medical prescriptions and 816 pieces of clothing, "the majority sewn by the ladies themselves." They raised 6,504 pesos by collecting alms in their local churches, soliciting their friends and neighbors, raffling off their handiwork, and contributing from their own pockets. They obtained donations in kind from local businesses. Their efforts were aided by 517 subscribers, 46 priests, and 4 Sisters of Charity, as well as by 74 doctors, 8 phlebotomists, and 6 laundresses who provided their services free of charge. The association did not neglect its religious duties, either. In addition to the devotions performed for the members' own "moral improvement," the "exhortations of the lady visitors" in Mexico City alone resulted in 911 confessions, 97 confirmations, 10 marriages, and 2 baptisms.[35] The provincial conferences reported similar activities, with the numbers growing exponentially in the next two years as the membership expanded (see table 3.4).

The Mexican Ladies of Charity did not confine itself to working with the sick and infirm, as prescribed by the original statutes. With its singular "knack for invention"[36]—and following the precedent of the male conferences—the association quickly enlarged its clientele to include healthy paupers. A revised Mexican edition of the bylaws published in 1864 explained that "in actuality, the Association of Ladies of Charity does not limit its aid to the sick poor, but extends its zeal to many other works of mercy, such as the protection of orphans, the adoption of abandoned children, the instruction of female prisoners, [and] the conversion of the neediest paupers."[37] Indeed, although the title of the 1865 *Memoria* still described its works as being "for the succor of the sick poor," later editions dropped that phrase in recognition of the expansion of the services provided by the volunteers (see fig. 3.2).[38]

TABLE 3.4. Activities of the Ladies of Charity, 1866–1911

	1866	1878	1892	1895	1902	1908	1911
Families visited		1,151	45,882	70,537	106,436	124,695	138,693
Sick	10,235	8,778	14,353	21,428	24,464	29,058	31,052
Burials	663	1,710	1,892	2,347	2,467	2,916	2,652
First commu-nions[*]	2729	14,705	1,398	2,917	8,223	7,622	8,454
Confirmations	312		145	279		86	225
Conversions[*]		11	60	182	7,119	569	260
Viaticums	705	2,913	1,595	2,933	3,318	3,480	—
Marriages	29	150	197	298	578	826	738
Baptisms	22	70	461	672	437	393	549
Devotional sacraments[*]	2,622	15,273	13,223	31,390	69,025	155,456	262,916
Ordinary rations[*]	135,900	385,110	315,581	1,036,588	1,366,034	1,692,497	1,750,287
Additional relief[*]	23,235	60,273	21,444	144,233	48,264	83,040	103,034
Prescriptions	43,157	50,622			116,952	119,963	123,836
Items of clothing	3,457	8,664			25,020	23,841	332,037
Income (in pesos)	39,900	52,194	67,174	105,986	166,746	244,077	283,299
Expenditures (")	29,669	49,243	61,539	96,206	155,742	208,812	250,206

[*] The category of "first communions" includes "communions" in 1866 and 1878. "Conversions" include "abjurations" in 1902 and 1908. In 1902, 7,023 of the reported *conversiones y abjuraciones* are from the Archdiocese of Guadalajara, a figure completely out of line with other years. "Devotional sacraments" are labeled *confesiones* in 1866 and 1878. Ordinary rations are labeled *vales* or *raciones* in many years. "Additional relief" is labeled *raciones extraordinarias* in 1866 and 1878, and *socorros particulares* in 1892–1911.

Sources: Asociación, *Memoria* (1866, 1878, 1892, 1895, 1902, 1908, 1911).

The early reports gave many examples of these activities. On Good Friday in 1864 the Ladies of the San Miguel parish in Mexico City served breakfast to three hundred children from the *escuelas gratuitas*. On Maundy Thursday the Ladies of the Sagrario parish organized a sumptuous dinner for one hundred paupers, twelve of whom sat at the head table with the parish priest. In Zinacantepec the "Lady president," Doña Agustina Bracamontes, personally instructed fifty children in Christian doctrine and reading. In Tenancingo the volunteers provided assistance to "all the poor families that presented themselves," and in San Agustín Tlalpam they provided meals for female prisoners, "served by the *socias* themselves," and obtained the release of several of the incarcerated. Members of the Morelia conference visited with female prisoners to instruct them in Christian doctrine. The Jalapa visitors found a safe house for a woman whose husband beat her "cruelly," and then they supervised the education of her five children "so the daughters would be good *madres de familia* and the sons would be good citizens." Several conferences paid the tuition for especially deserving girls to attend private primary schools.[39]

From the start the association also began constructing its own welfare institutions. For example, the largest Mexico City conference, in the Sagrario Metropolitano parish, established an asylum for orphaned and abandoned girls, the Asilo de la Caridad de Nuestra Señora de la Luz, built on land donated by Doña María Flores. By June 1864 it was sheltering ten young women under the care of an impoverished but honest woman. Despite the presence of a hired employee, the volunteers continued to be directly involved: "This small family was supervised by eight *Señoras socias* . . . who, rotating themselves in twos, provided lucrative and honest employment for the poor girls whom they educated and moralized . . . in order to remove them from the seductions of the world, even perhaps from prostitution, so that with time they will become excellent wives and tender mothers." By June 1866 the asylum was housing thirty-five girls.[40]

Although this shelter was the best known of the association's early foundations (and still functioned as late as 1912), it was only one of many.[41] Thus the Ladies of the Santa Veracruz parish opened a school for the local children. The Ladies of the San Miguel parish set up a cocina económica. The Ladies of the Señora de Guadalupe parish founded a small clinic. In San Luis Potosí, the conference established two *casas de misericordia* (houses of mercy) to care for over eighty orphans. As other conferences followed suit, the organization's asylums, orphanages, clinics, boticas (pharmaceutical dispensaries), soup kitchens, and schools proliferated throughout Mexico.[42]

The next available *Memoria* shows that the Ladies of Charity had become an even stronger force by 1878. During the year ending in June, the 3,003 volunteers cared for 10,488 sick and dying paupers, raised impressive sums of money, distributed large quantities of aid, and led numerous clients to take the sacraments (table 3.4). The statistical summary tells only part of the story. The reports of individual chapters indicate that the association reached thousands more paupers, including indigent families that were "habitually succored," orphans who were protected, repentant prostitutes (*arrepentidas*) who were rehabilitated, and children who were instructed in Christian doctrine, along with many others who attended the association's primary schools or found shelter in its asylums. The Central Council in Mexico City received a donation of ten sewing machines to provide work for impoverished women. A conference in San Luis Potosí established an employment agency to help its clients find jobs. A conference in the state of Mexico worked with the laborers in the La Colmena textile factory. In addition, the volunteers founded night schools for adults and workshops to train carpenters, shoemakers, and seamstresses. The reports also mention the regular visiting of prison inmates and patients in public hospitals. Thus, despite the militant separation of church and state that became the law of the land during the Restored Republic, the Ladies of Charity maintained a visible presence in public institutions as well as in the neighborhoods where its members visited the ailing poor and rescued the homeless who lived on the streets.

The organization's achievements mushroomed after the conferences recovered from the low point of the early 1880s. In 1895 the volunteers visited 70,537 needy families and 21,428 hospital patients. They distributed more than a million meals. In 1901 they ran "forty hospitals founded and sustained with association funds, where the sick receive meticulous care and are visited by the *señoras* themselves; over twenty cocinas económicas to feed impoverished families that cannot work; as well as free *consultorios* [medical clinics], *botiquines* [pharmaceutical dispensaries], asylums and so many girls' schools and other beneficent establishments that it would be tedious to list them all."[43] In 1909 the volunteers visited 135,334 families and 31,954 hospital patients. They distributed 1,779,843 meals, 132,481 prescriptions, and 27,024 articles of clothing. They managed an extensive national network of elementary schools, asylums, cafeterias, clinics, and dispensaries that included at least 32 hospitals, 20 schools, and 17 orphanages throughout Mexico—and probably more, since sixty conferences did not send news to the Superior Council that year. The 1909 report estimated that the schools alone reached some 25,000 students, with another 16,000 children attending the catechism classes. In addition, the women visited 28 prisons, where they worked with 5,606 prisoners.[44] They ministered to the needy in factories as well as on haciendas. In 1908 alone the Puebla volunteers taught the catechism to workers—both male and female—in ten factories, and those in San Luis Potosí regularly visited the La Fama cigar factory to instruct its female laborers in Christian doctrine "and inspire them to virtue."[45] In June 1911 the national association reported that during the preceding year its members had visited 138,693 families, distributed 1,750,287 rations and 103,034 prescriptions, and spent the enormous sum of 250,206 pesos (table 3.4). Thus, on the eve of the revolution, the expansion of the Ladies' good works continued unabated.

These benevolent activities gave the women's association a huge audience for its reform efforts. Indeed, a new set of bylaws published in 1911 applauded the diversification of the original mission precisely because it enhanced the volunteers' ability to contribute to "the glory of God and the health of souls." While noting that "Saint Vincent established the Association of the Ladies of Charity only to aid the sick poor and to succor the corporal and spiritual needs of impoverished families," the Reglamento commended the Mexican Ladies for taking additional opportunities "to moralize the populace," in particular praising their work in "establishing Catholic schools . . . to give a Christian education to indigent boys and girls who wander the streets and plazas exposed to their perdition."[46]

The statistics in table 3.4 show the extent of the volunteers' religious ministry, which not only consisted of reinvigorating the faith of those who were nominally Catholic but increasingly of converting Protestants as well. If their first conversion was in 1865—only five years after freedom of religion was established in Mexico—it was a rare achievement in the early years.[47] By the turn of the century the Ladies of Charity claimed to be converting hundreds of Protestants each year as well as saving people from "the farce of Spiritism."[48] The association also encouraged its members and clients to attend Mass and take communion, participate in spiritual exercises and devotions like Eucharistic adoration and the rosary, and venerate the growing cults of the Sacred Heart of Jesus and Saint Vincent de Paul.[49] Thus, while providing a broad range of social services to a large clientele, the organization promoted orthodox religious practices and contributed to the Catholic restoration. By forming habits of lay organizing, building institutions such as schools, hospitals, and asylums, and extending their reach into underserved regions, it also prepared the ground in which Social Catholicism would flourish.

Why the Conferences Appealed to Women

The phenomenal growth of the Ladies of Charity stems from many factors. One was the conscious church strategy of mobilizing women. The ecclesiastical hierarchy promoted the formation of female lay groups after the confraternities were outlawed in 1859 and, especially, after Mexican nunneries were closed in 1863.[50] Vincentian priests took up the call by founding the women's conferences, and the 1865 *Memoria* attributed their success during the first two years to the "zeal" of these missionaries.[51] The church intensified its efforts to recruit laywomen after the passage of the Organic Law in December 1874 that prohibited religious instruction in public institutions and suppressed the Sisters of Charity, who managed forty-three welfare institutions.[52] In their Pastoral Instruction of 1875, the archbishops of Mexico, Michoacán, and Guadalajara specifically called on "Catholic ladies" to join the conferences of Saint Vincent de Paul to continue the work of the sisters in providing for "the instruction of destitute children, the needs of ailing paupers in hospitals, and the relief of all sorts of misery."[53] According to the 1894 *Rapport* of the international Dames de la Charité, the Mexican chapter was the largest in "the world" (although this probably only meant outside of France) because the Mexican poor were "deprived . . . of the succor provided by the hospitaler communities."[54] Finally, the internal histories of the association correlate the heyday of the Ladies of Charity with the arrival of two new directors, Father Mariscal in 1882 and Father Moral in 1891.

Yet in explaining the success of the female conferences, we should beware of narratives that erase the agency of the women themselves. For if priests promoted the association, it was laywomen who enthusiastically joined. The women's initiative can be teased out of the self-effacing reports meant to portray them as mere followers of their priests. Already in 1865 the *Memoria* attributed the success of several conferences, such as the one in Mexico City's San Sebastián parish, "to the arduous work of its members, and principally the efforts of the *señoras presidenta, vicepresidenta,* and *tesorera.*"[55] Noting the women's fundraising abilities, the 1866 *Memoria* credited the "industrious charity" and "zeal" of two members for obtaining the locale for a central supply warehouse as well as the right to lottery income.[56] The 1870 *Memoria* provided additional examples of the volunteers' energy, commitment, and resourcefulness. Commending their dedication, the text stated that "it is admirable . . . to see these good Ladies of Charity out on the streets even at inconvenient hours bringing medicine, food, blankets, and other necessities to their beloved patients. When the city was under siege, without rest . . . they took grains and other aid to their ailing poor. It moves us to tears to see them . . . picking up the sick and destitute even from empty lots and taverns." They also risked their lives to nurse their charges through contagious illnesses, as did "one *socia* from Ocoyoacac" who, having caught a disease from a sick pauper, "in her delirium insisted that she faced death with contentment because she had been able to perform a work of charity."[57]

Moreover, the association's reports contained occasional hints that some conferences were not founded by priests at all but by some of the strong woman presidents. For example, the 1870 *Memoria* praised the "*presidenta* of the Association of Malacatepec" for "founding it herself, reviving the Toluca organization to the point of duplicating its members and its income . . . and today establishing a conference in Capuluhac."[58] A history of the Ladies of Charity in the Archdiocese of Guadalajara similarly attributes several chapter foundations to their female presidents.[59] Evidently, these women were not only willing handmaidens of the church, but also a driving force in the Vincentian lay movement.[60]

Since Mexican women joined the Ladies of Charity with such gusto, we should consider what this organization meant in their lives. Unfortunately, we know very little about the social background or life stories of the volunteers, and even less about their inner thoughts. The *Memorias* often listed the officers of the Superior Council and sometimes even of the conferences, but they rarely elaborated further. The available lists show that the volunteers were both married or widowed and single. And they were apparently drawn from a broad spectrum of the middle and lower-middle classes as well as from a small elite.

It is easiest to document the participation of upper-class volunteers. The 1863 bylaws noted that "the principal ladies of each town" were ideal members of the association because, having "no need to work for their subsistence like the women of an inferior class," they could devote their time to beneficent activities.[61] The only biography I have located of a Lady of Charity certainly fits this description. In her series on notable Mexican women, the journalist Laureana Wright de Kleinhans published a short biographical sketch of Nicolasa Luna de Corcuera (1820–1895).[62] After marrying a wealthy Spanish merchant at age twenty-three, Doña Nicolasa apparently devoted herself to her numerous children while they were infants, and then she threw herself energetically into the work of charity by founding the Guadalajara conferences when she was forty-four years old. Leading the Guadalajara Central Council while also participating in her own chapter in the Analco parish through her widowhood at age fifty-six until her death at age seventy-four, she is credited with making many substantial donations from her family fortune as well as with personally caring for the sick and helpless.[63]

The *Memorias* contain numerous indications of some Ladies' high social status, especially in the Superior and Central Councils (see table 3.1 and appendixes 2 and 4). The members included a few women with well-known surnames representing leading Mexican families, such as Señora Ana Furlong de Guerra, president of the first Superior Council, and Doña Vicenta Montes de Oca, treasurer of Mexico City's first conference in the Sagrario Metropolitano parish. Some women could evidently afford to contribute generously "from their personal wealth," as did Doña Antonia Frago de Tagle, who according to the 1865 *Memoria* shouldered all the costs of caring for her "adopted families"—including paying one family's rent—and the Señoras Pilar and Soledad Tijera, who hosted a special dinner for one hundred paupers in their spacious home.[64] In later years the Superior Council officers included women from the Escandón, García Pimentel, and Elguero families, the last two related to officers in the men's society.

Yet most of the members' surnames are unknown to historians of the period, and most of the individual donations praised by the annual reports are very small sums.[65] Indeed, the *Memorias* occasionally noted the modest social backgrounds of some of the volunteers. For example, the 1864 report observed that in Mexico City's twelve conferences "seamstresses are the majority of the *socias*," as were all seventeen members of the conference of San

Antonio de las Huertas in 1865.[66] The 1900 *Memoria* reported that in Guadalajara's Conferencia de Nuestra Señora de Guadalupe "most of *señoras socias* are poor." The members of chapters in small—and possibly indigenous—towns such as Izamal and Dzidsantún in Yucatán or Hecelchakán and Calkiní in Campeche were also unlikely to have belonged to high society.[67]

The women of the Ladies of Charity thus appear to have come from a similar range of backgrounds as the men who joined the Vincentian lay conferences. Since the male records sometimes list the occupations of the members, at least for the early years, we know that they included artisans, shopkeepers, and occasional manual laborers, along with members of well-to-do families. Although it is likely that few of the women held jobs and that most had servants to care for their homes and children while they engaged in charity work, this situation was characteristic of the middle classes as well as of the elites in nineteenth-century Mexico.[68] The conferences thus provided middle- and upper-class women, who rarely worked outside the home, with a socially acceptable way to serve the larger society beyond their families.

As female schooling increased and the ideal of feminine seclusion declined, many Mexican women sought outlets where they could apply their talents.[69] Female education improved considerably during the nineteenth century, particularly in the cities and major towns among the middle and upper classes—the very groups that supplied the Vincentian volunteers. In earlier generations women attracted to social service might have entered convents or joined a teaching or nursing order like the Sisters of Charity. However, these options were closed by the suppression of nunneries in 1863 and the expulsion of the Sisters of Charity in 1875. Even when new religious congregations were established during the late nineteenth and early twentieth centuries, Mexican women were no longer drawn to the convent to the same degree as before.[70] In fact, the population of nuns was already decreasing before independence, as the ideals of celibacy and enclosure diminished.[71] Consequently, Mexico did not experience the feminization of the clergy so widespread in Catholic countries like France, where female congregations attracted huge numbers of pious women.[72]

In nineteenth-century Mexico it was instead the lay organizations that women flocked to in droves. Many pious associations drew increasingly large majorities of female members, but they rarely provided opportunities for social service.[73] After its founding in 1869, thousands of laywomen joined the

Sociedad Católica de Señoras y Señoritas, which defended the faith by founding parochial schools and catechizing children; by 1873 its membership had reached some twenty thousand women. However, the apparent decline of the Sociedad Católica soon thereafter reduced that opportunity for women to contribute to social reform.[74] A few well-connected women found places on the boards of public welfare institutions or obtained positions managing them, but these were few and far between.[75] Thus filling a void, the Ladies of Charity gave Mexican women a structure for contributing to the common good without having to give up marriage and motherhood.

Nineteenth-century society was crying out for the association's attention. It is no coincidence that it grew rapidly not only after the arrival of the two new Vincentian directors but also after the Rerum Novarum encyclical of 1891 energized members of the laity who wanted to participate in the project for Catholic renewal. Devout women organized to resolve many problems in their communities. Hunger, sickness, unemployment, homelessness, and suffering increased with the pauperization that accompanied Porfirian modernization. Illiteracy was widespread. The Catholic faith was threatened by a shortage of priests and nuns, the decline of religious education, and the expansion of Protestantism and spiritism. By the end of the century, deepening social inequality and the doctrines of anarcho-syndicalism and socialism raised the specter of class conflict. Many women with a sense of civic duty welcomed the Vincentian conferences that permitted them to work for the salvation of society while simultaneously assuring their own.

Charity work allowed women to engage in "meaningful labor" without appearing to transgress traditional boundaries.[76] The imprimatur of the church gave their activities respectability. So did the highly gendered discourse that constructed the work of benevolence as a simple expansion of women's domestic roles. Far from appealing to the equality of the sexes, the justifications for women's volunteering emphasized their special (that is, different) female condition and qualities.[77] The Pastoral Instruction of 1875 that called on women to join the conferences noted the innate feminine disposition for serving the poor and sick.[78] So did the 1863 bylaws when they explained that, in addition to having "greater compassion for the sufferings of others," women were already "accustomed to carrying out certain types of chores in their houses, and could thus more easily exercise them to benefit strangers."[79] And the *Memorias* noted how women's selflessness and nurturing instincts prepared them to console their suffering charges with the "heart of a mother."[80]

Despite these attempts to naturalize their charitable endeavors, the Ladies were nonetheless engaging in a new type of female activism. Their volunteer work took them far from the safe spaces of home and church. The conferences may have held their weekly sessions in the parish church, but from there the women went out into public places where they were exposed to indelicate and sometimes dangerous situations. They may not have been alone while visiting the dingy—and "sometimes disgusting" and "fetid"[81]—rooms of their adopted families or the filthy wards of public hospitals and prisons, since they usually worked in pairs. Yet neither were they sheltered. In carrying out their good works, they might be subjected to shocking sights and rude insults. For example, the triumphal story of one lady who endured a dying patient's vulgar screams and after several tries succeeded in getting him to accept the last rites, was narrated in the 1865 *Memoria* as an inspiration to others.[82]

Moreover, although the male and female organizations were separate, the Ladies were not restricted to segregated female arenas. Their clients were male as well as female. The volunteers maintained close contact, not only with the priests who helped each conference, but also with the doctors, pharmacists, and lawyers who assisted them. Indeed, because these men were invited to attend the Ladies of Charity's annual general assembly, it was a mixed-sex gathering.[83] The officers of the women's association were also occasionally special guests at events organized by the male society, such as the Mass held in Guadalajara in 1888 to inaugurate a new altar donated by the men's Conferencia de San Vicente de Paul.[84] The women's fundraising efforts entailed not only organizing charity fairs and raffling off donated items such as jewels but also collecting alms in public plazas and approaching the leading men in the community, including a circus owner, Señor Chiarini, who in 1865 donated the 910 peso earnings of one performance to the association. The 1901 history lauded the volunteers for "leaving their comforts behind" and traveling far and wide—even venturing out to *ranchos, campos,* and mines—to solicit funds and reach people in need of assistance.[85]

It would therefore be a mistake to take at face value the rhetoric that the Ladies' good works were merely an extension of what Mexican women had always done. There were, to be sure, some precedents of individual women helping the poor and tending the sick, especially during temporary crises caused by warfare and epidemics. The Patriotas Marianas founded by royalist women in 1810—organized to defend the Spanish Virgen de los Remedios when the Mexican capital was under attack and then continuing to distribute aid to the wives and widows of royalist soldiers—may have been the first female group to systematically provide social assistance, but it only lasted a few years.[86] Vincentian charity not only lasted much longer but took large groups of women further afield.

Recognizing that the volunteers would be venturing into public spaces and interacting with men as well as women, the 1863 *Reglamento* defended them from potential critics by explaining that their "unimpeachable virtue . . . and spirit of true devotion, modesty . . . and benevolence" would protect them from scandal even when they "visited, consoled, and served the sick of the opposite sex."[87] The bylaws' very insistence on this point, however, underscores the novelty of these activities. Indeed, a chronicle of the original Hermandades de Caridad de Señoras de San Vicente de Paul in Spain explained that one reason for their decline in former times was "the repugnance of some fathers and husbands to having their daughters and wives visit the humble abodes of the poor where they would breathe the infected air of misery with risk to their health or to their decorum and dignity."[88] It appears that men's opposition had diminished by the nineteenth century—though, just in case, the 1864 bylaws required the volunteers to obtain permission from their husbands or fathers.[89] The 1901 history noted how surprising it had been at first to see Mexican ladies "mixing with prisoners" and sitting in church together with the innumerable *pobrecitos haraposos* they had succored. Something had evidently changed because, by the turn of the century, "similar scenes no longer attract our attention due to the frequency with which . . . they now take place."[90]

In addition to taking them out of the domestic sphere, the Vincentian conferences provided an arena where the members could become leaders, acquire new skills, and wield power. Whereas Mexican women were barred from voting and holding public office until the mid-twentieth century, they could do both as Ladies of Charity. Voting as equals in secret balloting, the members of each chapter elected a president, vice president, secretary, and treasurer.[91] Indeed, holding office was apparently so attractive to Mexican women that many conferences added second vice presidents, pro secretaries, and subtreasurers, as well as purveyors and librarians, to their rosters of officials (see

Figure 3.3. Page from a list of officers of the Guadalajara Archdiocese Ladies of Charity conferences, 1895. Arquidiócesis de Guadalajara, *Memoria* (1895). In AHAG, Sección Folletería, Serie Publicaciones Periódicas, Sociedad de San Vicente de Paul, 1897–1902, caja 2, no. 42.

—28—

Conferencias de Guadalajara.

NTRA. SRA. DE GUADALUPE.

Director, Sr. Cura D. Miguel Medina Gómez.
Presidenta, Sra. D. ª Antonia Mijares de Arce.
Vicepresidenta, Sra. D. ª Esther Bermudez V. de Gil.
Secretaria, Srita. Julia Godinez.
Prosecretaria, Srita. Dolores Martinez
Tesorera, Sra. D. ª Catalina Leñero de Moreno.
Subtesorera, Srita. Antonia Arce.

SAGRADO CORAZON DE JESUS.

Director, Sr. Magistral Dr. D. Luis Silva.
Presidenta, Sra. D. ª Felipa C. Negrete de Mora.
Vicepresidenta, Srita. Francisca Gutierrez.
Tesorera, Srita. Cecilia Tovar.
Secretaria, Srita. Margarita I. Matute.
Prosecretaria, Srita. Amalia Arce.
Celadoras, Srita. María Gonzalez.
        Srita. Concepción Mora.
Proveedoras, Sra. D. ª Aurora Ferniza de Cordero.
        Sra. D. ª Jesefa Arias de Gallardo.
        Srita. Angela Arreola.
        Srita. Rosalía Arreola.
        Srita. Margarita G. Esteves.
        Srita. Rita Padilla.
        Srita. Manuela de la Peña.

SMA. TRINIDAD.

Director, Sr. Prebendado Dr. D. Pedro Romero.
Presidenta, Srita. Dolores Gonzalez Palomar.
Vicepresidenta, Sra. D. ª Manuela Rivera V. de C. Negrete.
Secretaria, Srita. Vicenta Veréa.
Prosecretaria, Srita. Luisa Martinez.
Tesorera, Srita. Guadalupe Palomar.
Subtesorera, Srita. Concepción Gonzalez Palomar.

fig. 3.3).[92] Conference members also voted to approve the entrance of new volunteers. After a six-month trial,[93] the *aspirantes* who proved their capacity to perform the demanding work of serving the poor were inducted in the annual assembly whose ceremonies included the granting of a patent—complete with papal indulgences—to each new member. In the process of running their associations the volunteers also developed their organizational and financial expertise. Moreover, their charitable activities gave them social power, because their decisions about whom to help, in what way, and for how long could have a profound impact on the lives of people in their communities.

Although it is difficult to know how much influence was exercised by the parish priests, doctors, and lawyers with whom the Ladies of Charity collaborated, the documents contain occasional hints of the women's autonomy. For example, whereas the association's first report listed a male treasurer of the Superior Council, he no longer appeared in late nineteenth-century records.

Similarly, although the minutes of the 1864 and 1865 general assemblies were signed by a male secretary, the 1866 minutes were already signed by Secretary Agustina Castillo.[94] And by the turn of the century the male *procuradores* were often replaced by female *procuradoras* in the slate of conference officers. It thus seems that the women had proven that they could handle their own affairs.[95] In any case, even if they did not always run the conferences entirely on their own, the volunteers were increasing their "social capital": the skills, self-confidence, and moral authority that comes from taking part in an international organization, attending meetings, speaking in public, exercising suffrage, holding positions of responsibility, preparing reports, soliciting funds and managing budgets, designing and implementing welfare services, reforming the poor, and fortifying the commitment of the faithful.[96]

The conferences also provided new spaces for socializing. Meeting in their local chapters regularly, year after year, the volunteers formed friendships that must have been deeply satisfying. The few available membership lists show that some women participated in the same chapter for decades. For example, Señorita Soledad Paredes of the Mexico City conference of the Sagrario and Señora Angela Andrade de Ortega of the conference of San Miguel appeared in the *Memorias* for both 1865 and 1878. Señorita Paz Malagón, "a model for her *consocias*" because of her "ingenious ability to obtain resources for the poor," participated in the Conferencia del Divino Pastor in Salamanca, Michoacán, for some forty years until her death at age seventy-two.[97] Doña Nicolasa Luna de Corcuera of Guadalajara served as its Central Council president from 1864 until her death in 1894 and for thirty years hosted the council's monthly meetings—attended by the officers of each Guadalajara conference—in her home.[98] These gatherings would have provided entertainment and the basis for female camaraderie.

Through their benevolent activities the Ladies expanded their networks to include members of different social classes. Within each chapter the members appear to have shared similar backgrounds; indeed, they often joined in family groups, with mothers and daughters or sisters and sisters-in-law participating together (see, for example, fig. 3.3). Yet Vincentian charity also allowed the volunteers to interact with people they might not otherwise meet, not only among their social peers but also among their clients, as well as the employees they hired to staff their schools, clinics, and asylums. If the bonds forged with less fortunate individuals were paternalistic, they could at times be quite close. For example, Doña Josefa Valentín, who took three children into her own home and cared for them during the many months of their mother's illness, is unlikely to have ended the relationship when the children returned to their mother.[99] In fact, every year during Lent the visitors strengthened these ties by going back to take communion with the families they had helped. So the Ladies were deeply engaged with many different kinds of people in their local communities. This cross-class interaction had the added benefit of conferring social prestige on the volunteers and thus reinforcing their class status.

There are therefore multiple reasons why so many Mexican women joined the Vincentian conferences. They provided opportunities for sociability, prestige, and power. They offered respectable structures for women's participation in meaningful work and in community life. They allowed women to achieve personal fulfillment, engage in new kinds of institutional practices, and develop new skills. The religious element was also central to their appeal. The Ladies' volunteer work was closely tied to their identity as Catholics. The conferences constructed a community of believers that permitted their members to reinforce their faith while fulfilling their Christian obligation to care for the poor and helpless. As the volunteers worked to provide services for the needy, they also helped to bring about the Catholic revival.[100]

Conclusion

In the second half of the nineteenth century, Mexican Lady Bountifuls created one of largest branches of the Ladies of Charity in the world. Throwing their considerable energy and talents into helping the sick and poor while proselytizing and moralizing the popular classes, they set up an extensive network of local relief organizations that covered the length and breadth of Mexico and provided a wide range of medical, social, and educational services. With their characteristic modesty and tact, the Ladies did not attempt to upstage the much smaller male Society of Saint Vincent de Paul. Nonetheless, if the men's conferences perdured, it was the women's association that thrived in Porfirian Mexico.

The prominence of women in the Vincentian lay movement contradicts the stereotype of middle- and upper-class women's domesticity. Ironically, at the very moment when the prescriptive literature was exalting them as Angels in the Home, tens of thousands of women all over Mexico were stepping outside that realm to take on the problems of the world. In truth, despite

the rhetoric of republican motherhood that assigned women the task of raising good citizens, women—even mothers—were not really expected to dedicate themselves exclusively to the home. Although their charity work was
justified as a natural extension of women's domestic roles, it was far more
than that. It involved them in such new experiences as administering welfare
services, running voluntary associations, and disseminating Catholic doctrine to strangers. It enhanced the members' expertise by providing opportunities for them to become leaders, raise and manage large sums of money,
engage in democratic institutional practices, and acquire bureaucratic skills.
In the process of serving their communities, the volunteers thus entered the
public arena and exercised power beyond the family home.[101]

The Ladies of Charity were hardly rebels. They assumed these tasks without
overtly challenging social norms or claiming equality with men. Far from
asserting their independence, they joined the conferences with permission
from their husbands or fathers and worked closely with priests.[102] Still, their
charitable activities gradually increased the acceptable roles for women in the
middle and upper classes. Their volunteer work gave them new skills and self-
confidence. Their effectiveness in the "work of benevolence" drew from and
contributed to the emerging ideology of *marianismo* that defined women as
morally superior to men, thus subtly eroding gender hierarchies to pave the
way for the eventual improvement in women's status.[103] By the end of the nineteenth century, Mexican women were less often viewed as the *sexo debil* of
yore. As explained in the homily addressed to the Ladies in their 1895 general
assembly, with the grace of Jesus Christ their charitable endeavors had transformed "the weak cane of your sex" into "a strong and robust tree in whose
shade the miseries of humanity find refuge and protection."[104] Indeed, the
reports increasingly contained martial imagery that praised the women's
"valor" and depicted them as soldiers in an "Army of generous souls."[105]

The role of church fathers in enlisting the female volunteers—and thus
inadvertently contributing to social change—belies the view of the church as
an institution that solely victimized women or, in less value-laden terms,
upheld traditional values and opposed modernity. The reality was much
more complicated because the Catholic Church provided women with contradictory messages, and it was up to individual women to choose which
ones to heed.[106] While barring women from the priesthood, extolling their
role as wives and mothers, and preaching women's subordination to men, the
church also recruited them to engage in new activities and gave them safe

spaces to develop their talents. And it encouraged them to be strong and brave, as exemplified in the title of a book written by French bishop Jean-François-Anne Landriot, *La mujer fuerte* (1862), which was widely distributed in Mexico and still being read from in Ladies of Charity meetings as late as 1905.[107] Devoting one chapter to the female visitor of the poor, *The Strong Woman* made it clear that the church did not want women to be shrinking violets who stayed home and ignored social problems.

Because the crisis of nineteenth-century Catholicism required an activist laity, the impetus for changes in women's roles thus came from groups normally classified as "right wing," as well as from the "left."[108] Yet the mobilization and empowerment of Catholic women reveals the inadequacies of these labels. In adapting to new circumstances, the Mexican church employed the modern strategy of recruiting women, and the women who responded to the new opportunities both participated in and furthered modernizing processes.

The Ladies' role as indispensible agents of Catholic social reform also forces us to challenge the view of "politics" and the "public sphere" in this time period as exclusively male. The rhetoric of separate spheres for men and women was deeply rooted in Hispanic culture. After independence, republican discourse reinforced the masculinization of the public sphere by identifying citizenship with military service, electoral politics, and government service.[109] The Habermasian notion of a discursive public sphere similarly privileged male actors who worked to shape public opinion in formal venues such as newspapers, clubs, and civic societies.[110] Of course, even by this definition, some Mexican women participated in the public sphere by publishing in periodicals, joining literary societies, and pressuring the government on partisan issues. Indeed, 40,646 women signed petitions protesting the Organic Law of 1874—nearly as many as the 43,420 male signatories.[111]

Yet these definitions of the "public" and the "political" are unsatisfactory because the work of benevolence does not fit into the dichotomy between public/male and private/female spheres. Charity blurred the boundaries between the two because, once the female sphere expanded to include community service, it was no longer private. Nor is it easily contained in the category of "social." As Paula Baker argued for the United States, we "need to go beyond the definition of 'political' offered by nineteenth-century men" to include the many informal as well as formal ways in which women attempted "to affect the behavior of others."[112] Because the Mexican volunteers not only operated in public spaces but also formed public opinion by imposing their faith and moral convictions on people outside their family circles, Vincentian charity was both public and political.

Many historians of charity in other parts of the world have analyzed women's benevolent activities using the vocabulary of separate spheres. Some scholars characterized it as a "female dominion," where female philanthropists and reformers catered almost exclusively to needy women and children.[113] Others conflated the volunteers' politics with "maternalism" because they took mothers' concerns into the larger community.[114] Yet applying these paradigms to the Mexican Ladies of Charity is not only inaccurate but diminishes the volunteers' public contributions. Although Mexicans justified women's new roles with traditional gender notions, this was simply a rhetorical device to make them palatable.[115] Charity work was neither an extension of the domestic sphere nor was it exclusively female. The women shared their mission with male volunteers, collaborated closely with priests and male benefactors, and included men among their clientele. Nor can their politics be reduced to social maternity, because their agenda was much broader than helping children and promoting social welfare.[116]

The mission of the Ladies of Charity was, in fact, highly political even in the narrow sense of the term. As they worked to alleviate suffering, the volunteers took sides in the contentious debates of the day. At a time when the role of the church in society was a burning partisan issue, their religiously motivated philanthropy was a form of political activism. The volunteers not only functioned as social workers, educators, nurses, and pharmacists but also as lay leaders, missionaries, and reformers who spread their critique of secular liberalism, Protestantism, spiritism, and socialism along with their vision of Catholic renewal. By deepening the popular allegiance to the church, they expanded the social base for Catholic initiatives. They also challenged the Reform Laws directly by sponsoring public displays of piety, collecting alms outside of temples, and working to reinsert religion into popular education and public institutions such as hospitals and prisons. These activities manifested their discontent with official government policies that promoted the secularization of Mexico and sought to relegate religion to the private sphere. Therefore, although women were formally excluded from citizenship, the Ladies engaged in practical citizenship by trying to create a society that reflected the values they held dear.

4.

The Gendering of Vincentian Charity

THE DISPARITY BETWEEN the male and female voluntary associations begs explanation. Although the male Society of Saint Vincent de Paul was founded two decades before its female counterpart, the Ladies of Charity quickly surpassed its brother organization. Even as the Catholic restoration picked up steam at the end of the nineteenth century and the women's association grew by leaps and bounds, the male society stalled. On the eve of the revolution, the predominance of women in the Vincentian lay movement was overwhelming. With many more members covering a much larger area of Mexico, the women were far more successful in mobilizing volunteers and supporters; providing health care, education, and poor relief for the needy in their communities; and winning hearts and minds for the church.

Because the conferences attracted so many more women than men, it is tempting to argue that Mexican piety and charity were feminized. The feminization thesis has dominated the study of European religion and benevolence for several decades and is now being applied to Latin America as scholars begin to study these subjects.[1] Yet it is not persuasive for the Mexican case—and has indeed been recently challenged by European scholars as well.[2] It is certainly true that Liberals denigrated the church by associating it with women and Conservatives glowingly praised women as the *sexo devoto*. If we move beyond the discourse, however, and place the conferences in the larger context of the Catholic revival, another explanation becomes apparent. Mexican Catholics had developed a sexual division of labor, with women prevailing in some religious organizations while men prevailed in others. Because women specialized in routine hands-on caregiving, Vincentian charity was increasingly viewed as "women's work." Meanwhile, pious men put their efforts into other—often more public—activities to support the Catholic cause, or they supported the female volunteers from behind the scenes. Many devout men practiced a male variant of charity that consisted of large-scale fundraising, founding asylums and schools, and providing free medical and legal services. Generous shopkeepers, pharmacists, and owners of factories and agricultural estates also donated goods for the poor. Even those men who participated in the conferences tended to engage in different sorts of activities than the female volunteers. Thus Mexican men as well as women were both religious and charitable, although often in complementary ways.

The Feminization of Piety?

A comparison of the male and female groups might at first appear to suggest that women were more pious than men. Although the available statistics are approximations because some chapters failed to report and comparable data are not always available, the feminization of the Vincentian lay movement is evident in a variety of measures. The women began outnumbering—and outperforming—the men soon after the Ladies of Charity was founded in 1863. Over time the gaps between the male and female organizations widened considerably.

One striking difference was in the number of volunteers, as highlighted in figure 4.1. Already by June 1864, at the end of their first year, the 566 female volunteers had equaled the number it had taken the men nearly a decade to recruit. In 1865, at the end of their second year, the women had overtaken them with 997 active members compared with only 791 men. The Ladies briefly lost their lead during their low point in 1885, but in subsequent years, as the female association rebounded while the male society languished, the women's organization far outstripped the men's. By 1895 there were only 1,536 men active in 121 conferences, compared with 9,875 women active in some 400 chapters.[3] The women had thus mobilized over six times more volunteers than the men. In 1908 (one of the few years when national statistics are available for the struggling men's organization) there were 18,180 female volunteers compared with only 1,613 men—a ratio of more than 11:1.

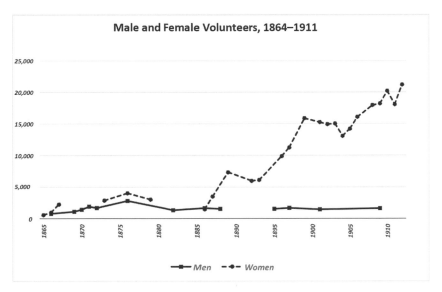

Figure 4.1. Based on data in tables 2.1 and 3.2.

The discrepancies are even more marked in the numbers of honorary members, including subscribers. The Ladies quickly developed a much larger network of individuals contributing money to their charitable projects. In 1865 they were already backed by six times more supporters than the men; by 1895 they had mobilized some thirty times more. In 1908, when the men only listed 78 honorary members, the women had 23,343—nearly three hundred times more than their male counterparts. By then the gap between the two groups had become a chasm.

A similar pattern occurred with the geographic coverage. By 1895 the Ladies of Charity was much more widely distributed across the national territory. With the exception of six chapters in Mérida and one in Oaxaca, the men's society was concentrated in a band across the center of Mexico (see map 1). The Ladies of Charity was in twelve additional states, including all the northern states as well as the remote southern regions of Chiapas and Campeche (cf. tables 2.2 and 3.3). Although the location of the men's chapters is not available after 1895, the leveling off in the number of male volunteers indicates that—even as the society expanded into Tabasco at the turn of the century—it had basically stopped growing. Meanwhile, the number of female

TABLE 4.1. Male and Female Conference Visiting and Expenditures, 1875–1910

	Families Visited				Expenditures			
	Men		Women		Men		Women	
	No.	%	No.	%	No.	%	No.	%
1875–79	714	38.3	1,151	61.7	23,793	36.0	42,243	64.0
1893–97	1,130	1.5	75,855	98.5	48,800	33.2	98,253	66.8
1906–10	727	0.6	130,015	99.4	69,717	24.3	217,253	75.7

Note: Because there are so few years when data are available for both the men's and women's conferences, I have presented the annual average within each five-year range in order to highlight chronological trends.

Sources: Sociedad, *Reseña*, 47; Sociedad, *Boletín* (May 1887), 142; Sociedad Guadalajara, *Boletín* (July 1909), 152; Asociación, *Memoria* (1878, 1895, 1896, 1898, 1906, 1908, 1909), "Estado general," n.p; ibid. (1902), 11; De Dios, *Historia de la familia vicentina*, 2:642–46.

volunteers doubled, and they continued moving into many new areas. By 1908 the Ladies of Charity had chapters in nearly every state of Mexico (see map 2). Its conferences extended out from major urban centers to small towns and villages. The only areas they did not penetrate were Quintana Roo and Baja California.[4] By taking the conferences far beyond where the men had gone, it was consequently the women who gave the Vincentian lay movement a truly national presence.

The women's charitable activities eclipsed the men's as well. The statistics in both organizations' reports show dramatic contrasts. Two crucial indicators are summarized in table 4.1. By the end of the nineteenth century, the Ladies were visiting some sixty-seven times more families than the men. These differences increased in the next decade as the female organization experienced explosive growth while the male society stagnated, and on the eve of the revolution the gap had nearly tripled. Conducting more than 99 percent of all the home visitations in Mexico, the women had become the main providers of the core Vincentian service. Their good works also accounted for 76 percent of the conference expenditures. Indeed, the women outspent the men by 139,095 pesos—and the disparity would have been even greater if the totals had included the value of donated goods and services.

Other categories showed similar trends (cf. tables 2.4 and 3.4). For example, in 1895–1896 the Ladies visited 21,428 patients while the men only visited 1,071; in 1908 the female volunteers had increased their patient visits to 29,058 while the men's had decreased to 172. That year the Ladies arranged 7,622 first communions, 826 marriages, and 393 baptisms compared with the men's 226, 35, and 20. The text of the 1908 reports also noted that the society's schools only enrolled 1,102 students, while the women's association reached some 25,000.[5]

The contrast between the male and female conferences was fully recognized by contemporary observers. As early as 1870 it was mentioned in a heated polemic between José María Plancarte, member of a fervently Catholic family, and Father D. I. Aguilar. Defending his hometown of Zamora from the cleric's charge that the decadence of the "conferences of charity" showed the lack of piety, egotism, and materialism of the city's elite, Plancarte pointed out that, although the male chapters had dwindled, the "abundant" success of the Señoras' conferences revealed his compatriots' deep faith and charity. The "men should learn from them," he wrote, because the Ladies were "like an independent tribe of Christian Amazons" and the true repositories of Zamora's Catholic values.[6]

Why were women in the vanguard of the Vincentian lay movement? Margaret Chowning and Pamela Voekel have shown how, in an attempt to discredit the church, liberals identified it with women. Frequently portraying the Reforma as "a rational masculine force pitted against a superstitious and feminized enemy," they ridiculed devout women as the mistresses of priests or as fanatic *beatas*—by the nineteenth century a derogatory term that loosely translates as "church mice." Conservatives also stereotyped women by praising the deep faith and selfless generosity of the female sex. As Edward Wright-Rios noted, they "framed local clashes of good and evil as contests between moral women in league with clergymen against depraved secular men."[7] Yet despite women's reputation as the sexo devoto, I am not convinced that Mexican women were much more religious than Mexican men.

To begin with, the feminization of piety has only been posited for the urban middle and upper classes, for no one has questioned the faith of most men who lived in rural hamlets—as did the majority of Mexicans in the nineteenth century.[8] Yet even among many well-educated elites there is considerable evidence of the persisting strength of Catholicism. While women predominated in some organizations such as the Vincentian conferences,

Sociedades Católicas, and Vela Perpetua, male piety flourished in other areas. In the second half of the nineteenth century, committed laymen published Catholic periodicals and joined numerous devotional and mutual aid associations. In the early twentieth century they engaged in multiple endeavors inspired by Social Catholicism, such as Catholic workers' circles and confessional trade unions. Devout men from all over Mexico gathered in Catholic congresses to find solutions to the country's social problems. In 1911 they proclaimed their religious fervor publically by founding a Christian Democratic political party, the Partido Católico Nacional.[9] Moreover, thousands of men joined the pilgrimages and huge religious celebrations of the late Porfiriato, such as the coronation of the Virgin of Guadalupe in 1895 that marked the return of Catholicism to public life.[10] And several times from the Reform to the revolution, male militants took up arms and risked their lives to defend the church.[11] Thus, for many Mexican men, religion was a source of social identity and even, as Robert Curley argued for Jalisco, "a fundamental aspect of citizenship."[12]

Could it be that, despite their devotion, pious men shied away from the society because of careerism? After anticlerical Liberals won the Reform Wars, some ambitious men might have concluded that their professional advancement would be hindered by membership in a Catholic organization with close ties to the defeated Conservatives. Certainly, the female association was not similarly tainted, since the Ladies' very anonymity and supposed lack of interest in politics insulated them from the partisan fray. Yet if the male conferences lost some of their earlier attraction, it was not because of political persecution. During the Restored Republic, the society not only recovered fully from the difficult period of the Reform Wars but experienced the best years in its history. The political climate was even more favorable to the lay groups during the Porfiriato, when President Díaz carried out a policy of conciliating the church and encouraging private philanthropy. The reasons for the disproportionate success of the Ladies of Charity thus lies elsewhere.

The role of the church played a part, since it explicitly tried to recruit women and maintained close ties with the women's association that, unlike the male society, was directed by priests. Yet despite the relative autonomy of the male conferences, clerics also reached out to Mexican laymen with far less success. The pope and archbishops offered the male volunteers indulgences similar to those granted the Ladies of Charity.[13] The 1875 Pastoral

Instruction encouraged male as well as female parishioners to join the conferences, as did subsequent instructions in 1907 and 1910.[14] Paulist priests and other ecclesiastical officials repeatedly tried to revive the men's society throughout the Porfiriato.[15] The society also benefited from strong lay leaders like Joaquín García Icazbalceta, who presided over the Superior Council from 1886 to 1894. Nonetheless, the male conferences kept falling further behind the women's.

A more compelling reason for the differences is that men had many other ways to defend their faith, serve others, and reform the modern world. They could do so through work, government service, or—for the most devout—the priesthood. They also had many alternate sources of prestige, sociability, and power, such as the Masonic lodges, mutual aid associations, cultural and scientific societies, social clubs, and political parties that were becoming increasingly numerous in the nineteenth century. In contrast, most of these options were closed to their wives, mothers, sisters, and daughters.[16] Because there were few comparable outlets for upper- and middle-class laywomen who wanted to support Catholicism and improve their communities, many pious women channeled their energies into the Vincentian voluntary organization.

The Feminization of Charity?

The salience of women in the Vincentian lay movement might indicate that it was charity, rather than piety, that had become feminized. Yet a close look at the activities of the male and female volunteers suggests that the explanation is considerably more complicated. Although it is true that the conferences became feminized in the sense that women outnumbered men, it was not because Mexican men were not charitable. Instead, it was because the practice of charity had become gendered, with men specializing in certain kinds of activities while women specialized in others.

To begin with, many men were deterred from joining the society because of the kind of commitment and activities required. The time-consuming nature of volunteer work was one obstacle. The Ladies of Charity 1863 bylaws noted the female advantage by pointing out that Mexican ladies "are always at home and less distracted than the men, who are ordinarily occupied with their business and frequently out of the house and even the city."[17] Another obstacle was that, in the highly gendered world of nineteenth-century Mexico, the demands that the volunteers have regular contact with poor people and provide care with their own hands were considered more suited to women than to men. The task of nursing the sick in particular had come to be viewed as women's work, even though in the colonial period it had been a perfectly respectable activity for the male members of hospitaler orders.[18]

The male volunteers had from the start preferred to operate at a higher level, managing institutions and citywide projects while leaving the day-to-day labor of caregiving to the Sisters of Charity or to female board members and employees. Until the Restored Republic, the men's society played a prominent role in Mexican public life. After 1867, when its partnership with municipal authorities was ruptured, the men continued gravitating to high profile and supervisory activities—or they shunned the conferences altogether. For many Mexican men who wanted to participate in civic life openly, the newly restricted mission of the organization must have made it less appealing.

These preferences even affected the men who chose to join the conferences. The low level of visiting the poor had always been a problem for the men's organization. After promising the French headquarters to increase this activity, each early volunteer only managed to visit an average of 0.45 families per year by 1855. When the Mexican Society of Saint Vincent de Paul began printing aggregation forms for new chapters in the 1860s, it felt the need to explain, in a footnote to the section where each conference was to list its activities, that "the obra of visiting poor families in their domiciles, is the first one that should be listed because it is the fundamental and characteristic obra of the Society of Saint Vincent de Paul and the only truly essential one. The others, such as the rehabilitation of illicit unions, . . . the patronage of children and apprentices, the instruction of workers, soldiers, and prisoners, the visitation of hospitals, etc., are secondary."[19] Despite such admonitions, the rate of visiting fell to only 0.25 families per volunteer in 1875. In 1887 Superior Council President García Icazbalceta complained that "conferences in the *campos* and pueblos, generally composed of poor people with little education . . . who do not understand the bylaws, fail to give home visits the capital importance they hold among us."[20] The difficulty appears to have been more widespread than he admitted, however. If under his tutelage visiting by 1894 reached 0.72 families for each active member, it dropped back to its old level after his death in November of that year. In 1908 each male volunteer was on average again only visiting 0.45 families.

In contrast, the women's conferences took visiting to heart. Each female volunteer visited an average of seven families in both 1895 and 1908. Their rate of home visiting was thus fifteen times higher than the men's. And these statistics may underestimate the discrepancy. The 1909 *Boletín* of Guadalajara's Central Council referred to the worrisome practice in at least one of the male chapters where "families are not even visited; instead the poor have to go to the volunteers' houses to pick up their aid from the hands of the gentlemen who should instead be taking it to them"—probably in the form of vouchers that they could take to local businesses. These families nonetheless appeared in the society's statistics in the same category as those that were visited.[21] The Ladies' greater involvement with destitute families is also reflected in the much larger number of marriages, baptisms, and first communions that they listed on their organization's annual reports, since these were obtained through prolonged face-to-face interaction with individual clients. Other categories that appeared in the women's reports but not the men's, such as the number of rations and prescriptions distributed, likewise reflect the women's emphasis on visiting ailing families and hospital patients.

Even when the women founded institutions, their dedication to personal service distinguished them from their brothers. The *Memorias* of the Ladies of Charity repeatedly noted that the female volunteers themselves served the food in their cafeterias, taught the Sunday school classes, sewed clothes and washed bed linens, cared for the sick, and—even when they paid employees to work in their hospitals, schools, and asylums—visited the institutions on a regular basis. These visits were not solely limited to brief inspections, presiding over special holiday meals, or awarding prizes for graduating children (the limit of many men's involvement with their foundations). For example, in one of their Michoacán hospitals, "each day, two of the *señoras socias* dedicate themselves to cleaning the establishment and assisting the patients; four of the youngest members are charged with preparing the medicines . . . and others are commissioned to provide the spiritual reading and religious instruction every Thursday and Sunday."[22] In several hospitals, the women applied poultices, administered injections, and assisted the medical doctors when they performed surgeries.[23] The Ladies thus appear to have remained directly involved in the daily functioning of their foundations.

The men, it seems, preferred ministering to groups of paupers rather than providing personal care or building relationships with individuals. For example, their prison ministry usually consisted of delivering Sunday lectures to assembled prisoners. Even when the unusual male volunteer taught the catechism to children, as did the president of the male conference in the town of San Pedro Tlaquepaque, he did so by gathering a crowd of students from the municipal school in the corridors of his house every Thursday afternoon.[24] When the men reached out to moralize workers, it was, at least by 1913, by lecturing to hundreds of workers in a San Angel theater.[25] The Guadalajara chapter boasted of its successful—but even more impersonal—antivice campaign achieved when its members, "saddened by the scandalous intemperance that frequently occurs during Holy Week, obtained the closure of *cantinas* and *tabernas* on Maundy Thursday and Good Friday."[26]

The men's reports did not mention certain practices that recur in the Ladies' *Memorias*, such as occasionally taking an ailing individual into their own homes—or, in 1909, the "excellent custom" instituted in "eight or nine places" of inviting a pauper to dine at their tables each day.[27] Instead, the male society's *Boletínes* often praised the selflessness and sacrifice of impoverished women, usually former clients, who sheltered and cared for people who were more in need than themselves.[28] One particularly memorable example comes from Mexico City in 1895, when a woman who had been helped by the Monserrate conference, upon learning that a desperate mother was trying to sell her young daughter, gave her two pesos and then raised the child as her own.[29] The male volunteers rarely established such close connections with their charges.

Another notable difference was the degree to which the female conferences dominated the provision of medical services—not only by nursing the sick but also by founding medical clinics, hospitals, and pharmaceutical dispensaries, as well as by paying the salary of the attending physician when their hospitals became large enough. The reports of the men's conferences almost never mention these activities. Indeed, a few late nineteenth-century documents asserted (though it was not entirely true) that the male volunteers concentrated on aiding the healthy poor while the women concentrated on aiding the sick.[30]

Where the male volunteers outshone the women was in per capita fundraising. Because of their superiority in numbers, the female volunteers collected much more money in total than their male counterparts—nearly four times as much in 1875 and some three times in 1908 (table 4.1). In proportion to their small membership, however, the men were more successful fundraisers. In 1900 each male volunteer on average took in approximately 37 pesos for each woman's 10. Maintaining the same ratio, in 1908 each active male volunteer raised an average of some 43 pesos compared with only 11.5 for his female counterpart.[31] The women made up the difference by contributing their labor.

To some extent, the men's conferences by the end of the nineteenth century functioned more like pious associations than like providers of caregiving services. With ever fewer members, they used the funds they raised to support elementary schools, night schools for artisans, catechism classes, and other welfare institutions staffed by paid employees. They made large donations to local churches, as when the Orizaba conference of the Purísima Concepción purchased "a magnificent carriage for the Sacred Viaticum," and the Guadalajara conference of El Corazón de Jesús built an altar to Saint Vincent de Paul in the Church of San Felipe, decorated with an image purchased in Paris at the cost of 1,273 pesos. Even as their work with ailing paupers diminished, the Vincentian gentlemen maintained the devotional exercises and spiritual retreats meant to deepen their faith. By the early twentieth century they were organizing pilgrimages to the cathedral in honor of the Sacred Heart of Jesus at the end of June and to the Sanctuary of the Virgin of Guadalupe in December. The Superior Council also regularly published the society's monthly *Boletín*, which contained news and sermons from the international organization, an expensive undertaking meant to edify the volunteers rather than directly benefit the poor—and also designed to raise funds to support the Superior Council, since each chapter paid a small fee for the subscription. In addition, the men's society periodically contributed to international relief efforts or to help celebrate milestones of the church in Rome.[32]

The Vincentian conferences had thus developed a roughly gendered division of labor. While the men concentrated on raising money and spending it on highly visible works of mercy, the women went into the community to work one on one with the destitute. While the men focused on educating, catechizing, and moralizing groups of healthy paupers, the women tended to the sick. And while the men put much of their energy into their own spiritual development, the women dedicated themselves to their charitable endeavors. The specialization was never complete, since some men continued visiting the needy even after the Ladies' association was established, and women also engaged in devotional activities, raised impressive sums of money, founded numerous schools and asylums, supported their neighborhood churches, and ministered to the healthy poor. Yet the different emphases were conspicuous.

The reason for the much greater size and activity of the women's organization is not so much the feminization of charity, then, but the feminization of the kind of hands-on poor relief that was central to the mission of the Vincentian conferences. Moreover, the prominence of women may have been particularly marked in Mexico because of the political context. Despite the anticlericalism of liberals throughout Latin America, Mexico stood alone in having a church that was defeated in a bitter war and where convents were suppressed and Catholic instruction outlawed in public schools. In other Latin American countries where nuns continued to provide nursing, welfare, and educational services, laywomen did not need to mobilize to the same degree. These circumstances may explain why there was apparently less disparity between the female and male volunteers in other Latin American countries where these groups have been studied.[33]

The rhetoric of the feminization of charity hides the extent to which Mexican men were also charitable. The records of the women's conferences reveal many examples of male charity. For instance, instead of actively volunteering with the male society, many men supported the women volunteers from behind the scenes. In addition to the priests who served as spiritual directors for the female chapters, some laymen devoted themselves to helping the women run their associations. For example, the Guadalajara Central Council listed male as well as female secretaries and pro secretaries, and the local chapters sometimes included a male *procurador* as part of the slate of officers (see appendix 4 and fig. 3.3). Numerous other men assisted the Ladies' clients at no cost. Thus physicians collaborated with the conferences or set aside a few hours of their practice each week to treat the indigent, lawyers took on cases pro bono, and shopkeepers and pharmacists donated goods or provided them at a reduced price. Although they are only occasionally listed in the association's reports, the number of professionals who contributed their services appears to have been substantial. The *Memoria* presented at the first general assembly of 1864 reported that 74 doctors and 8 phlebotomists aided the new conferences, and the 1866 *Memoria* listed 150 doctors and 11 phlebotomists.[34] For the end of the nineteenth century, Laura Díaz Robles found that many of Jalisco's best doctors—including the famous writer Mariano Azuela of Lagos—helped the women volunteers care for the sick paupers of their communities.[35] The 1901 history of the Ladies of Charity includes men who aided the women in other ways, from wealthy businessmen donating large sums of money to tailors sewing clothes for the destitute.[36] A 1908 *Memoria* praised the "generosity of some *señores agricultores*" who donated products from their haciendas.[37] These men were practicing a distinctively masculine type of charity.

The gendering of charity is also illustrated by comparing the obituaries of three well-known volunteers. Nicolasa Luna de Corcuera was praised not only for her large donations to works of mercy but also for "deriving special satisfaction from personally assisting the sick with her own hands, without ever showing repugnance toward any task, no matter how lowly."[38] In contrast, the men's obituaries did not mention similar acts of caregiving. Instead, José María Andrade was lauded for sustaining several parish schools and poor churches as well as for supporting the less fortunate members of his extended family, including his sister and his deceased brother's widow and children.[39] Joaquín García Icazbalceta's visiting of the poor was only mentioned once, in the eulogy delivered by Bishop Ignacio Montes de Oca to the general assembly of the society, in the brief phrase "he visited the houses of the poor and aided them generously." Other eulogies and biographies instead saved their effusive praise of this "perfect" Christian gentleman for such good deeds as using his considerable fortune to fund Catholic schools and for treating his workers well, indeed setting up—and funding—a savings account (caja de ahorro) for each of his employees, from the top administrator to the lowest peon on his Morelos estates.[40]

Although some of the differences between the male and female volunteers were real enough, they were exaggerated by these accounts. García Icazbalceta had, after all, campaigned to persuade his fellow society members to visit the poor, and he himself did so for some forty years. Yet his home visiting received little notice. By the early twentieth century, ideas about the feminization of charity had become so deeply rooted that García Icazbalceta's biographers felt it necessary to justify his engagement in the society by explaining that he did it to compensate for the emptiness he felt after the death in child-birth of his beloved wife—a false allegation, since he already served as trea-surer of the conference of Monserrate at least five years before she died in 1862.[41] No such explanation would have been required had García Icazbalceta been a woman.

If we look beyond the conferences to survey the larger panorama of pri-vate philanthropy, a similar picture emerges. The charitable activities of middle- and upper-class women were expanding and gaining public recogni-tion. Women had come to dominate certain kinds of benevolent works. For example, Victor Macías-González noted the increasing popularity of charity bazaars and raffles sponsored by politicians' wives that, when timed to coin-cide with national holidays and presidential inaugurations, helped legitimate the Porfirian regime.[42] Wealthy women also founded major welfare institu-tions such as the Asilo Colón, Hospital Concepción Béistegui, and Colegio Luz Saviñón in Mexico City.[43]

Doña Carmen Romero Rubio, wife of President Porfirio Díaz, personified the importance of women in the charitable arena (see fig.4.2). She is well-known for benevolent acts such as establishing the Casa Amiga de la Obrera, an institution that provided day care and education for the children of work-ing women.[44] Less well-known is that she served as honorary president of the Association of Ladies of Charity and of its Superior Council from 1895 to approximately 1905.[45] The role of the First Lady shows the degree to which the reconciliation of church and state had progressed by the 1890s, as well as the degree to which the regime valued the contributions of the private sector. Yet it is significant that it was the president's wife rather than the president himself who served on the board and that it was the women's association rather than the men's society that received the regime's symbolic approval. A male politician representing an ostensibly liberal regime could not have served on the board of a religious organization. Doña Carmelita's participa-tion in the female group shows the degree to which women—and their orga-nizations—provided a middle ground where church and state and Liberals and Conservatives could come together. It demonstrates the degree to which the role of presidential spouses had come to include overseeing welfare initia-tives.[46] Moreover, it highlights the wide recognition that the female volun-teers had earned for providing social services. The relationship was mutually beneficial: the Porfirian regime could demonstrate its commitment to

Figure 4.2. Portrait of First Lady Carmen Romero Rubio de Díaz (1864–1944), honorary president of the Association of Ladies of Charity from 1895 to approximately 1905. Gelatin print in the Casasola Archive, Fototeca Nacional, Mexico City. Reproduction authorized by the Instituto Nacional de Antropología e Historia.

addressing the needs of its poorest citizens, while the administration's indirect support helped legitimate the Ladies of Charity and may have contributed to its runaway success in the late Porfiriato.

The visibility of women's charity does not mean, however, that men ceded the charitable realm to women. The names of men are prominently scattered throughout the few available studies of late nineteenth-century philanthropy, often as institution builders or major donors to benevolent enterprises. Examples include Gabriel Mancera, Francisco Díaz de León, and Olegario Molina.[47] Medical doctors are also praised for their generosity in caring for the poor without charge,[48] and businessmen for giving regularly to the beggars who each Saturday crowded the doors of their homes, offices, and commercial establishments.[49]

These men have entered the history books as "philanthropists" who practiced a supposedly secular and masculine version of charity. Yet the distinction is often artificial and inaccurate.[50] Indeed, the fragmentary documentation on the male society reveals that some of the great philanthropists were also members of the Vincentian conferences. One was Francisco Díaz de León, the noted publisher and city councilman who founded an asylum for beggars, the Asilo de Mendigos, to great fanfare in 1879. Although the institution was not overtly linked to the Society of Saint Vincent de Paul, it turns out that Díaz de León was (at least by 1902) the president of the conference of the Purísima Concepción in Mexico City. Donors to his project included his "business partner" Joaquín García Icazbalceta, who was in fact a fellow Vincentian volunteer. Moreover, the archbishop as well as the city council provided support for the institution, and Catholic rituals were an integral part of its internal routine.[51] Another example is the Colegio Jesús de Urquiaga, a charity school for girls in Mexico City's San Angel neighborhood. Although its ties with the society have hitherto remained hidden, its founder was Jesús Urquiaga, the organization's longtime Superior Council secretary, and his relative and fellow society member Francisco Urquiaga was involved in the school's administration.[52] It is probable that additional connections will emerge as more lists of society members come to light. And, even for those institutions that were not related to the Vincentian organization, the existing chronicles often indicate that many of the men who built Porfirian welfare institutions were inspired by their faith and commitment to Christian charity.[53] Consequently, the discourse that labeled what men did as "philanthropy" and what women did as "charity" is not a reliable description of what Mexican men and women were doing.

Conclusion

Nineteenth-century texts are replete with rhetoric that implied that religion and charity were feminized. These stereotypes came both from misogynist liberals belittling the church by identifying it with women and from conservatives romanticizing the Angel of Mercy. Yet this was part of an ideological discourse that, in effect, excluded women from the supposedly secular and masculine public sphere by portraying their good works as religious, social, or a mere extension of the private sphere. These rhetorical distinctions attempted to maintain the fiction of separate spheres even as women were increasing their participation in the public domain.

This discourse is highly misleading. There were many charitable men in Porfirian Mexico, hidden behind the respectable cloak of philanthropy. And although it is true that women predominated in the Vincentian lay movement, it is not because men were less pious or charitable. What had happened was that Mexicans had developed a rough sexual division of labor where men and women often manifested their faith in different ways and engaged in complementary forms of charity. At the risk of overstating the differences, we could say that men left many of the routine tasks of serving the poor and helpless to the female volunteers, while they operated at a higher—or sometimes simply more indirect—level.

The degree to which men and women worked as a team can be seen by examining the scope of activities that occupied many of the men outside of their conferences. Without complete membership lists, we can only piece together a partial picture of their endeavors. It indicates that, if the male volunteers did not spend as much time working with needy individuals, it was because many were simultaneously involved in other activities to defend their church and religion. For them, charity was just one part of a much wider project of Catholic activism.

Just as they had before the Reforma, many society members worked as publicists for the Catholic cause. In the middle of the century José María Andrade (1807–1883) and at the end of the century Francisco Díaz de León (1837–1903) owned publishing houses that printed Catholic texts, including issues of the society's *Boletín* as well as the bylaws and instruction manuals for both the Vincentian lay organizations.[54] In 1881 Díaz de León also published Juan de Dios Peza's book *La beneficencia en México*, an indication of his commitment to improving Mexican social welfare. Joaquín García Icazbalceta authored studies of major church figures and compiled and printed devotional literature that circulated widely.[55] Another important publisher was Victoriano Agüeros (1854–1911), founder of the Catholic newspaper *El Tiempo* (1883–1912), who became a member of the Superior Council in 1897.[56] Trinidad Sánchez Santos (1859–1913), who joined the capital's conference of Nuestra Señora de la Luz in 1895, published the Catholic newspapers *La Voz de México* (1892–1897) and *El País* (1899–1912), the official organ of Social Catholicism.[57] Members of the Vincentian organization were thus at the helm of the leading Catholic newspapers in Mexico City. A similar situation occurred in Jalisco. Dionisio Rodríguez (1810–1877), a founding member of the men's conferences in Guadalajara in the 1850s and a counselor to the Ladies of Charity Central Council in the 1860s, owned a publishing house that printed many Catholic works.[58] A half century later, from 1904 to 1909, society member Daniel Acosta published the Catholic periodical

El Regional.[59] These men were deeply engaged in inserting Catholic voices into the public sphere.

Several society members also participated in more overtly political activities. For example, in 1877 Juan B. Alamán, José María Andrade, and Joaquín García Icazbalceta ran for office on the Conservative Party ticket.[60] Although in the next few decades Catholic activists shied away from electoral politics, by the end of the nineteenth century a new generation was joining the myriad Social Catholic organizations that flourished in the wake of Rerum Novarum. Trinidad Sánchez Santos was a prime example. In addition to publishing *El País*, he traveled the country giving lectures on the need for Catholic reform and served as an officer in the Círculo Católico de Obreros de Oaxaca, founded in 1906.[61] The male conferences were officially represented in some Social Catholic initiatives. In 1903, for example, they sent delegates to the first National Catholic Congress that met in Puebla to discuss how Catholics could address the Social Question.[62] In 1911 many society members helped form the Partido Católico Nacional and served on its first executive board, Manuel Amor and Manuel F. de la Hoz as vice presidents and Luis García Pimentel (son of Joaquín García Icazbalceta and president of his father's Conferencia de Monserrate) as treasurer. Party leaders also included Francisco Elguero in Morelia, Carlos Salas López in Aguascalientes, and for a short time, at least, Trinidad Sánchez Santos.[63]

However admirable, these activities diluted the attention of the male volunteers and distracted them from the work of Vincentian charity. As Social Catholicism gained force in the first decade of the twentieth century, pious men were even less attracted to the society than before—not because they weren't religious or charitable but, on the contrary, because of how religious and charitable they were. As they gravitated toward the increasingly militant organizations that flourished throughout Mexico, they left women to shoulder the everyday work of tending to the needy. Yet the men did not step back until they saw that the labor-intensive work of the conferences was in women's competent hands.

To some degree, we could say that while women labored in the shadows, men provided the public face of the Catholic restoration. The Ladies' contributions to that project were nonetheless essential: while women rarely joined the new Social Catholic organizations, they helped prepare the ground in which these thrived. For the female volunteers were instrumental in building the infrastructure of Catholic social works and in forging personal connections with people outside their social circles. It was they who more often wiped the brow of feverish patients, held vigils by the bedside of the dying, took food and clothes to the destitute, taught children the catechism and prepared them for their first communions, persuaded Protestants to return to the church, and worked to convince adults to abandon their "immoral" ways. It was more often the women, too, who founded the conferences' schools, hospitals, orphanages, and other welfare institutions. Although some men joined their sisters in these efforts, the male volunteers tended to engage in different types of activities. Many other men who did not join the society backed the Ladies from behind the scenes by contributing money, goods, and services. This division of labor freed committed men to serve the Catholic cause in other ways. The feminization of the Vincentian conferences does not thus mean that women had a monopoly on piety or charity or that men monopolized the decidedly political task of restoring religion in the public sphere.

5.

Jalisco

A Case Study of Militant Catholicism

HISTORIANS WHO STUDY the Catholic revival of the late nineteenth century have repeatedly noted its strength in the central region of Mexico that Manuel Ceballos Ramírez dubbed the *eje geopolítico católico*.[1] Although this "Catholic axis" included several states, especially Guanajuato, Michoacán, and Puebla, its heart was in Jalisco, a large and relatively prosperous state in central-western Mexico that boasted the country's second largest city, Guadalajara. This state emerged as the mainstay of the National Catholic Party in 1912 and of the Cristero Rebellion against the revolutionary government in 1926–1929. These militant Catholic movements built on many decades of growth for the church in the Archdiocese of Guadalajara—roughly coterminous with the state of Jalisco.[2] During the second half of the nineteenth century, the archdiocese developed an extensive parochial infrastructure and a cadre of dedicated priests who helped mobilize the laity by promoting the foundation of Catholic schools, devotional associations, and mutual aid societies.[3] The Vincentian conferences were part of this dense web of Catholic organizations. Although the male Society of Saint Vincent de Paul and the female Association of Ladies of Charity were both founded in Mexico City, by the 1880s their strongholds had shifted to Jalisco.

This case study of Jalisco fills in the picture already pieced together for the nation as a whole. While confirming many themes of the larger story, it also illuminates new ones. The relatively rich documentation for this area, especially for the women's groups, provides additional insight into the experiences of conference members. By revealing their overlapping social and organizational networks, it suggests that the volunteers in this region—perhaps more than in other areas—were part of a broad collective effort to strengthen Catholicism and care for the needy in their communities. The political implications of their charitable activities also come into sharp relief. The regional concentration of the conferences helps explain how a new political party, the Partido Católico Nacional, could come out of nowhere in 1912, just one year after its founding, to capture the governorship of Jalisco and rule its major municipalities. By defending the church in Reforma Mexico, the volunteers contributed to the Catholic restoration. On the eve of the Mexican Revolution, their mission took on additional political significance because, in the process of establishing contacts with poor people, they helped create a mass constituency that could be used for partisan purposes. And, as in other parts of Mexico, the overwhelming majority of these volunteers were women.

Recent works on the revolutionary period recognize the significant female contribution to the Catholic movement, as women flocked to the ranks of the Damas Católicas, a social action organization founded in 1912,[4] took to the streets by the thousands to protest anticlerical policies in 1918 and 1919, participated in massive petition drives and boycotts, and provided critical support for the Cristeros and the embattled church in the 1920s.[5] Yet these works largely present women's activism as a new and unusual phenomenon. The crucial role of women in constructing a Catholic base before the revolution has also been overlooked by Laura O'Dogherty Madrazo in her fine book on the National Catholic Party in Jalisco. Although she notes that the PCN built on networks established by Catholic lay organizations—and refers to the conferences of Saint Vincent de Paul in a few sentences—she portrays them as exclusively male.[6] An examination of both the male and female conferences in the Archdiocese of Guadalajara suggests that this view of the Catholic revival as a masculine project, with women only entering the scene in 1913 when mobilized as a counterrevolutionary force, requires revision.[7] The important role of the Jalisco Ladies of Charity in building not just schools and asylums, but also hospitals and infirmaries, further suggests that women need to be included in the history of the modernization of Mexican medical services. For, if the Vincentian conferences were feminized, they were not marginalized from major developments of the Porfirian period.

The Men's Conferences

The Jalisco branch of the Society of Saint Vincent de Paul was founded in 1852, seven years after the organization appeared in Mexico City. It is difficult to piece together a portrait of the male conferences in the region because the information is quite sparse, especially for the first few decades. Although Guadalajara's Central Council began publishing its own bulletin in 1898, it rarely included information on the local conferences. Particularly useful are two brief histories written to commemorate the fiftieth anniversaries of the founding (1852 to 1902) and aggregation (1857 to 1907) of the first Guadalajara conference, as well as occasional national reports published by the Superior Council in Mexico City.[8]

These records show that the society got off to a slow start in Jalisco, flourished during the Second Empire, and was then badly hurt during the Reforma that was virulently anticlerical in that state. Recovering from its time of "tribulations" in the 1880s, the organization grew steadily until, around the turn of the century, it suffered a steep decline. This pattern mirrors some of the trends experienced by the male conferences in the rest of Mexico, though the Guadalajara conferences did not share in the rest of the country's expansion during the Restored Republic, and they grew much more during the 1880s and 1890s, when the chapters in some other areas were already waning.

The first conference was founded in the Sagrario parish of the city of Guadalajara, capital of the state of Jalisco, when several "honorable Christian gentlemen . . . motivated solely by the divine spirit of charity" met in the chapel of San Francisco Javier and, "with prior approval from the ecclesiastical and civil authorities," created the Conferencia del Santísimo Sacramento on September 8, 1852. It must have been successful at first, because in 1853 one of its members, Dionisio Rodríguez—a wealthy publisher and industrialist who was "one of the greatest benefactors of Guadalajara"—left to establish a second Guadalajara conference, the Conferencia de la Purísima Concepción. But then the association apparently stalled. In 1907 José Tomás Figueroa—a member of the Santísimo Sacramento conference whose father, José María Figueroa, was one of its founders—wrote that the early conference had ceased functioning for a while before being reinstalled in 1855 and finally receiving the formal aggregation of the French société in 1857. The group nonetheless enjoyed some stability because of the commitment of its members. Its founding president, Don Manuel María Palomar, and its first secretary, Don Agustín F. Villa, were "both well-known and highly esteemed in this city for their great virtues, enlightenment, and social influence." Steering the group through its rocky early years, Palomar remained its president until his death in 1870.[9] Nonetheless, these two chapters were the only ones in the region for the next decade.

The situation improved markedly during the Second Empire. After a ten-year lull, new conference foundations resumed under the safe umbrella of the imperial regime—and with the particular encouragement of the new archbishop, Pedro Espinosa y Dávila, appointed when Guadalajara was raised from a diocese to an archdiocese in 1863.[10] The effect was immediate. Five new chapters were founded in the city of Guadalajara in 1864, and a Particular Council was established to govern its seven conferences. The organization also began expanding into the countryside with a chapter in the faraway Villa de Encarnación in the northeastern corner of the state. In 1866 it created a second distant *conferencia foránea* (as chapters outside the state capital were called) in Autlán to the southwest.

By then the Jalisco volunteers stood out for their dedication and number.[11] In 1865 the Superior Council in Mexico City noted how "pleased and filled with hope" it was by the news from the province. So many men had joined the society in the state capital that its ranks swelled to 252 active members. Moved by the misery of refugees from the war-torn countryside, which was compounded by harvest failures and food shortages, the volunteers inaugurated several works of mercy that included a cocina económica run by the Sisters of Charity, a pharmaceutical dispensary, and a laundry and sewing workshop to employ destitute women.[12] In fact, Guadalajara's charitable gentlemen represented 32 percent of all the Vincentian volunteers in Mexico in 1864. Over the next three years the growth in the region was so impressive that it accounted for a quarter of the male conferences founded in Mexico during the Second Empire.[13]

The fall of the Empire in July 1867 abruptly ended this expansion and indeed threatened the very existence of the organization in Jalisco. Controlled by "exalted" Liberals, the state government outlawed the Vincentian conferences on July 3, 1868—the only state of the nation to issue such a harsh decree. Some chapters continued to function sub rosa as the secular Sociedad de Misericordia, with a new set of bylaws approved by state officials. Yet others disappeared or, like the original conference of the Santísimo Sacramento, suspended their activities.[14] Although the ban was lifted in October of 1869,[15] the difficulties continued. The Superior Council reported that "since the extinction decree was issued by those who exercise power in the State of Jalisco," the volunteers had "suffered tribulations over tribulations."[16] In 1869 only three conferences remained in the city of Guadalajara, with a total of seventy-three volunteers. They managed to aid thirty-five families, patronize two boys, and instruct three hundred prisoners and workers, but had no marriages, dying assisted, or burials to report. In 1870, as the conference of the Santísimo Sacramento resumed its activities, the total number of active members in the capital rose to ninety-two. They had stopped instructing prisoners and workers, however, probably because these activities were barred by the local government. A year later the number of volunteers dropped to eighty-one, a sign that the city's conferences were still struggling.[17] The society's decline in the archdiocese was so out of step with the rest of the nation that by 1871 it only accounted for 10 percent of the Vincentian volunteers in Mexico.

While the city of Guadalajara remained hostile territory for Catholic organizations, the conferences outside the state capital apparently fared better. In 1869 the Superior Council reported that the chapter in the Villa de la Encarnación was beginning to recover under the name of the Sociedad de Misericordia. Its thirty-four active members "continued practicing home visitations to the poor that it assists, promoting religious teachings in the prisons, placing some children in schools and distributing aid in kind." By the next year it counted 157 volunteers who helped twenty-six families "composed of seventy-six people who have received, in addition to the ordinary rations of food, sixty-three *varas* of *manta*, five of *jerga*, two blankets, six *rebozos,* and various other items of new and used clothing."[18] New conferences were founded in Tizapan el Alto in 1869, Tapalpa in 1870, and Pihuano in 1871. The 1870 *Noticia* reported that the chapter in Tizapan had thirty-nine active members who, in addition to visiting sick and imprisoned paupers, had buried four cadavers. The new Tapalpa conference already had 105 *socios activos* "who work with such zeal in promoting the works of our Society, that it has penetrated . . . the nearby towns as well."[19]

Despite the few glimmers of light outside the capital city, the 1870s remained dark days for the society in Jalisco. The number of volunteers fell precipitously. The Pastoral Instruction of March 19, 1875, encouraging the formation of Vincentian conferences had little effect, even though Guadalajara's Archbishop Pedro Loza y Pardavé was one of the three signatories and the church granted substantial indulgences to those who answered the call.[20] A few months after the instruction was published, on November 21, 1875, a group of men formed a conference in the state capital, but that was the only

new chapter in the entire archdiocese until 1881, when another was established in Zapopan. Moreover, conference foundations tell only part of the
story, since we do not know how active they were or how long they lasted. By
1895, when the Superior Council compiled a list of existing conferences, only
two of those founded in the Jalisco countryside between 1864 and 1881 apparently remained, in the villas of Encarnación and Autlán.[21] Unfortunately, no
information is available about the date when the others folded. A more reliable indicator of the organization's health is thus the number of active members, which bottomed out at 39 in 1875, rose to 116 in 1877, and then dropped
off again and fluctuated between 64 and 78 for the next six years—a far cry
from the 252 volunteers of 1864 (fig. 5.1).

As late as 1882 the national *Boletín* lamented that the Guadalajara section

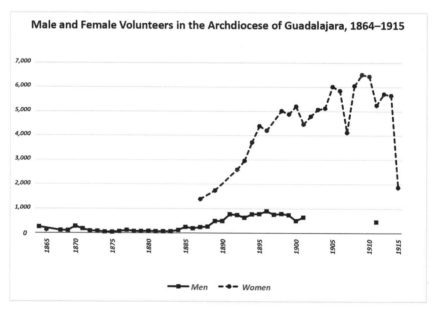

Figure 5.1. Statistics on the men's conferences from De Dios, *Historia de la familia vicentina*, 1:535–36; Sociedad, *Noticia* (1868–1870); Sociedad, *Memoria* (1871); Sociedad Guadalajara, *Boletín* (September 1902; December 1911, 206); Sociedad Guadalajara, *Informe*, 9.
Statistics on the women's conferences from Asociación, *Memoria* (1865 and 1904);
Arquidiócesis de Guadalajara, *Memorias*; Arquidiócesis de Guadalajara, "Caridad Cristiana," 7. Note that where there are discrepancies among the sources, I follow the 1902 list
for the men and the Guadalajara rather than national reports for the women.

was still in a sorry state. The "fervor" and "charitable impulse" of the volunteers was declining each day. Although the number of conferences in the state capital had risen to seven, two of them were barely functioning and, indeed, suspended their activities during the rainy season. It was only with great difficulty that the city's sixty-five volunteers managed to aid forty families, serve as patrons to four girls, and bury two cadavers. The chapter in the Villa de Encarnación was still active but only helped twelve families—less than half the number it aided in 1871. The other conferences in the countryside—if they still existed—failed to report that year.[22]

The organization began to turn the corner in the mid-1880s. The climate for Catholic lay groups improved as Porfirio Díaz's conciliation policy took effect and a more tolerant state government came to power. The Vincentian conferences also benefited from the arrival in 1882 of the new, energetic visitor of the Congregación de la Misión, Father Felix Mariscal, and from the "encouragement, or more accurately, push" they received from members of Guadalajara's ecclesiastical hierarchy, who promoted the society by instructing local priests to establish conferences in their parishes and by contributing to their expenses. From 1885 until he left to become archbishop of Michoacán in 1892, Father Atenógenes Silva of the cathedral chapter worked to strengthen the lay organization by holding monthly spiritual retreats to inspire the volunteers and by presiding over the meetings of the Particular and (after 1889) Central Councils—an unusual practice in the nominally secular society.[23]

By the late 1880s new conference foundations were burgeoning. In 1884 four more were added in the state capital and one in the provincial town of Atoyac. Sixteen additional chapters were established in the next five years, most of them in the countryside. By 1889 the conferences were so numerous that they had outgrown the old capital-centric structure where the only governing body was a Particular Council overseeing the chapters in the city of Guadalajara. Thus, in 1889 the society created the first Central Council in Mexico to supervise the chapters throughout the Archdiocese of Guadalajara. Expansion continued with twenty-eight more foundations by 1895. Although some of these were short-lived, by 1897 the society had nineteen functioning conferences in the capital and at least sixteen in other areas of the state, up from nine and six only one decade earlier (table 5.1).[24] The membership showed a similar increase. With 261 volunteers throughout the archdiocese in 1888, the organization surpassed its previous record from 1864. It

TABLE 5.1. Men's Conferences in the Archdiocese of Guadalajara, 1894, 1897, 1911

	Exists 1894	Number Volunteers 1897	1911
Guadalajara City			
Santísimo Sacramento (1852)	Yes	28	10
Purísima Concepcion (1853)	Yes	12	10
Nuestra Señora de Guadalupe (1864)	Yes	10	4
Divina Providencia (1864)	Yes	14	7
Señor San José (1864)	Yes	13	9
Jesús, María y José (1864)	Yes	13	5
Sagrado Corazón de Jesús (1864)	Yes	22	10
Nuestra Señora del Refugio (1875)	Yes	12	7
Santísima Trinidad (1884)	Yes	8	
Patrocinio del Señor San José (1884)	Yes	5	7
San Luis Gonzaga—jóvenes (1884)	Yes	20	8
San Francisco de Asís (1885)	Yes	15	6
Señor de la Penitencia (1886)	Yes	15	7
Sagrado Corazón de Jesús—niños (1887)	Yes		
Nuestra Señora de Guadalupe—niños (1891)	Yes	20	14
San Felipe de Jesús—niños (1891)	Yes	18	12
Santa Cecilia (1891)	Yes	5	15
Sagrado Corazon del Seminario (1893)	Yes	17	
Nuestra Señora de Belén		17	30
San Juan de Dios [Fábrica de Atemajac]	Yes	8	8
Total socios activos		*272*	*169*
	19 conferences	19 conferences	17 conferences
Foráneas (outside capital)			
Villa de Encarnación (1865)	Yes	20	30
Autlán (1866)	Yes	40	
Atoyac (1884)	Yes		
Zapotlán el Grande [Cd. Guzmán] (1886)	Yes		32
Cocula (1887)	Yes	24	
San Martín (1887)	Yes		
Tepatitlán (1887)	Yes	13	8

Table 5.1 continued

	Exists 1894	Number Volunteers 1897	Number Volunteers 1911
Foráneas (outside capital)			
Ixcuintla (1889)	Yes		
Teocuitatlán (1892)	Yes	29	
Estipac (1893)	Yes		
Tecatitlán (1893)	Yes		
Atotonilco (1893)	Yes	62	30
San Juan de los Lagos (1894)	Yes	35	35
Zapotlán (1894)	Yes		20
Arandas		40	57
Ameca		43	24
Ocotlán		26	
Santa María del Oro		15	
Tala			6
Teocaltiche			45
Colima (3 conferences)[*]		120	
Aguascalientes (2 conferences)[*]		34	
Total socios activos		*501*	*287*
	14 conferences	16 conferences[†]	10 conferences

Note: Foundation dates in parenthesis. The boys in the *conferencias de niños* were preparing for their first communion. The *jóvenes* were aspiring members.

[*] Colima and Aguascalientes left the Archdiocese of Guadalajara in 1881 and 1900, but they were still counted in the 1897 statistics.

[†] This number is too low because the August 1898 *Boletín* noted that there were ten additional *conferencias foráneas* that failed to report to the Central Council; it is unclear how many of these still existed. Sociedad Guadalajara, *Boletín* (August 1898), 27.

Sources: Sociedad, *Reseña*, 50–60; Sociedad Guadalajara, *Boletín* (August 1898, 26–28; December 1911, 200–206).

then continued to grow until 1896, with the number of active members more than tripling to reach 895.

The Jalisco conferences were the pride and joy of the Mexican sociedad during this time period, accounting for half its volunteers in 1894 as well as approximately half the chapters founded nationwide between 1884 and 1894 (32 of 66).[25] A comparison between the cities of Guadalajara in 1897 and Mexico in 1898 (the dates of available statistics) highlights the strength of the organization in Jalisco: with less than a third the population of Mexico City—approximately 100,000 in 1900 compared to Mexico City's 345,000[26]—the city of Guadalajara had both more chapters (19 versus 16) and more active members (272 versus 206) than the much larger Mexican capital (table 2.5).

The reports of Guadalajara's Central Council proudly boasted of the volunteers' activities. They visited 314 families in 1890 and 350 in 1896; during the same period, their spending on good works rose from 6,707 pesos to 11,587.[27] The catechism classes for children were their most successful venture; in 1898 a single Guadalajara chapter, the conference of the Sagrado Corazón del Seminario, taught 1,088 children.[28] The Jalisco volunteers also visited hospitals and, especially, prisons. Although the prison ministry thrived throughout the archdiocese, it especially flourished in the capital's penitentiary between 1886 and 1890 "because of the tolerance of the Government and the good will of the intendant of this Establishment, who was a good Catholic." The prisoners prayed, confessed, took communion, and "gratefully received the religious instruction provided by a member of the Conferences." The volunteers brought them clothes, blankets, cigarettes, catechism books, and rosaries. On religious holidays they treated the inmates to special meals. The men also managed to obtain the release of some who had been wrongfully imprisoned.[29]

In addition, a few conferences founded schools and other institutions to benefit the poor in their communities. In 1886, for example, the conference of San José in the city of Guadalajara founded the Escuela de Adultos del Sagrado Corazón, which gave primary instruction—as well as a religious formation—to illiterate adults. In 1890 another school for adults was founded in the city's Analco neighborhood, but it closed in 1895 when the local conference decided to fund a workshop, the Taller Guadalupano, to manufacture socks instead. Inaugurated to coincide with the coronation of the Virgin of Guadalupe as Patroness of Mexico, the workshop started out with seventeen machines and by 1897 had twenty-two machines providing employment for young women in the families attended to by the volunteers. Both of these foundations lasted into the twentieth century, the Taller Guadalupano until at least 1907 and the Escuela de Adultos until at least 1911.[30]

For a while Jalisco bucked the trend of so many Mexican regions where the male conferences were in decline, but by the turn of the century it too joined the downward spiral. Figure 5.1 shows that membership started to dip in 1897 and then fell precipitously. By 1901 there were only 644 members in the entire state, down 28 percent from the peak only five years earlier. Figure 5.2 shows that their spending dropped by 22 percent, with the sum of 9,045 pesos further eroded by the high inflation of the period. Other indices reflected the same trend. The volunteers visited 269 families, 81 fewer than in 1897. Although the Central Council of the archdiocese published its own bulletin from 1898 until at least 1912, many other activities were suspended, including the visits to hospitals and prisons, which, according to the 1902 report, "in the last few years have been as if forgotten by the Conferences"—apparently because the local government in 1894 prohibited the volunteers from entering the Penitenciaría and Hospital Civil.[31]

Only one new welfare institution is listed in the records, the Orphanage of San Vicente, established by the conference of the Sagrado Corazón de Jesús in January 1899. After three years in a small house, the asylum was scheduled to

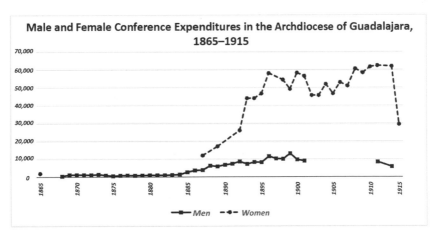

Figure 5.2. Based on sources used for figure 5.1.

move to a sumptuous locale built with a generous donation from society member Francisco Godínez, owner of the Gran Fábrica Guadalupana de Órganos. Following instructions in his will, the new building was to contain a concert hall for the children that could double as an oratory. It is unclear whether the move ever took place, however, because the asylum disappeared from later reports. Another apparently short-lived work of mercy was the obra initiated by several volunteers from the Guadalajara conferences of the Santísimo Sacramento and Santa Cecilia who traveled to nearby indigenous villages to teach the inhabitants the Christian Doctrine. Unable to keep the project going, the society had by June 1900 spun it off as the independent Society of Catechists of Santo Domingo de Guzmán under clerical supervision.[32]

The "decadence" of the conferences was recognized by the Central Council officers when they commemorated the Guadalajara society's fiftieth anniversary in a special assembly on September 8, 1902. In his address to the hundred gathered men, Secretary Teófilo Loreto remarked that the recent drop in membership and resources meant that "our ability to attend to the necessities of our poor brethren, which grow each day, has diminished."[33] In 1904 and 1905 members of the ecclesiastical hierarchy lamented the state of the men's organization and debated strategies to revive it.[34] In an effort to stem the decline, the society even merged with the remnants of the old Sociedad Católica.[35]

These efforts nonetheless failed to reinvigorate the male conferences. The prison and hospital ministries were evidently reestablished, for in 1911 the volunteers reported visiting 1,560 prisoners and 671 hospital patients. But the membership had dropped even further, to 456 active members, and many conferences were reduced to a handful of socios (table 5.1). Their good works had declined commensurately, with the volunteers only visiting 185 families and instructing 374 children and 200 artisans throughout the archdiocese. In addition, they assisted 33 dying paupers and arranged for the burial of 38 cadavers.[36] In the city of Guadalajara, where reliable statistics are available for 1913, the slide continued: by then the state capital only had 131 active volunteers, down from 169 in 1911. The number of conferences in the city had dropped as well, from 19 in the late nineteenth century to only 16.[37]

At the 1902 general assembly, Secretary Loreto blamed "our apathy and tepidity" for this lamentable situation. President Carlos Tapia attributed the conference deficits to the financial crisis, scarcity of silver, inflation, and food shortages that led to "our demoralization" and the consequent "desertions in our ranks." The departure of Father Silva in 1892 did not help: although other ecclesiastical officials stepped in to protect the conferences, Silva's transferal to Michoacán spelled the end of the regular *retiros espirituales* that had fortified the faith of the volunteers.[38]

These explanations for the weakness of the men's society missed some of its principal causes, however. Even in the fertile Catholic ground of the Archdiocese of Guadalajara, where pious associations flourished, there had been a disparity between the male and female organizations since at least the 1880s, when statistics become available for the women's conferences. By the turn of the century the feminization of the conferences was even more marked (see figs. 5.1 and 5.2). Guadalajara was a hotbed of Social Catholic initiatives inspired by the Rerum Novarum encyclical of 1891 and the First Provincial Council of Guadalajara of 1896. Many socially committed Catholic men sought solutions to the Social Question by attending national Catholic congresses, publishing Catholic periodicals, and founding mutual aid societies and vocational schools for workers. The pace of these initiatives increased during the first decade of the twentieth century, with the notable foundation of the Asociación Guadalupana de Artesanos y Obreros Católicos in 1902, the hosting of the Third Catholic Congress in the city of Guadalajara in 1906, the publication of the *El Regional* newspaper beginning in 1904, and the formation of the Operarios Guadalupanos in 1909. By 1911 some prominent men from Jalisco were also involved in organizing the National Catholic Party to bring the goals of Social Catholicism into politics.[39] As many devout men moved on to these new projects, Vincentian charity became even more the domain of women. Yet it was still as necessary as ever, given the poverty and suffering of so many Jalicienses.

The Women's Conferences

The Jalisco branch of the Señoras de la Caridad de San Vicente de Paul was created in the spring of 1864, less than a year after the national association was established in Mexico City.[40] Although no documents survive from the first two decades, it is possible to reconstruct a hazy picture of the early years from a retrospective history published in 1922, as well as from the national *Memorias* of 1865, 1866, and 1878.[41] The picture comes into sharper focus for the period after 1887, when the region's Central Council began publishing its own *Memoria*. These records show that the women's conferences were far more successful than the men's. By the 1880s the female chapters in the

Archdiocese of Guadalajara also surpassed those in other areas of the Mexican republic and remained the stars of the national Ladies of Charity throughout the Porfiriato.

We know little about the role of women in founding the Ladies of Charity in Guadalajara. The clerical histories present the early conferences as a creation of the new archbishop and Paulist priests, as well as of the Sisters of Charity who directed the chapter in the state capital's Analco neighborhood.[42] Founding members of the men's conferences also helped the association.[43] Yet there is more to the story. The speed with which the female conferences multiplied shows that the region's laywomen welcomed the organization with enthusiasm. Indeed, the 1922 history credits several women for expanding the conferences in the countryside. Señora Nicolasa Luna de Corcuera, the Guadalajara Central Council president, is praised for "personally establishing" three chapters through her "direct intervention": in the Villa de San Pedro in October 1865, the Fábrica de Atemajac in April 1886, and her own Hacienda de Estipac in 1884. Another foundation, on the Hacienda de Bellavista in 1894, is attributed "directly to the influence of Señora Isabel Remus, owner, in part, of the hacienda."[44]

Although there are some minor discrepancies between the founding dates given in the 1922 history and in the national *Memorias*, both show that the women's chapters quickly outnumbered the men's. Six female conferences (possibly seven) were founded in the city of Guadalajara during the first year, as was the Central Council of Guadalajara. Its first report in July 1865 informed the Superior Council in Mexico City that 136 volunteers had already signed on. Four *conferencias foráneas* were founded the next year in Encarnación, Etzatlán, Zacoalco, and Zapotlán; Arandas and Atoyac were added in 1867. In contrast, the men's society had by then only founded eight conferences since its first chapter was established fifteen years earlier. Thus, even in the propitious climate of the Second Empire, the Guadalajara Ladies outdid their brothers. The differences widened over the next decade, as the women's association added another twenty-five conferences during the Restored Republic, compared with only five for the men's society.

Yet the situation was not all smooth sailing, especially for the volunteers in the countryside. Many of the thirty-seven conferences founded in small towns throughout the archdiocese between 1865 and 1872 did not send regular reports to the Central Council. Although some may have continued functioning, many others did not. The 1922 history mentioned that a few of the early conferencias foráneas had folded, and it implied the same fate for others that were "reestablished" between 1882 and 1898. New foundations dipped following the expulsion of the Sisters of Charity in 1875 and the death of the visitor of the Congregación de la Misión in 1877; indeed, only one chapter was created between 1873 and 1882, in Amatitán in 1876. Nonetheless, the Ladies appear to have weathered the times of tribulations far more easily than the men, particularly in the state capital, where all of the original female conferences survived these difficult decades.[45]

The Ladies of Charity conferences resumed steady growth in 1882, with the reestablishment of a chapter in the town of San Pedro. In 1884 another three conferences were created and three were reestablished. In 1886 the trickle turned into a flood. By 1895 the Central Council reported that sixteen conferences had been reestablished outside the state capital and thirty-one new ones founded; in addition, five new chapters appeared in the city of Guadalajara. Mirroring this expansion, the association's membership tripled between 1887 and 1896 to reach 4,209 active volunteers (fig. 5.1). During that same decade its spending on good works quadrupled, to reach 46,729 pesos (fig. 5.2). Thus, although the late nineteenth century was a time of prosperity for both the male and female conferences, Jalisco's Ladies of Charity dwarfed their male counterpart even during the best years of the men's society. At its peak in 1896, the male volunteers were outnumbered by a factor of five.

Then, as the men's organization contracted, the women's association continued to expand. By 1909 it counted 6,521 volunteers. Its conference foundations proliferated until that year as well; no conferences were created in 1910, and the last reported foundation was in 1911, when the Zapotlanejo chapter was reestablished and the one in Mezquital del Oro sent its first annual report (though it is unclear when it was established).[46] Even as conference foundations slowed at the end of the decade, however, the organization was still thriving, with 5,250 active volunteers in 1911 and 5,716 in 1912. Numerous special chapters for young girls, designed "to foment the spirit of true charity in the tender hearts of the *niñas socias*," suggest that the organization was preparing to grow further in the next generation.[47] For example, Guadalajara's Conferencia de la Santa Inocencia, although dating to 1889 and reestablished in 1892, swelled to 1,042 members in 1911—all of them girls under the age of fifteen.[48] Thus, despite facing the same economic crises and changes in the ecclesiastical hierarchy that the men blamed for their decline, the women's conferences thrived until the Mexican Revolution arrived in Jalisco. Indeed, by 1911 the women outnumbered the men by a factor of more than ten.

The Guadalajara Ladies of Charity also stood out when compared with those in other regions of Mexico. In the first decade after the national association was founded in 1863, most women's conferences were in or close to Mexico City. In 1865 Guadalajara's new Central Council (one of four in the nation) provided only 14 percent of Mexico's 997 active *socias*.[49] When good national statistics again became available two decades later, the largest concentration of female volunteers was in Jalisco. In 1887 the Archdiocese of Guadalajara provided 39 percent of Mexico's active socias, and the proportion had risen to 42 percent by 1892.[50] That year Jalisco's Ladies of Charity conferences earned special praise from the editor of the national *Memoria* for their religious and philanthropic activities: "The conferences of Guadalajara tower above all others in the Republic because of their activity and the large quantities they have collected and distributed among the poor. They continuously offer notable aid to the indigent, sick, and children of both sexes; celebrate the imposing ceremony of the *lavatorio* on Holy Thursday, when they give clothes and money to the needy and provide them with a holiday meal; and take special care in celebrating with pomp and solemnity the feast of Saint Vincent, as well as those of their secondary patrons."[51] Guadalajara was alone among Mexico's twenty-three Central Councils in being singled out for such recognition.

The region's preeminence persisted for the next two decades. As Ladies of Charity conferences spread to new areas of the republic, the percentage in Jalisco declined but remained disproportionately large. In 1911, for example, when Guadalajara was only one of twenty-eight Central Councils reporting to the national association, it provided 25 percent of all the Mexican volunteers, raised 22 percent of the funds, and distributed 53 percent of the rations and 54 percent of the prescriptions. In 1909 the Archdiocese of Guadalajara alone sustained twenty of the association's thirty-two hospitals.[52] Jalisco thus accounted for the lion's share of the activities tabulated by the national association.

The strength of Jalisco's female association can be measured not only by its membership but also by its geographic coverage. Table 5.2 shows that in

1892 the city of Guadalajara counted twelve female conferences with 1,515 active members, while fourteen regional chapters reported 936. By 1901 there were fourteen conferences in the capital with 1,640 volunteers, and thirty-one in the rest of the state with 2,827. The expansion was thus particularly impressive in the countryside, where the number of conferences had more than doubled in nine years and their membership tripled. Although the chapter total did not increase after 1901—a sign that a few conferences disappeared even as new ones were created—the number of volunteers continued to grow, to 2,182 in Guadalajara city in 1911 and (even without counting those in the nine conferencias foráneas that failed to report that year) to 3,068 outside the state capital.[53]

Thus, by the beginning of the twentieth century the conferences were no longer a primarily urban phenomenon. To be sure, their density was highest in the state capital where the Central Council—as well as a quarter of Jalisco's population[54]—was located. Yet the majority of chapters were scattered across the countryside, in provincial towns small and large, as well as in tiny villages and haciendas. Those on haciendas may have been the least permanent. The longest lived was on the Hacienda de Estipac, founded in 1884 by Central Council president Nicolasa Luna de Corcuera on her own family estate; it seems to have lasted seventeen years, and its last report, submitted in 1901, shows that it outlived her by at least five years. Several other hacienda conferences came and went, with four established between 1894 and 1903. Of those only the one on the Hacienda de Bellavista, led by the "beneficent Lady proprietor of that hacienda," reported to the Central Council in 1911; by 1913 it too had folded, apparently because of "the high turnover of the residents of that Hacienda who could have become socias."[55] Yet the organization's rural presence was larger than what appeared on the Central Council's list because some conferences had branches that did not file separate reports; for example, the San Gabriel conferencia de cabecera (head conference) by 1910 had sucursales (branches) in Jiquilpan, the Hacienda de San Antonio, and the Hacienda del Jazmín.[56] The volunteers consequently ministered to peasants and peons as well as to residents of cities and towns.

The vitality of the Jalisco Ladies of Charity is also reflected in the organization's increased fundraising and spending. The sums collected by the reporting conferences quickly rose from 27,305 pesos in 1892 to 48,625 in 1895, remained in that vicinity for a few years, and then resumed growth to

TABLE 5.2 Women's Conferences in the Archdiocese of Guadalajara, 1892, 1901, 1911

Guadalajara City	Members 1892[*]		Members 1901		Members 1911	
	Active	Honorary	Active	Honorary	Active	Honorary
Beata Margarita (1896)[†]			208	136	454	225
Santísima Trinidad (1887)	40	103	127	54	46	64
Nuestra Señora de Guadalupe (1864)	130	635	170	328	105	85
Sagrado Corazón de Jesús (1886)	384	140	274	nn	140	90
Señor San José y Santa Teresa (1906)					75	96
Madre Santísima de la Luz[†]			199	549	12	4
Dulce Nombre de Jesús (1864)	491	25	20		48	20
Nuestra Señora del Pilar (1864)	148	46	70	30	50	7
Nuestra Señora del Auxilio (1864)	20	44	50	20	30	15
Señor de la Penitencia (1864)	30	8			100	33
Purísima Concepción (1864)	24		50	15	22	2
Santa Inocencia—niñas (1889/1902)[†]	48	5	135	22	1,042	
Sagrado Corazón de María (1886)[†]	24	30	20	10	10	8
Señor San José de Analco (1864)	24	35	100	20	48	24
San Vicente de Paul (1898–1906)			136	30		
Nuestra Señora del Socorro	152	46	81	30		
Total socias activas	*1,515*	*1,117*	*1,640*	*1,244*	*2,182*	*709*
	12 conferences		14 conferences		14 conferences[‡]	

Table 5.2 continued

| | Members 1892[*] | | Members 1901 | | Members 1911 | |
	Active	Honorary	Active	Honorary	Active	Honorary
Outside capital						
Ahualulco (1868)	48	91	98	11	50	27
Ahualulco (2d conference)			56	15		
Amatitán (1876)			185	67		
Ameca (1891)			80	160	118	48
Atotonilco (1891)			76	154	127	196
Arandas (1867)			162	410	194	463
Atoyac (1867)	83	64	105	22		
Ayutla (1907)					150	442
Cocula (1887)	72	206				
Cuitzeo (1889)			70	60		
Cuquio (1889)	144	92	112	nn	30	49
Degollado (1904)					20	15
Encarnación (1865)	60	157	98	485	114	96
Etzatlán (1865)	70	70	104	109	92	107
Hacienda Bellavista (1894)					32	5
Hacienda de Estipac (1884)			38	nn		
Ixtlan	113	484				
Jamay (1900)			115	12	272	27
Juanacatlán (1903)					72	15
Juchitlán (1893)	23	231			70	74
La Barca (1884)			28	72	80	nn
Lagos (1893)			73	104	54	97
Nochistlán (1887)			142	200		
Ocotlán (1868)	193	92	100	111		
Poncitlán (1889)			46	50		
San Gabriel (1871)			136	278	861[‡]	72
San Juan de los Lagos (1871)			100	110	80	150
San Martín Hidalgo (1888)			45	4	53	10
Tala (1893)			236	48		
Tamazula (1871)	nn	nn	56	nn		

Table 5.2 continued

Outside capital	Members 1892[*]		Members 1901		Members 1911	
	Active	Honorary	Active	Honorary	Active	Honorary
Tapalpa			35	nn		
Tecolotlán (1869)	57	552	40	60		
Teocaltiche (1872)			30	100	86	200
Tepatitlán (1861?)	30	25	57	25	200	58
Tlajomulco (1898)			93	24		
Totatiche (1909)					98	32
Tototlán (1861?)	43	34				
Tenamaxtlán			30	6	44	7
Unión de Tula (1903)					30	160
Zacoalco (1865)					66	37
Zapopan (1900)			40	nn	15	nn
Zapotlán (1865)	nn	nn	241	1,898		
Zapotlanejo (1911)					60	nn
Total socias activas	936	2,098	2,827	4,595	3,068	2,354[‡]
	14 conferences		31 conferences		26 conferences[§]	

Note: Foundation dates in parenthesis, from Arquidiócesis de Guadalajara, "Caridad cristiana." I question the early dates for Tepatitlán and Tototlán because they do not appear in the national *Memorias* of 1865 or 1866, or in the 1901 history that mentions scattered conference foundations preceding the creation of the national association in 1863.

[*]In order to make the statistics comparable over time, I removed four conferences from the 1892 statistics because by 1901 they reported to the Central Council in Tepic, part of the new Diocese of Tepic: one each in the cities of Tepic, with 49/114 members, Compostela, 40/208; San Pedro Lagunillas, n.n.; and Santiago Ixcuintla, 51/116.

[†]Also known as Santa Margarita, Nuestra Señora de la Luz, Dulce Nombre de Jesús Niñas, Purísimo Corazón de María. The members of the Santa Inocencia/Dulce Nombre conference were girls under fifteen preparing for their first communion.

[‡]Column does not add up, but I left the numbers as in the original because I do not know whether the mistake is in one of the conference sizes or in the total.

[§]The national report specified that nine active conferences failed to report that year (Sayula, Tequila, Tototlán, Tecolotlán, Atoyac, Tala, Zapotlán, plus two "from the parish"), so there may in fact have been thirty-three conferencias foráneas and sixteen in the capital. In addition, some conferences had *sucursales* (branches) that did not report separately. San Gabriel had three, which helps explain its large membership in 1911.

Sources: Arquidiócesis de Guadalajara, *Memoria* (1892, 1901, 1911); Arquidiócesis de Guadalajara, "Caridad cristiana" (including foundation dates in parenthesis); Asociación, *Memoria* (1911), "Estado" no. 2., n.p.

reach 62,915 in 1911; expenditures rose in similar proportion (fig. 5.2). Although these figures are not corrected for the inflation that eroded their value in this period, it is a testament to the volunteers that they could raise so much money in the first decade of the twentieth century when the Mexican economy was in a tailspin and lamentations of "the poverty and difficult circumstances confronting the Republic" were a constant refrain.[57] Moreover, these figures do not include the many gifts in kind referred to in the *Memorias*, which laud pharmacists who dispensed free medicines, merchants and owners of factories and estates who donated clothes, food, bedding, and furniture, as well as other benefactors who contributed parcels of land for building hospitals, asylums, and schools.

The expansion of the organization's religious ministry follows a similar pattern. The annual *Memorias* reveal a huge jump between 1892 and 1895. For example, the volunteers arranged 248 baptisms and 950 first communions in 1895, compared with only 64 and 134 barely three years earlier. Another leap had occurred by 1902, when the women arranged 3,514 first communions. In that single year they reported achieving 7,023 conversions and abjurations of heresy, though that figure seems implausible because no other year came close. The *sacramentos por devoción* also skyrocketed, from 582 in 1892 to 5,011 in 1895, where they then leveled off for a few years. A new category that appeared in 1909, *visitas al Santísimo Sacramento y a la Santísima Virgen*— where the volunteers took turns visiting these shrines daily—reached 5,685 by 1911. By then the *sacramentos por devoción*, which may have included devotions practiced by the members as well as by their clients, numbered 40,890 (see fig. 5.3).[58] The Ladies of Charity were thus key agents in disseminating orthodox religious practices among the populace.

The female volunteers also stood out because of their contribution to building the infrastructure for Jalisco's public health system. Individual conferences repeatedly reported beginning with home visitations of the sick, then opening a small clinic with a handful of beds, and—in the more prosperous towns— eventually establishing a hospital with separate wings for different types of patients, operating rooms with the latest medical equipment, pharmaceutical dispensaries, gardens, and a chapel furnished with statues of Saint Vincent and the local chapter's other patron saints. One of the earliest hospitals was in Zapotlán, where by July 1867 the conference established two years earlier had already assisted 120 patients. Eventually adding "an operating room, a *botiquín*, and seventeen beds furnished with all that is necessary," it still functioned in the early twentieth century.[59] Most hospitals were founded in the 1880s and 1890s, when the association was expanding rapidly. By 1909

ESTADO del Consejo Central de Guadalajara, de 1910 á 1911.

ASOCIACIONES DE ESTE CONSEJO.	Socias Acti- vas	Socias Hono- rarias	Enfer- mos	Visitas	Vláti- cos	Muer- tos	Bautis- mos	Abju- racio- nes	Confir- ma- ciones	Conversio- nes	Prime- ras co- munio- nes	Matri- monios	Sacra- mentos por de- voción	Socorros parti- culares	Rece- tas de copa	Piezas de ropa	Raciones	SUMAS Entradas	SUMAS Salidas
Consejo																		1,196 69	1,042 52
Santísima Trinidad	46	64	295	9,430	16	10	1		47				5,807		22,339	584	140,196	12,227 06	12,125 15
Beata Margarita	454	225	128	2,286	13	11			3				4,678	32	11,129	995	208,852	11,252 15	11,246 34
Nuestra Señora de Guadalupe	105	85	1,184	758	32	37			27				8,345	12	5,816	225	173,464	8,441 01	8,615 62
Sagrado Corazón de Jesús	140	90	133	161	6	6							2,127		5,177	290	136,795	4,851 01	4,829 99
Señor San José y Sta. Teresa	75	96	151	127	1								2,516	14	6,308	186	17,773	4,586 29	4,586 29
La Madre Santísima de la Luz	12	40	7										672	1	120		22,040	1,212 75	1,200 00
Dulce Nombre de Jesús	48	20	67	516	4	14							348	65	128	147	8,187	378 25	376 50
Nuestra Señora del Pilar	50	7	35	381	2	9							107		245	40	1,047	183 71	124 14
Nuestra Señora del Auxilio	30	15	13	109		1							324		66	121	3,583	174 11	173 44
Señor de la Penitencia	100	35	145	402	31	11			3			334	1,142	146	525	148	1,796	115 35	114 10
Purísima Concepción	22	2	35	103	8	8							48		85	40	576	82 48	77 28
Santa Inocencia	1,042		10	60					52						236	112	2,641	483 81	453 81
Purísimo Corazón de María	10	8	29	54											106		1,271	113 48	118 28
Señor San José	48	24	107	503									50		634		75	208 43	103 12
Atotonilco el Alto	127	196	215	1,307	23	19			108				4,593	121	1,042	52	18,290	5,769 96	5,735 72
Arandas	194	463	35	414	28	15	4		26			820	449	3	161	20	10,950	1,973 70	1,973 70
La Barca	80		49		14	7						385	114		1,095	20	730	1,668 00	1,943 89
Ameca	118	48	61			17											1,037	37 1,037 37	37
San Gabriel	861	72	58	222	4	2	6		19				93	418	278	12	794	45	339 82
Ezatlán	92	107	73	154	20	11						772	297		2,119	3	2,470	726 27	641 22
Lagos	54	97	68	100		23									787	65	5,142	653 86	615 24
Teocaltiche	86	200	34	368	17	7	2		146		5	365	820	43		31	3,260	636 83	631 33
Degollado	20	15	186	288	8	7							70	13		8	114,860	561 23	561 25
Tepatitlán	200	58	46	845	59	13			200		1		729		740	60	3,585	539 73	544 11
Cuquío	30	49	50	480	8	8			20			168	3,500	398		134	1,080	464 00	480 00
Zacoalco	66	37	107	133	16	10	1					384	270	50	1,325		2,135	244 07	219 07
La Encarnación	114	96	15	140	15	4			144			366	366			6		145 70	132 87
Totatiche	98	32	9	92		4	1	1	47							104	6,163	224 81	204 56
Bellavista	32	5	30	220	14	8			13			365	138	78		63	574	210 43	131 45
San Martín Hidalgo	53	10	29	74		9								57		293	200	85	299 83
Jamay	272	27	25	457	17	10	2		125		1		950	250	53	116	5,101	177 09	148 83
Zapotlanejo	60		9	300	30	4			30				876		20			175 77	173 61
Juchitlán	70	71	34	13	2	4	1		61			166	156	2		18	4,360	80 18	59 57
Unión de Tula	30	160	10	300	4	2	2		20			128	108	60	90	30	1,348	74 43	54 53
Ayutla	150	442	4	50		4			20			422	400	14		23		59 18	56 12
Tenamaxtlán	44	7	8	8			5				10	200	500	125			560	57 44	44 63
Zapopan	15		10	30	2	2									100			40 71	36 02
San Juan de los Lagos	80	150	50	60	4	8				30	2	50	50	20	5,600		2,500	360 00	370 00
Juanacatlán	72	15	50	18	10				36		2	780	98	5			80	46 96	46 96
Ahualulco	50	27	48	192	30	15							40	20	450			48 72	63 72
TOTALES	**5,250**	**3,095**	**3,637**	**21,081**	**477**	**310**	**25**		**2,151**	**30**	**21**	**5,688**	**40,890**	**1,947**	**67,078**	**4,031**	**921,689**	**62,915**	**63,150 65**

Figure 5.3. Chart summarizing the membership and activities of the Guadalajara Archdiocese Ladies of Charity, 1911. Asociación, *Memoria* (1911), "Estado del Consejo Central de Guadalajara, de 1910 á 1911." In AHAG, Sección Folletería, Serie Publicaciones Periódicas México, San Vicente de Paul, Años 1892–1960, caja 4, no. 21.

Guadalajara's Central Council reported that the Ladies of Charity supported twenty hospitals, five of these in the state capital. Indeed, four of Guadalajara's modern hospitals—the Sagrado Corazón de Jesús, Guadalupano, Santísima Trinidad, and Beata (or Santa) Margarita—were originally founded by the local women's conferences in 1886, 1887, 1890, and 1896 respectively.[60]

By the turn of the twentieth century, the delivery of medical care was becoming increasingly professionalized. Although volunteers continued the home visitations and staffing of small clinics, they turned some of the larger hospitals over to trained members of the new nursing orders, such as the Servidoras de los Pobres, who took over the Santísima Trinidad Hospital in 1895, or the Hermanas del Refugio, who took over the Hospital Guadalupano in 1913.[61] In the smaller establishments charitable doctors offered their services gratis; in the larger hospitals the Ladies often paid the physicians' salaries as well as the cost of the priest who officiated in the chapel. The amateur volunteers had not yet bowed out, however. Although 1,338 patients were treated in the association's hospitals in 1909, many more (2,501) received care at home. One parish in Zapotlán el Grande was so poor that the women took most of the ailing paupers into their own houses, where they could at least be guaranteed "breakfast, lunch, and supper."[62] And even when nuns took over the Ladies of Charity's hospitals, the volunteers continued in a supervisory and funding capacity.

Not content to stop there, the women "extended their obras to address the most imperious needs of the age in which we live."[63] Most widespread was the instruction of boys and girls, either in Catholic elementary schools or—if the parish was too impoverished—in Sunday schools where the volunteers "teach the Christian doctrine, with which they achieve an immense gain for our religion."[64] By 1912 the conference in Ameca alone ran five parochial schools and thirty escuelas dominicales, covering all the barrios of the town. The Ladies of Charity throughout the archdiocese regularly distributed food and clothing to the indigent and unemployed and often took meals and consolation to prisoners. Some chapters established orphanages and asylums for the elderly (including penniless priests) or for repentant prostitutes known as arrepentidas. They opened lending libraries with uplifting texts and created workshops where young women were taught such marketable skills as sewing, embroidery, ironing, and making artificial flowers. By 1900 a few reports were mentioning the founding of cajas de ahorros where workers could save their earnings, as did the orphaned girls who took in laundry at the Asilo de la Caridad de Nuestra Señora de la Luz in the city of Guadalajara.

When necessary, the volunteers rallied to provide emergency relief. Thus, when the epidemic of fiebre agripada spread through Jalisco in 1890, the conference of Nuestra Señora de Guadalupe rented a house for the overflow patients who did not fit in its hospital.[65] In 1911, as soon as they heard the news of a tragic train derailment at Paso Blanco, the members of the conference of Beata Margarita sought permission from the state government to bring the injured children to their hospital in Guadalajara, where the young victims were healed, prepared for their first communions, and then placed in orphanages if they had no surviving relatives.[66]

While the Ladies dedicated themselves with exemplary "zeal" to helping "the sick poor, orphaned children, desolate widows, and needy families," they also worked to strengthen Catholicism in many ways that do not appear in the statistical tabulations.[67] They took special care to organize community celebrations of religious holidays, especially the feast of Saint Vincent on July 19, the Days of María in December, and Easter Week. One of their emblematic activities was to sponsor a splendid Holy Thursday ceremony where, after the homily, the women washed the feet of twelve paupers and then served dinner and gave coins and articles of clothing to anywhere from a dozen to several hundred indigents. By the turn of the century their *Memorias* also mentioned distributing toys to children at Christmastime. In addition, conference members attended spiritual exercises, retreats, and pilgrimages to deepen their own faith, and they often convinced their clients to join them.

Internal Vincentian reports recognized the importance of the Ladies' "true apostolate."[68] The 1909 *Memoria* observed their "transcendental importance" as "efficient auxiliaries" who helped priests provide "religious instruction, foment piety, and moralize the people." Praising the volunteers' valor and dedication, the 1910 *Memoria* noted that "the innumerable personal services . . . they offered to the . . . sick, both in hospitals and in humble shacks; to the inmates of foul prisons; to the forsaken infants in orphanages; to the children and youth in diverse educational establishments" often came "at the cost of heroic sacrifices, privations, and even danger to their lives."[69]

To be sure, the men's conferences also contributed to the Catholic project, but they were greatly outnumbered: in 1911 there were 5,250 active female volunteers throughout the archdiocese but only 456 men. A comparison of the activities listed in their 1911 reports shows the degree to which the men had taken a back seat to their sisters.[70] The male volunteers only visited 185 families and 671 patients compared with the women's 21,031 and 3,637, only prepared 52 children for their first communion compared with the women's 1,151, only arranged 38 Christian burials compared with the women's 310, and only spent 8,428 pesos compared with the women's 62,385. The women mobilized far more supporters: 3,093 compared with the men's 518. In addition, the Ladies of Charity were far more effective in penetrating the Jalisco countryside: 65 percent of the female conferences with 3,068 active members were foráneas, compared with only 37 percent of the men's conferences with 287 active members. Women consequently accounted for 91 percent of the volunteers in the countryside (and probably more, since the nine nonreporting female conferences are excluded from these figures). The real action—especially outside the state capital—was thus with the Ladies (see map 3).

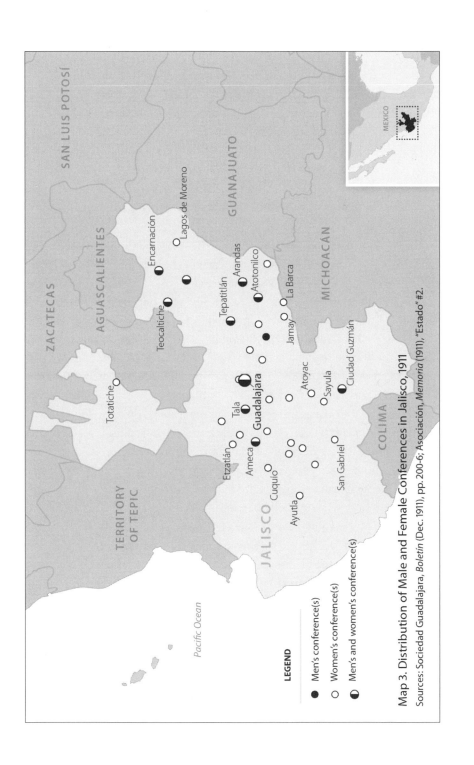

Map 3. Distribution of Male and Female Conferences in Jalisco, 1911

Sources: Sociedad Guadalajara, *Boletín* (Dec. 1911), pp. 200–6; Asociación, *Memoria* (1911), "Estado" #2.

LEGEND

● Men's conference(s)

○ Women's conference(s)

◑ Men's and women's conference(s)

The Politics of Charity

In the first decade of the twentieth century, the Vincentian volunteers—
mostly Ladies of Charity with some help from the much smaller male society—constituted a redoubtable Catholic Armada that labored to defend the
church while providing schooling, health care, shelter, vocational training,
job placement, and other indispensable social services. Although the
Jalisco conferences continued to prosper throughout the "democratic
spring" of Francisco Madero's short rule in 1911 and 1912, this rosy chapter
in the association's history ended with the civil war that followed his mur-
der in February 1913.

The years of violence when anticlerical forces targeted Catholics as enemies
of the revolution were difficult for all Catholic organizations. The Central
Council of the Ladies of Charity still reported 5,657 active members throughout the archdiocese for the year ending in July 1913, but the membership fell
thereafter. The men's society was already decimated by December, with only
131 volunteers left in the city of Guadalajara. By then the figures from the
countryside were unreliable. At least one conference, in Teocaltiche, "was
forced to suspend its meetings for four months when the revolutionaries
attacked the population."[71] After that the situation deteriorated dramatically
and written records disappeared. The 1922 report described the "mortal persecution" Catholic activists suffered at the hands of Carranzista forces in 1914,
which included the confiscation of some of the Vincentian hospitals, orphanages, and schools. Many of the rural conferences were "paralyzed" because of
the "continuous alarm and insecurity in the countryside," while others "continued their activities with true heroism."[72] Some militant families fled to
Mexico City or the United States. The civil war also spelled the death of the
National Catholic Party that had blossomed in Jalisco in 1912.

Despite the triumph of "the anti-religious revolution," the Jalisco conferences staged a weak, and apparently short-lived, recovery. Beginning in 1915
some of them resumed their work "in silence," and their Central Council
held its monthly meetings "in secret." Still, there were only 1,869 active
female volunteers by July 1915—apparently an increase from the low point a
year earlier. Scattered information from later years suggests that the women's
association slowly regained membership, with 2,640 volunteers in 1918 and
3,869 in 1920.[73] These numbers were nonetheless smaller than before the revolution, when over 6,000 volunteers were counted.[74] The men's society had a

harder time bouncing back, and in 1921 it had only 174 volunteers in the entire Archdiocese of Guadalajara.[75]

The Ladies' association thus seems to have lost its prerevolutionary vigor and the foundering men's society continued to struggle. In addition to operating in a hostile political environment, the Vincentian lay groups faced competition from new social action organizations that stole some of their thunder.[76] Then, like all Catholic associations, they were forced to lower their profile when the Cristeros lost their fight with the revolutionary government in 1929.[77] Later, with the expansion of the public health and education systems in the 1930s and 1940s, as well as the professionalization of nursing and social work, Vincentian charity lost much of its raison d'être.

Yet the dramatic crises of the revolutionary years and the subsequent decline of the conferences should not allow us to forget what came before. Nor should the eventual defeat of the Catholic movement obscure the links between the volunteers' benevolent activities and political developments in Jalisco. By defending the church in post-Reforma Mexico, the ladies and gentlemen of the Vincentian conferences had for decades served as soldiers fighting the culture wars of the day. As they reached out to the poor at the beginning of the twentieth century, the volunteers were also creating networks that contributed to the capacity of Catholic movements for rallying the masses. When they embarked on their good works they could not have foreseen that their efforts would pave the way for a political party and eventually an armed resistance movement. On the eve of the revolution they had nonetheless reached a huge number of people who could be mobilized when the need arose. Because of the feminization of the conferences, the Ladies of Charity must be front and center in any discussion of the political implications of Vincentian charity.

It is difficult to quantify the scale of the association's potential constituency because the statistics in the annual reports are only the tip of the iceberg. Although the tabulations omit many of the people who were aided, occasional notations indicate their numbers. The Ladies of the Guadalajara archdiocese instructed 8,887 children in 1909 and 11,000 in 1911, for example.[78] They treated 61,430 paupers to special holiday meals in 1911.[79] That same year a new public cafeteria (*comedor público*) in Ameca alone fed 800 to 1,000 people daily.[80] Moreover, the networks of the Ladies' conferences included not only the paupers who received assistance but also their families, not only the children in their charity schools but also their parents, not only the new members recruited to join the organization but also the employees who staffed their institutions and the benefactors who supported them. Presumably these networks included the volunteers' servants and relatives as well. And annual figures must be compounded to include the people who had been aided or influenced in previous years, with whom the volunteers often maintained ongoing relationships.

The annual reports contain some hints of how to measure the broader impact of these charitable activities. In 1911 Guadalajara's male conferences specified that their 185 adopted families were composed of 646 people; using this multiplier, when their female counterparts conducted 21,031 home visits that year, they would have worked with 73,605 people.[81] Anecdotes from individual conference reports provide further glimpses of the size of their clientele. For example, in 1909 the Ladies of Charity in Tala celebrated the feast of Saint Vincent with great "splendor." After the local curate officiated at a solemn mass, the volunteers served dinner to 280 paupers, with musical accompaniment provided by the municipal band. The next day the women distributed 250 articles of clothing to the needy and then proceeded to elect their conference dignitaries.[82] The festivities organized by the local conference therefore drew the entire community together. The Ladies' sponsorship of centennial celebrations of independence in September 1910 (in possible violation of laws mandating the separation of church and state) had a similar effect, when several conferences inserted a religious element into the civic ceremonies, and following the model of religious holidays, served a feast and gave presents to the town's paupers.[83]

The Ladies of Charity likewise increased the presence of the church through its hospital foundations. For example, when the Conferencia del Señor San José y Santa Teresa in the state capital built a "magnificent" hospital in the periphery of the city for curing eye diseases, it included a chapel that was open to the public as well as to patients. Because "the *pobladores* of a barrio so distant from the temples in the center now had a sacred place where they could go to fulfill their religious duties," this outlying area gained access to a neighborhood church.[84] The inauguration ceremonies of the association's hospitals also reinforced the faith of local residents. For example, when after years of fundraising and construction the Ladies of Cocula enlarged their small hospital, the newly renovated establishment was "solemnly blessed" in a special Mass "attended by the majority of the population."[85]

The volunteers' broad geographical distribution meant that their influence reached far and wide. Working in some sixteen conferences in the capital and thirty-three foráneas in 1911, the 5,250 members of Ladies of Charity
were active in nearly half the parishes in the Archdiocese of Guadalajara.[86]
The men's society increased the Vincentian coverage, with some 456 additional volunteers distributed among seventeen conferences in the state capital and ten scattered throughout the state, usually in the same locales where
the women's chapters existed (see map 3; cf. tables 5.1, 5.2). In the early twentieth century, several of the conferences expanded into the countryside by
establishing rural branches and founding *círculos rurales* (rural study
groups) to teach Catholic doctrine to the inhabitants of nearby rancherías
and pueblos. The conference of Cuquío alone boasted twelve *círculos rurales*
in 1905, twenty-two in 1909, thirty-two in 1910, and thirty-three in 1912, a sign
that the rural ministries were growing rapidly on the eve of the civil war.[87]

The Vincentian conferences had thus constructed a network that incorporated hundreds of thousands of people throughout Jalisco. Although most of
the volunteers were middle and upper class, they reached out to servants,
seamstresses, employees, artisans, workers, farmers, and peons. Their activities touched entire communities and not just the needy they aided. They helped
link far-flung villages and towns to major cities. Indeed, the centralized organization of the Vincentian conferences provided a unifying structure, and the
annual meetings drew volunteers from all over Jalisco to the state capital. The
circulation of the men's *Boletín* and the women's *Memoria* also facilitated communication within the archdiocese.[88] Thus bridging the rural-urban divide,
the conferences also crossed social classes and generations.

The Vincentian volunteers were not alone in their endeavors: they formed
part of a much larger—and often overlapping—web that encompassed priests
as well as many other lay activists. Together, they created the constituency that
helped propel the National Catholic Party to prominence in impressively short
time. Because of this large Catholic network, the Partido Católico Nacional
founded in May 1911, a few days before the dictator Díaz resigned, was uniquely
poised to take advantage of the return of democracy. When universal male
suffrage was established shortly thereafter, politicians had to reach beyond the
narrow social and geographical circles that had sustained them in the past. In
the days before radio (which reached Mexico in the 1920s and was used to great
effect by Lázaro Cárdenas in building his mass party in the 1930s), it was

difficult for a candidate to recruit followers. Despite the presence of a few rail-road lines after 1888, Jalisco's large size, rugged terrain, and generally poor transportation made organizing people outside the major urban centers par-ticularly challenging; indeed, on the eve of the revolution it still took five days to travel from Colotlán to Guadalajara.[89] Political movements therefore depended on social networks that utilized the relationships among family, friends, and patrons with their servants, employees, and clients. As O'Dogherty Madrazo explains, though all politicians of the time tried to enlist support among their subordinates, what distinguished the PCN was its ability to engage in "corporative mobilization" that relied on its ties with the church, which had a strong presence throughout the archdiocese. In addition to utiliz-ing parish structures to found party cells, the PCN obtained support from "the networks of ecclesiastical influence": schools and benevolent organizations, pious associations and mutual aid societies, and the Catholic press. Indeed, many party members had themselves founded or participated in these institu-tions. Their close association with the church and lay organizations not only gave the party legitimacy but also provided communication channels and an extensive social base that could translate into campaign workers and votes.[90]

It is difficult to document the links between the party and the Vincentian conferences, especially because the PCN's membership lists have been lost and the male society's reports rarely include the names of its members.[91] Some well-known examples of male volunteers who joined the PCN come from other parts of Mexico, as discussed in chapter 3. In Jalisco, O'Dogherty Madrazo discovered that in Ciudad Guzmán (formerly Zapotlán el Grande) party activists Ricardo Hernández and Francisco Arias were members of the local conference.[92] Perhaps not surprisingly, this city—which Elisa Cárdenas Ayala described as a bastion of Catholic Social Action—gave more than 90 percent of its votes to the PCN in the election of January 1911.[93]

Many of the connections, especially those between Jalisco's Ladies of Charity and the PCN, are largely circumstantial. Although the correlation was far from perfect, the party gained offices in many of the same locales where the conferences functioned, such as the towns of Jamay and Zapotlán.[94] These were also places where local clerics promoted the party. Indeed, in the city of Guadalajara Father Miguel de la Mora—who had for years collaborated closely with the conferences—instructed parish priests to help establish the PCN.[95] He most likely sent the word out for conference members to support it as well. Another potential link was through a shared ideology. Both the conferences and the PCN wanted to create a space for the church to function openly, with freedom of speech, freedom of association, and the right of Catholic organizations to operate schools and own property.[96]

In addition, shared surnames suggest family ties between the party leaders and the volunteers. Notable was Palomar, surname of party leader and later Cristero activist Miguel Palomar y Vizcarra, as well as of several officers of the Ladies of Charity conferences in the state capital. The Palomar women included the vice president and treasurer of the Central Council (Concepción Corcuera de Palomar and Catalina Palomar, *viuda de Verea*), the *proveedora* and *ropera* of the conference of the Santísima Trinidad (Dolores González Palomar and Concepción González Palomar), and the secretary and treasurer of the conference of the Sagrado Corazón de María (Concepción González Palomar and Mercedes González Palomar).[97] The women's surnames also suggest connections with other Catholic activists such as Efraín González Luna, a Cristero militant who later founded the Catholic National Action Party (PAN) in 1939.[98]

The recurrence of certain surnames within the conferences illustrates the importance of kinship in the Vincentian organizations (see fig. 3.3 and appendix 4). The Central Council of the Guadalajara Ladies of Charity, for example, had for decades been dominated by Corcuera, Palomar, and Verea women, members of Guadalajara's leading families that were interrelated by marriage. Its first president was Señora Nicolasa Luna de (that is, married to) Corcuera, who was succeeded in 1895 by her daughter Señora Antonia Corcuera de Moreno, who was succeeded in 1910 by Señora Concepción Corcuera de Palomar, who was succeeded in 1919 or 1920 by Señorita Vicenta Verea, who was succeeded after her death in 1933 by Señora Catalina Palomar de Verea, daughter of Doña Concepción Corcuera de Palomar.[99] The Central Council members belonged to an individual conference as well, and for the Palomar women it was either the conference of the Santísima Trinidad or the Sagrado Corazón de María in the city of Guadalajara. Many members of chapters throughout the archbishopric had similar connections through blood or marriage. For example, Arce women clustered in the capital's conference of Nuestra Señora de Guadalupe, as did Mora women in its conference of the Sagrado Corazón de Jesús. Outside the capital, Avelar women served together in Nochistlán, as did De la Torre women in Tepatitlán and

San Juan de los Lagos, to name just a few.[100] The continuous presence of members of the same families in the Ladies' conferences suggests their commitment over generations to the "family project" of charity, an essential part of the identity of many of Jalisco's Catholic upper and middle classes.

The stability of the volunteers' networks is also evident in the length of individual women's participation. It was not only in the Central Council that officers held the same position for decades, as did its first president Nicolasa Luna de Corcuera, who served from 1864 until her death in 1894. In Guadalajara's conference of the Santísima Trinidad, for example, Señorita Vicenta Verea became secretary in December 1887, was elected president to succeed Señorita Dolores González Palomar in 1897 or 1898, and remained in that post until her death in 1933. A 1934 report praised her as "the soul of our association, to which she devoted her entire life."[101] Señorita Mercedes Morfín Silva similarly served as secretary of the conference of Nuestra Señora de la Luz (directed by her relative, possibly brother, Father Enrique Morfín Silva) from at least 1898; by 1909 she had joined the Central Council as its pro secretary, and she continued to hold both positions until at least 1913.

The interlacing of Catholic networks can be seen in the volunteers' often multiple affiliations. For example, Catalina Palomar de Verea not only served the Central Council for some forty years, first as its treasurer from 1896 to at least 1932 and then as its president from at least 1934 to 1937,[102] but by 1931 also presided over the new Luisa de Marillac conference in Guadalajara city.[103] Moreover, she (like many other members of the Ladies of Charity) simultaneously joined the new Unión de Damas Católicas when it was founded in Guadalajara in 1913 and served as its president from at least 1918 until 1923.[104] An earlier example of overlapping affiliations comes from the 1870s, when Nicolasa Luna de Corcuera joined the Sociedad Católica de Señoras de Guadalajara as a *consejera* (adviser) while retaining her position as president of the Guadalajara Ladies of Charity Central Council.[105]

Similar patterns can be found in the male society's conferences. Many men volunteered for decades, as did Carlos Tapia, who joined the Society of Saint Vincent de Paul as a young aspiring member in 1865, became president of Guadalajara's Central Council in 1897, and served in this capacity until at least 1902.[106] The conferences' members included generations of male relatives, such as father and son José María and José Tomás Figueroa of the Santísimo Sacramento conference in Guadalajara city. They often belonged to multiple lay associations; for instance, the younger Figueroa was an engineer and central figure in the cultural society El Ateneo, as well as a founding member of the Operarios Guadalupanos, which helped establish the Partido Católico Nacional.[107] In Ciudad Guzmán, Ricardo Hernández and Francisco Arias were simultaneously members of the local conference and of the Sociedad Arias y Cárdenas, which had ties to Social Catholic mutual aid associations.[108]

The Palomar family provides the best example of long-standing family loyalties to the conferences. Don Manuel María Palomar was the president of the first male conference in Guadalajara, established in 1852. One of the organization's most generous benefactors was Don José Palomar, grandfather of Catholic activist Miguel Palomar y Vizcarra.[109] José Palomar was also linked with the Vincentian conferences because both men and women had chapters in his textile factory, the Fábrica de Atemajac.[110] Recurring last names like Palomar further suggest that some of the male volunteers were husbands or sons of women in the female conferences. Catholic activists thus shared associational bonds as well as family, friendship, and faith.[111]

We can only assume, then, that when Miguel Palomar and other political leaders sent out the call to support the new Catholic party in 1911, the message was relayed through their relatives as well as through lay organizations that included the conferences of Saint Vincent de Paul. O'Dogherty Madrazo labels Jalisco the "laboratory of the PCN." After sweeping electoral victories in October 1912, the party captured the governorship of Jalisco, dominated the state Congress, and ruled most major municipalities—though not the capital, where it was hotly contested by Liberals.[112] This overlapping geography seems far from coincidental.

The meteoric rise of the National Catholic Party in Jalisco (and, later, the strength of the Cristero rebels in its countryside) is difficult to explain without understanding the vibrant base constructed by lay activists—men and, above all, women—who for many decades did the "work of ants": the time-consuming task of making contacts and spreading their ideological message, one person at a time, beyond the confines of their homes and neighborhoods into *arrabales*, barrios, rancherias, haciendas, *aldeas*, and pueblos throughout Jalisco. In the context of post-Reforma Mexico, the faith-based charity of the Vincentian volunteers was never apolitical. By strengthening Catholicism in their communities, they created the environment in which the later political initiatives flourished. As the Mexican Revolution approached they played the additional role of helping to establish and maintain the networks that were essential to the PCN's success. And, because of the preponderance of the female conferences, it was mostly women who constructed this foundation while engaging in Vincentian charity. As the pious Ladies quietly went about their business, they may have been unremarkable to many observers. Yet the self-effacing volunteers were in the thick of the partisan battles of their day, unwittingly—or perhaps deliberately—functioning as grassroots organizers for the militant Catholic movement. Although Catholic politicians downplayed the degree to which they relied on women, the revolutionaries remembered their effectiveness when they withheld women's suffrage until 1953 for fear that it would strengthen the hand of their enemies.

6.

Charity for the Modern World

Concluding Remarks

AUSTEN IVEREIGH'S EDITED volume, *The Politics of Religion in an Age of Revival,* helps rescue Latin America from the distortions of liberal historiography by showing that much of the region shared in the Catholic revival sweeping through Europe in the nineteenth century. Yet the chapters on Mexico give the impression that it did not participate in the Catholic movements that mobilized society elsewhere.[1] On the contrary, the history of the Vincentian conferences suggests that the Mexican Catholic Church was far from a decadent, retrograde institution rescued for modernity only by Rerum Novarum in 1891. Decades earlier, Mexican activists established a new kind of lay association that dedicated itself to helping the poor as a way to defend Catholicism. The male Society of Saint Vincent de Paul, founded in 1845, was the first branch of the French organization in the American hemisphere; the Association of Ladies of Charity of Saint Vincent de Paul, founded in 1863, was not only one of the earliest (though it followed the US branch by six years) but also the largest outside of France.[2] With the help of the conference volunteers, the Mexican Catholic Church experienced a dramatic resurgence during the Porfiriato despite the midcentury anticlerical Reforma. Although the recuperation of the church has been termed a Catholic restoration, however, it did not represent a simple return to an older status quo.

The innovative nature of Vincentian charity is not always readily apparent because it had many "traditional" as well as "modern" characteristics. These terms are problematic, to be sure. For one thing, they can be defined in many different ways. For another, it is difficult—and, indeed, misleading—to draw sharp distinctions between the two because they were so often intertwined, with modernity drawing from, and coexisting with, many deeply rooted colonial traditions.[3] Yet these categories are nonetheless useful for examining continuities and changes. And change there was. As Sol Serrano noted for Chile, "nineteenth-century charity . . . was far from being . . . a 'traditional praxis.'"[4] The form and purposes of both the male and female conferences show that Mexican Catholics shared in many contemporary trends. They contributed to the creation of modern systems of public health, education, and social welfare as well as to the development of novel associative and administrative practices. They disseminated democratic and capitalist values, and they helped expand women's roles. Moreover, they were the harbingers of a new lay militancy that paved the way for the progressive Catholic movements of the late nineteenth century.

A New Sociability

The nineteenth century was a golden age for voluntary associations as new social clubs, Masonic lodges, scientific and literary societies, mutual aid organizations, and political parties emerged throughout Mexico. Viewing this trend as part of the modernization of the independent nation, scholars such as François-Xavier Guerra and Carlos Forment linked membership in these groups to the rise of civil society and democratic life.[5] Although Catholic lay groups are usually overlooked in studies of the development of civic culture, they shared many similarities with their secular counterparts and provided an alternate site for sociability, identity formation, and the shaping of public opinion.

The conferences do not fit neatly into historical categories. As Sarah Curtis noted for France, the Vincentian movement "reinvented" models from the Catholic Reformation for a new age.[6] In particular, the idea of organizing society into functional groups followed the plan proposed in 1822 by the Catholic thinker Félicité Robert de Lamennais to reconstruct the corporations of the Ancien Régime in order to counter the evils of individualism. Ozanam, who heard Lamennais lecture in 1831, took this idea to heart when he created the Conférence de la Charité two years later.[7] So did his compatriots when they formed Catholic study circles, mutual aid associations, and workers' organizations in the decades that followed. The project to promote new Catholic collectivities was particularly relevant in Mexico, where Bourbon reformers had already weakened the confraternities and abolished the guilds before independence and where Liberals mounted a sweeping attack on the corporate system during the Reforma. The Mexican conferences thus became part of a broader corporatist strategy to incorporate all the faithful into associations structured by age, gender, and class, an approach meant to regenerate society as well as to help the church recover its lost prestige and influence.

Aside from the defensive and reformist purposes that set the new Catholic organizations apart from the old, in many ways the conferences can be viewed as a revival of the confraternities that had formed the cornerstone of colonial civil society.[8] The ideal of creating a fraternal community was central to both groups. As Asunción Lavrin noted, the confraternity was, "after the parish church, . . . the vehicle most often used by people at all levels of society to organize themselves socially outside of their families. It was also an association that gave a special direction to the members' lives, in practical as well as spiritual matters, permitting them to channel their energies toward administrative, charitable, or pious goals."[9] In a Catholic society, membership conferred prestige or, as Peter Guardino noted, "at least recognition of one's piety."[10] Underscoring these similarities, the chapters of the Ladies of Charity were often referred to by their centuries-old name of *cofradías* as well as by the more modern terms *conferencias* or *asociaciones*, and members of both the men's and women's chapters were occasionally called cófrades as well as socios and socias.

Like the confraternities, the Vincentian organizations had close ties with the church. In the case of the female association, the connection was official and open. In the case of the men's it was unofficial and sometimes hidden, especially during the Reforma, when the society insisted that it was an independent secular organization. With the rapprochement between the church and state during the Porfiriato, these ties became more visible. Thus, the fiftieth-anniversary review published by the society in 1895 proudly proclaimed that its "adhesion and submission to the church have been absolute and invariable since the first day."[11] Although this statement cannot be verified on the basis of available records, it is certainly true that even though the male conferences did not have clerical directors, they maintained a special relationship with the Paulist Fathers and—until their suppression in 1875—with the Sisters of Charity. The volunteers worked hand in hand with the church in promoting the Catholic cause, and they never hid their devotional and proselytizing goals.

Like the confraternities, both the men's and women's organizations provided a locus for reinforcing the faith of their members. Indeed, the bylaws of the male society insisted that its principal goal was "the zeal to save souls, above all those of its members," using works of charity as the means to this end.[12] In order to achieve their sanctification, conference members worshipped together just as the cófrades had. Their annual assemblies included a sermon and closed with a prayer. They practiced special devotions, such as celebrating the feast day of Saint Vincent de Paul on July 19. Some of the chapters donated and decorated chapels to honor the saint, and many took his name rather than that of the local parish. They promoted regular sacramental practices and group spiritual exercises. The volunteers and benefactors earned indulgences by participating. (Just like the confraternity members of yore, the Ladies of Charity even received patents that outlined these spiritual benefits.) In addition, both organizations strengthened the ties between the church and the faithful.

The conferences also functioned like confraternities by praying for sick and deceased members. Although this practice was part of the women's association from the start, it was not apparently customary in the early French men's organization.[13] By the 1850s, however, annotated versions of the Society of Saint Vincent de Paul's bylaws were explaining that "we have introduced the custom of asking . . . after any sick member . . . to pray in common for him at the end of the session. The president appoints one of the members to visit the sick or afflicted socio. In the same session we pray the De Profundis when we learn that one of our brothers has died, in addition to the Mass that we will celebrate for him later."[14] Indeed, when the society's founder, Dr. Manuel Andrade, died in 1848, fellow conference members carried his body on their shoulders from the center of Mexico City to the distant cemetery of Santa Paula.[15] These practices were still being observed as late as 1913.[16] In caring for their fellow members in sickness and in death, the Mexican conferences thus followed colonial traditions of mutual aid in guilds and confraternities.

Yet they represented a departure as well. Unlike the confraternities, the conferences did not exist primarily to protect a particular church or religious image, or to care for their own members or their survivors in times of need.[17] Instead, the Vincentian volunteers devoted themselves to helping total strangers on a regular basis. To be sure, some confraternities had aided hospital patients and prisoners, but their assistance to the public had more often been episodic, as when they helped victims of a natural disaster or epidemic.[18] While both organizations focused on the spiritual development of their members, the conferences also reached outside their own group to moralize and catechize the masses. Because of this goal, the conferences largely excluded the poor except as clients, unlike the confraternities, which included people at all levels of society as members—though usually in groups segregated by class or ethnicity.

The Liberal government recognized some of these differences when it exempted the conferences from the abolition of confraternities in 1859. Clarifying its reasoning in a report of May 1, 1861, the director of the Dirección General de los Fondos de Beneficencia, Marcelino Castañeda, explained that "the conferences of Saint Vincent de Paul are not of ancient origin; they are a modern creation, representing the philanthropy of the century and the spirit of practical charity that does not seek public applause . . . [and] that alleviates suffering without expecting recompense." Moreover, he noted that the conferences complied with the "fundamental laws of the Republic" concerning religious toleration because, although of Catholic origin, they helped the needy of all faiths and political persuasions.[19] Of course, Castañeda conveniently ignored the degree to which the lay groups formed part of a larger Catholic project. Yet his emphasis on their modernity was not entirely off the mark.

In many ways the conferences resembled what Guerra labeled "modern sociabilities." Although he has been rightly criticized for using an overly rigid binary model that sees modernity and tradition as polar opposites,[20] Guerra's discussion of nineteenth-century associationism is useful for analyzing some of the distinctive characteristics of the Vincentian lay groups. To begin with, in contrast to "traditional" sociabilities like the family, community, or guild, adhesion to the conferences was voluntary. Their members were not even required to pay the entrance fees or dues that were normally mandatory in confraternities—indeed, some of the poorer conferences were entitled to receive subventions.[21] And membership was based on ideological affinities, for if Catholicism was customary in Mexico, this particular brand of Catholic activism was not. In particular, the practice of home visiting had to be learned. In a country without a tradition of organized outdoor relief, it was far easier (especially for elite men) to simply give money to the poor rather than donating their time and personal service. For most laywomen, active participation in community service and administration of welfare organizations were not customary practices either. Moreover, the very act of joining a conference made a statement about where the volunteer stood on one of the major political issues of the day. In the context of Reforma Mexico, working to restore the presence of Catholicism in everyday life constituted a challenge to official policy. Just like the Masonic lodges, cultural and scientific societies, and political parties, the conferences therefore qualify to be considered "societies of thought" based on shared beliefs and often constructing their identity in opposition to the liberal state.[22]

Hilda Sábato has noted that in nineteenth-century Latin America voluntary associations enjoyed enormous prestige as "beacons of civilization and the breeding ground, as well as expression, of a modern, free, and democratic society."[23] Like their secular counterparts, the conferences were sites where the volunteers could develop important civic skills. Governing themselves according to written rules, they elected officers and voted as equals. The bylaws of the Ladies of Charity even required that their elections be held by secret ballot.[24] Each chapter engaged in collective discussions when formulating its activities, choosing new members, and deciding which clients to adopt. Forment's conclusion about other voluntary organizations thus applies just as much to the conferences: they were "enclaves of democracy" where many Mexican men and women "practiced self-rule . . . for the first time in their lives by participating in meetings, voting for officials, making those officials accountable to other members of the group, deliberating about common concerns, . . . [and] enforcing the norms and statutes of the group."[25] To be sure, Forment exaggerated the novelty of these associative practices, since colonial confraternities also had written constitutions and elected officers—and, because their membership was voluntary, might qualify as "modern" by Guerra's definition. These continuities do not, however, lessen the importance of the Vincentian lay groups—along with many other Catholic lay organizations—in helping to shape republican citizenry.

If their model of internal governance was not entirely new, their complex national and international structure was. The Vincentian conferences differed from the autonomous localized confraternities by being part of hierarchical, centralized organizations. Both the men's and women's groups were branches of transnational associations governed by charters written in France and approved by the Vatican. They had central and regional governing bodies, held annual assemblies that brought all national members together, and maintained regular communications across the entire network.

Of course, the system did not always work as planned. Both the male society and women's association occasionally failed to hold their assemblies or publish reports, especially during periods of political difficulties and institutional weakness. The national headquarters sometimes lost contact with provincial conferences that were scattered far and wide across the Mexican countryside at a time when primitive transportation systems made contact difficult. Some local chapters must therefore have had considerable independence from the Superior and Central Councils, just as the Mexican conferences had from the General Council in Paris.

Yet the various governing bodies consistently attempted to impose uniformity on their affiliated chapters. The bylaws established rules to standardize their governance and activities. So did the training manuals and practical guides such as the *Manual de la Sociedad*, *Guía práctica de las Conferencias*, *Instrucción a los presidentes*, and other publications that were circulated among the members (fig. 6.1). Meeting times were regularized and publicized, with each conference setting a recurring day of the week and place for its reunions (fig. 6.2). Meetings of the Central and Particular Councils also followed a predictable schedule. (For example, while Señora Nicolasa Luna de Corcuera was president of the Ladies of Charity Central Council in Guadalajara, it met the first Tuesday of every month in her home.[26]) In an effort to achieve transparency and accountability to their donors, both the male and female organizations gathered information on printed report forms and then tabulated statistics that were published in the annual reports.

The conferences also sought to standardize assistance by specifying the composition of the rations they offered. In 1890, for example, the Central Council of Guadalajara defined a ration as a one-cent loaf of bread, six tortillas, four ounces of meat, two ounces of rice, one egg, and half a *cuartillo* of milk.[27] The association's 1911 bylaws defined the normal ration as "rice, beans, and salt in sufficient quantities to sustain a person" as well as a

OBRAS que se hallan de venta en la Secretaría de la Sociedad, situada en la casa núm. 7 de la calle de los Medinas.

Manual de la Sociedad.............................$	1 0
Reglamento de la Sociedad con notas explicativas .	0 1¼
Guía práctica de las Conferencias.................	0 1
Instruccion á los presidentes......................	0 1
Idem para fundar Conferencias....................	0 0¼
Obra de las Santas Familias......................	0 1
El Visitador de los Pobres	0 2
Boletin de la Sociedad, cada número..............	0 1
Circulares del Consejo General, á la holandesa.....	1 2
Idem á la rústica	1 0
Circulares de los presidentes del Consejo Superior de México.............	0 2
Vida de San Vicente de Paul, dos tomos en un volúmen, á la holandesa........................	1 4
Idem á la rústica................................	1 2
Lectura y consejos para las Sociedades de caridad, á la holandesa................................	1 0
Idem á la rústica	0 6
Manual de caridad, á la holandesa	1 0
Idem á la rústica...	0 6
Novena de San Vicente	0 1
Estampas de San Vicente de Paul, en medio pliego de marca, grabado........	0 6
En cuarto, idem, idem, idem................	0 1¼
Medallas de la Purísima y San Vicente de Paul:	
En metal blanco fino............................	0 1½
En idem amarillo..................	0 0¾
En idem, idem, menor tamaño..............	0 0½

Por docena valen las primeras $ 2, las segundas 87 centavos y las terceras 18 centavos

Figure 6.1. List of publications and religious prints sold by the Society of Saint Vincent de Paul. Sociedad, *Boletín* (February 1887), back page. In AHAG, Sección Folletería, Serie Publicaciones Periódicas México, Sociedad San Vicente de Paul, Años 1887–1978, Caja 1, no. 47.

five-cent loaf of bread, two *tablillas* of chocolate, and, if possible, candles, charcoal, and soap. The gravely ill were entitled to additional items like milk and chicken, following a doctor's order.[28] The general principle of treating each pauper equally was enunciated in the 1858 edition of the male society's bylaws when it insisted that no pauper should be favored because of the importance of the visitor.[29]

It is difficult to know whether these rules were always followed. An unusual run of minutes available for the Ladies' Central Council in Culiacán from 1894 to 1912 and for a men's conference in Culiacán from 1897 to 1898 are so formulaic that they provide little insight into local practices except to show that those chapters met regularly and adhered to an established format. The minutes of the Central Council listed the day, time, and place of its meetings—every month in the Cathedral at 4:30 or 5:00 p.m. They noted whether the clerical director was present or not—he almost always was, and if not, the *señorita presidente* ran the meeting. The sessions opened "with the customary prayers," passed the collection plate, conducted business, and closed with a reading from an inspirational text. Although the minutes consistently reported that those of the previous meeting were read and approved, and that news from individual conferences was presented, they gave few particulars.[30] Those of the male chapter in Culiacán were even briefer and less useful.[31]

The only other minutes I have located, for a small men's conference in Coyoacán (Federal District) for the first year after it was founded in June 1912, are more detailed.[32] They contain information on the handful of paupers adopted by the conference, with heart-wrenching tales of a crippled father with five children, three of whom were blind; two elderly sisters who cared for their thirteen-year-old epileptic niece; and a pregnant woman with

SOCIEDAD DE SAN VICENTE DE PAÚL.
CUADRO DE LAS CONFERENCIAS DE ESTA CAPITAL.

CONFERENCIAS	PUNTOS DE REUNION	DIAS Y HORAS	CARGOS	NOMBRES Y APELLIDOS	DOMICILIOS
Nuestra Señora de los Dolores	2ª del Factor 2	Viernes á las 7 de la noche	Presidente	Sr. D. Luis G. Palma	Aguila 5.
			Vicepresidente	„ „ Luis G. Arnaldo	2ª del Factor 2.
Purísima Concepción	San Andrés 2	Miércoles á las 6 de la tarde	Presidente	„ „ Fr. Javier. Irisa de León.	San Angel.
			Vicepresidente	„ „ Manuel Beltrán	Asilo de Mendigos.
Nuestra Señora de Guadalupe	Sacristía de la Iglesia de Regina	Miércoles á las 7 de la noche	Presidente	„ „ Angel de la Peña	Hijos de San Agustín 1.
			Vicepresidente	„ „ Julián Tellez	Calle de la Merced, Tinp⁴ La Abeja.
Nuestra Señora de la Luz	Secretaría del Consejo	Miércoles á las 7 de la noche	Presidente	„ „ Leoncio Rego	2ª de Humboldt 1.
			Vicepresidente	„ „ Enrique Ricov	2ª de Mesones 22.
Santo Niño de San Juan	Escalerillas 8	Martes á las 5 de la tarde	Presidente	„ „ Juan B. Alzúcar	Tacuba 20.
			Vicepresidente	„ „ Manuel Amor	4ª de Lumumur 1,828.
				„ „ Manuel Arisoc	Donceles 5 y 6.
Señor San José	Callejón de las Ratas 4	Miércoles á las 7½ de la noche	Presidente	„ „ J. R. Lozano Berasueta	Encarnación 6.
			Vicepresidente	„ „ Vicente de P. Bustos	Escalerillas 8.
				„ „ Luis Torres Ansorena	Aguila 25.
Anunciación de Nuestra Señora	Sacristía de la Iglesia de Balvanera	Martes á las 6½ de la noche	Presidente	„ „ Francisco de Trujillago	Medinas 7.
Nuestra Señora de Monserrate	Donceles 9.	Viernes á las 7 de la noche	Vicepresidente	„ „ José Orvañanos	Callejón de las Ratas 4.
			Presidente	„ „ José M. Silva	D. Juan Manuel 12.
			Vicepresidente	„ „ Luis García Pimentel	Corazón de Jesús 7.
				„ „ Ignacio de la Hidalga	Donceles 9.
				„ „ Manuel Elguero	Donceles 8.
Sagrado Corazón de Jesús	Chavarria 10	Jueves á las 7 de la noche	Presidente	„ „ Manuel Luna Menocal	Vesero 9.
			Vicepresidente	„ „ Jesús Alvarez Leal	Chiconautla 3.
Santísima Trinidad	Sacristía de Santa Catalina de Sena	Martes á las 7 de la noche	Presidente	„ „ Emilio Lozano	Puente del Cuervo 6.
			Vicepresidente	„ „ Agustín Pérez	Callejón de los Gobias 4.
Santísimo Sacramento	Secretaría del Consejo	Martes á las 7 de la noche	Presidente	„ „ Néstor Rubio Alpuche	3ª del Reloj 9.
			Vicepresidente	„ „ Antonio Buerk	Estampa de Jesús Mario 6.
			Presidente	„ „ Ignacio Rubiel	Montealegre 3.
			Vicepresidente	„ „ Arcadio Norma	6ª de Alzato 0.
				„ „ Claudio Limón	Calle de los Medinas X.
Inmaculado Corazón de María Santísima	2ª de la Pila Seca 7 R.	Martes á las 7 de la noche	Presidente	„ „ Juan de la Orta	Villa de Guadpe, Calle del Arco 1.
			Vicepresidente	„ „ J.M.Sánchez del Castillo	2ª de la Pila Seca 7 R.
Nuestra Señora de la Consolación	Parroquia de San Cosme	Miércoles á las 6½ de la tarde	Presidente	„ „ Jesús G. Camacho	3ª de San Lorenzo 1.
			Vicepresidente	„ „ Manuel F. de la Hoz	2ª del Chopo 2.
				„ „ José Zubieta	1ª de la Ribera de Santa María 12.
				„ „ José Burbide	Calle de la Paz 445.
				„ „ Ignacio Solares	Santa Clara 4.
				„ „ José Ortega y Fonseca	Calle de los Medinas X.
Nuestra Señora de los Angeles	Secretaría del Consejo	Viernes á las 6 de la tarde	Presidente	„ „ Manuel Ramírez	1ª de la Ribera de Santa María 6½
Nuestra Señora del Rosario	2ª de la Pila Seca 7 R.	Jueves á las 7 de la noche	Presidente	„ „ José M. Saldaña	Cruz Verde 3.
			Vicepresidente	„ „ Antonio Gómez	Polilla 3.
Patrocinio de Señor San José	Callejón de San Antonio 2 ó 240	Martes á las 7½ de la noche	Presidente	„ „ Fortino Aguilar	Callejón de Pajaritos 8.
			Vicepresidente	„ „ Luis G. Antuñano	3ª de Mina 4.
				„ „ Eduardo Rodríguez	Cerrada de la Misericordia 1 y 2.

Figure 6.2. Male conference officers and meeting places, Mexico City, 1902. This list is unusual because it is one of the few documents to include the names of the society's officers. In Sociedad, *Boletín* (December 1902), "Cuadro de las Conferencias de esta Capital." In AHAG, Sección Folletería, Serie Publicaciones Periódicas, Sociedad San Vicente de Paul, Años 1897–1902, caja 2, no. 42.

three small children who was evicted from her home while her husband was in prison, losing most of her possessions when they were thrown onto the street. The minutes show that the visitors coded the names of their clients— as the Familia de la Transfiguración or the Familia del Santo Niño de Praga, for example—a practice not mentioned in the early bylaws but prescribed by the 1911 version of the Ladies of Charity's *Reglamento*.[33] The volunteers were therefore following the by then established procedure to ensure that the needy retained their anonymity, and thus presumably their dignity. The minutes also reveal a bitter conflict with the parish priest that led the group to move its weekly meetings from the local church to the conference president's home in protest over the cleric's attempts to control their activities.[34] Since the male conferences were officially independent from the church, however, this separation did not violate the bylaws.

The society's published reports contain hints of some variation in practice. For example, in 1864 its Superior Council scolded the Particular Council in Guadalajara for creating a laundry to employ women, in violation of the rules prohibiting the men from patronizing young members of the opposite sex. This discrepancy from the société's practice was apparently so widespread that in 1900 the Mexican sociedad's *Boletín* explicitly stated that, unlike the French conferences, the Mexicans did not restrict themselves to only serving men and boys.[35] In contrast, when other differences were discovered, the governing councils tried to bring the noncompliant chapters into line with Vincentian guidelines. Thus in 1887 Superior Council president Joaquín García Icazbalceta attempted to have all the Mexican chapters give home visitations the importance they deserved.[36] And, at least in Jalisco, too much independence could prevent a local conference from becoming affiliated with the parent organization.[37]

Another instance of this urge to homogenize comes from 1900, when the Mexican Ladies' association revised its decades-old *Reglamento*. In a preface, the organization's director, Father Ildefonso Moral, explained that the new edition clarified the confusion caused by occasional discrepancies in previous editions and incorporated a few modifications that had been introduced in response to changing conditions. The goal was "to regularize the practice of charity among the numerous associations and make it uniform throughout the country . . . and have it conform to the Association of the Mother House [in Paris]."[38] This standardization was characteristic of increasingly bureaucratized nineteenth-century organizations, as was the insistence on careful recordkeeping.

Their production and dissemination of published texts was also part of the trend to emphasize written communication that scholars associate with the transition to modernity.[39] In addition to the bylaws, reports, and training manuals that circulated among their members, the conferences distributed Catholic almanacs, missals, and edifying works among their clients. The Culiacán Actas reported that the Ladies of Charity Central Council also distributed a newspaper, *El Josefino*, which it described as a *periodiquito católico*.[40] After opening the first lending library in 1858, the men's society created the position of conference librarian, and the reports occasionally noted how many volumes were owned with great pride.[41] In a sign of its significance, one of the few details consistently provided in the Culiacán minutes was the title of the reading used in each meeting, which included *Los pecados de la lengua, La vida de San Vicente de Paul, La mujer cristiana, La imitación de Jesucristo, El combate espiritual, La tribulación, La humildad,* and *La mujer fuerte.* The conferences also promoted popular education by founding night schools for adults as well as elementary schools for children, and even catechism courses often served as "de facto adult literacy centers."[42] Thus, contrary to the widespread view that, unlike Protestantism, Catholicism did not foster the culture of literacy, the Vincentian lay associations clearly did.

Another facet of the modernity of the Vincentian lay movement was its contribution to the expansion of women's roles. The Ladies' association did not set out to change the status of women—indeed, when its early twentieth-century records referred to "the legitimate emancipation of women," they meant the ability of women to sustain themselves with their own labor.[43] Yet, in adapting to new circumstances, the church and the laity used modern strategies, for the idea that women should leave home to improve society was quintessentially modern. By recruiting middle- and upper-class women to defend the faith and serve the poor, the conferences gave them a base from which to move beyond home and family, to develop practical organizational and leadership skills, and to exercise power within their communities. While delivering social services, the volunteers also became important political actors helping to further the project of Catholic reform.

The widespread mobilization of women and their participation in the public sphere, usually dated to the Mexican Revolution of 1910—or, in religious histories, to the Catholic Action organizations of the following decade—had thus begun under Catholic auspices as early as the 1860s. It had reached an impressive dimension by the first decade of the twentieth century, when tens of thousands of women joined the ranks of the Vincentian volunteers. As women responded enthusiastically to the new opportunities—while devout men gravitated to more visible and overtly political, or at least less "hands-on," activities—the female voluntary association became preeminent. The success of the Ladies of Charity reveals how Mexican Catholics both participated in and helped advance modernity, for, despite the gendered rhetoric that attempted to naturalize the work of benevolence as an extension of traditional female roles, Vincentian charity represented a new kind of experience for Mexican women.

Precursors to Social Catholicism

The Vincentian approach to solving social problems exhibited a similar mixture of traditional and modern elements. The rhetoric in the bylaws and reports recalled the centuries-old Catholic discourse that emphasized imitating Christ, loving the poor, and showing compassion, humility, and abnegation. The volunteers engaged in charity not only out of a desire to help others but also to gain their own salvation, aided by the indulgences granted to those who joined the organizations. The Ladies regularly engaged in such traditional Catholic practices as inviting twelve paupers to dine on Maundy Thursday and washing and kissing their feet. Moreover, a large part of their efforts went to providing the Seven Acts of Mercy: feeding the hungry, housing the wayfarer, dressing the naked, giving drink to the thirsty, attending the sick, caring for orphans, and burying the dead. These older types of assistance characterized the work with hospital patients and prisoners. Much of the thrust of home visiting also offered only temporary remedies to destitution and suffering.

Yet the works of the Vincentian lay groups should not be dismissed as mere throwbacks to traditional Catholic charity.[44] Coexisting with the older approaches were more modern notions of poor relief. Instead of accepting poverty as a normal condition and merely relieving its symptoms, the conferences often tried to treat its causes. The emphasis on providing

elementary schooling, adult education, vocational training for youths—
even music lessons so that a blind man could support his family as a musician[45]—aimed to prevent their clients' future destitution. The curriculum
in their schools not only included Christian doctrine but also history, science, music, calculus, and line drawing that prepared the students for
employment.[46] The *cajas de socorro mutuo* (mutual savings funds) were
designed to combat usury and help their clients achieve financial independence. The job placements and provision of tools and sewing machines likewise went beyond palliative measures.

The Liberal Marcelino Castañeda highlighted these differences in building his argument for permitting the conferences to continue their beneficent
activities. In addition to praising their work in providing for the immediate
needs of ailing families, prisoners, orphans, and the elderly, his 1861 report
noted that the volunteers "gave children the means to learn and work, including books to those who need them for their studies," established trade schools
to train youths and night schools to educate adults, placed impoverished
children as apprentices, maintained "well-stocked workshops," and founded
popular lending libraries and savings associations.[47]

Unlike traditional almsgivers, Vincentian volunteers did not hand out aid
indiscriminately. In providing home relief the chapters usually responded to
petitions from destitute families.[48] Before adopting them, however, a visitor
investigated their situation and reported back to the conference, which discussed each case and voted on whether to take it on.[49] As an 1859 *Boletín* of
the male society explained, the conferences "form a kind of police . . . to
assure that assistance will go to the truly needy and avoid the theft perpetrated by the lazy."[50] This sentiment was echoed in 1907 when Guadalajara's
Boletín denounced "the false poor who deceive us . . . without genuinely
requiring our aid."[51] Indeed, some Ladies of Charity chapters had a *calificadora*, an officer in charge of "scrupulously examining the recommended
families, to verify that no aid is given to those without real need."[52] As the
demand for assistance increased in the late nineteenth century, this officer
appeared more frequently on the list of conference dignitaries. Moreover, a
conference officer was charged with revisiting the adopted families—every
three months in the women's association, once a year in the men's society[53]—
not only to make sure that they were being properly cared for but also to
determine whether their circumstances still warranted assistance. For home

relief was meant to be temporary, lasting only until the crisis of illness or unemployment had passed. Those with chronic conditions that required long-term attention were supposed to be placed in hospitals or asylums whenever possible (although these placements could take many months because of the high demand for limited places in such institutions).[54]

The conferences thus accepted the distinction between the "worthy" and "unworthy" poor that set enlightened poor relief apart from the traditional distribution of alms to all who begged. The society's future Superior Council president Joaquín García Icazbalceta elaborated on the Vincentian critique of traditional charity in his 1864 report on public welfare in Mexico City. He insisted that those who were capable of earning a living on their own—or who had relatives who could support them—should not receive aid because that would encourage idleness, foster dependence, and divert resources from the "truly needy." Moreover, he advocated the rounding up and rehabilitation of beggars to rid the streets of "that plague." Tolerating "public mendicity," he explained, was to "authorize vagrancy [because] many beggars are not *verdaderos pobres*, but rather men who have found a means to live without working" and who steal "incredible sums" that should be applied to those who deserve them.[55] The society's fiftieth-anniversary review confirmed that beggars were rarely among its clients "except when there is some hope that we can convert them into useful members of society."[56]

Beyond these general guidelines, the criteria used to distinguish the "deserving" from the "undeserving" poor were rarely spelled out in detail. The reports of both the men's and women's organizations indicate that, except in the prison ministries, the volunteers considered the elderly, sick, disabled, orphans, and widowed or abandoned mothers—the traditional objects of charity—as particularly worthy.[57] Occasional descriptions of their clients in terms such as "a decent but stricken family" suggest that the home-relief programs favored respectable people fallen on hard times.[58] The focus on families with fixed abodes, as well as on those who could read the literature they distributed, reveals a preference for the *pobres vergonzantes* who were too proud to beg. Indeed, as late as 1910, the Culiacán Actas used the old term for the "shamefaced poor" when noting that a *familia vergonzante* had been adopted.[59]

Yet their desire to uplift the Mexican poor meant that the conferences could not apply overly rigid criteria in selecting their clients. Although they may have preferred "docile" paupers with "good habits and honorable conduct," they worked with many others. They did not favor Catholics, for example, because they wanted to convert Protestants, spiritists, and atheists. For the same reason, they did not totally exclude alcoholics, those who lived in concubinage, or those who abandoned themselves to other "grave vices." On the contrary, "rebellious" families were to be treated with the "utmost benevolence . . . in the hopes of bringing them back to the righteous path."[60] These people were nonetheless assisted on a conditional basis. As the 1911 bylaws of the Ladies of Charity explained, families "of notorious immorality" or "who live in suspicious houses" could occasionally be adopted "out of charity," but only "if they give hope of being reformed." Home relief was supposed to be discontinued for those who refused to mend their ways.[61]

This goal of changing popular culture was another factor distinguishing Vincentian poor relief from traditional charity that exalted the poor, and aside from tending to their corporal needs, largely left them alone. A central part of the Vincentian project was to reinvigorate the Catholic faith in a population characterized by "ignorance . . . and indifference on the subject of religion."[62] Yet the desire to transform the poor went beyond saving their souls to encompass a broader *acción civilizadora*, or "civilizing mission."[63] The visitors tried to moralize their charges by pressuring them to end illicit relationships, conciliating divided families, persuading the debauched to give up drinking and fighting, encouraging children to respect their parents, and providing separate beds for the boys and girls. They taught the importance of cleanliness and hygiene. They gave moral and practical, as well as religious, instruction to the students in their schools, the orphans, homeless, and wayward youths in their asylums, and the prisoners, patients, apprentices, and workers they aided. In an attempt to counter the "indolence and a certain aversion to work" of a large portion of the Mexican people,[64] they placed children in school, instilled the work ethic, and provided employment so that the youths they patronized would not turn to begging, prostitution, or crime. The conferences also worked to counter "the pernicious influence of the novel and newspaper."[65]

Their charitable activities were thus part of a strategy to discipline the poor. Indeed, their emphasis on industriousness, temperance, savings—and even punctuality[66]—shows the important role of Catholic organizations in shaping the capitalist ethos.[67] The similarity of the values and behavior encouraged by the Vincentian volunteers and those promoted by secular reformers is another indication of the considerable overlap between Catholic and Liberal projects that was often lost in partisan polemics.

The volunteers nonetheless insisted that their concern for the "whole person" distinguished their approach, not only from traditional almsgiving but also from modern philanthropy and public welfare. Thus in 1895 Agustín Rodríguez, the president of the society's Superior Council, proclaimed Vincentian charity as far superior to *beneficencia pública*, which "is haughty . . . and leaves the poor in the isolation, indifference, and oblivion that offend him more than his material deprivations."[68] In 1892 the *Memoria* of the Ladies of Charity explained that "modern philanthropists . . . do not sincerely love the poor" because they "only provide corporal assistance to those who live in misery and indigence, while leaving an immense vacuum to fill, because they absolutely neglect to alleviate the needs of the soul, which are always more pressing . . . than those of the body. In contrast, . . . [the] conferences are not content with merely alleviating poverty, but surround it with respect, honor, . . . [and] dignity."[69]

From today's perspective, we might denigrate Vincentian charity as paternalistic and controlling, since self-righteous visitors tried to impose their ideology on those they assisted. We might also condemn it for accepting the hierarchical class structure. Although a few conferences occasionally supported the upward mobility of selected clients—as when they paid for the secondary schooling (or entrance into the priesthood or convent) of a particularly talented (or pious) child—these cases were few and far between. By helping those who suffered temporary setbacks due to accidents, illness, or unemployment, the home relief helped others avoid the downward mobility that often accompanied these crises. Yet García Icazbalceta likely represents the sentiments of many volunteers when he insisted that the education of paupers should be geared to their station.[70] Such was clearly the case, for example, with the widespread obra of finding placements for impoverished women as domestic servants.[71] The goal was simply to prepare them to be self-supporting, productive members of society, not to challenge social inequality.

Still, the Vincentian project was not merely designed to reinforce the status quo. Instead, the volunteers were reformers combating the major ills of their time. They were troubled, not only by the increasing poverty, hunger, homelessness, and sickness that they saw around them, but also by the progress of luxury, vice, immorality, and the loosening of social ties.[72] And they proposed an integrated approach for social renovation that went to what they believed was the root of these problems: the loss of faith.

In many ways, their analysis was profoundly antiliberal, for they blamed the French Revolution for unleashing the secularizing forces that led to the moral degeneracy, materialism, egoism, alienation, and class conflict of the nineteenth century. This philosophy is evident in the organizations' reports that repeatedly condemned the "horrific" revolution whose ideas "have rapidly propagated throughout the world, perturbing spirits and corrupting customs."[73] It is also manifested in the writings of two of the male society's volunteers. As Superior Council president Luis Gonzaga Cuevas explained in his 1851 book, *Porvenir de México*, "the errors that are dragging us into the abyss" stemmed from "breaking the ties between religion and public power."[74] Half a century later, Trinidad Sánchez Santos presented a similar analysis in his numerous speeches and newspaper articles that called for restoring the influence of Christianity through Catholic education and charity.[75]

Because of their opposition to the French Revolution and to the Liberal Reforma, the mid-nineteenth-century conferences could be labeled as Conservative in the Mexican political spectrum. Yet their concern for civil liberties makes it difficult to dismiss them as entirely reactionary. They consistently defended their right to assemble and publish. For example, in calling for Mexicans to join the lay associations, the 1875 Pastoral Instruction emphasized that "the Constitution of the Republic formally and expressly recognizes the right of all Mexicans to associate for any honest and licit end."[76] Ironically, it was the Liberals who tried to restrict the conferences' freedom of association in 1861 and 1868, and who as late as 1893 limited their right to publish by insisting that the society's reports could only be distributed to its own members.[77] In promoting Catholic education, the volunteers also insisted on freedom of conscience and instruction. By resisting the authoritarian tendencies of the liberal state and by disseminating democratic principles, the conferences were thus part of Mexico's modernizing process.[78]

The conferences were also very much a part of the modern world because their activities were formulated as a direct response to contemporary problems. Because the volunteers were deeply immersed in their local communities as well as influenced by transnational trends, different concerns came to the fore in different time periods. In the 1840s and 1850s they focused on improving public health by managing hospitals and providing emergency relief during warfare and epidemics. During the Reforma, they rallied to defend the church from new anticlerical attacks, and after freedom of religion was introduced in 1860, they turned their attention to countering Protestantism and spiritism. After 1874, when religious education was outlawed in public schools, they emphasized the creation of parochial schools and catechism classes. Over time they incorporated new devotions into their repertoire, such as the group spiritual exercises and adoration of the Eucharist that reflected the Romanization of religious practice.[79] By the turn of the century they were railing against socialism and class hatred. They also exhibited new ideas about the link between public hygiene and disease by adding soap to the standard rations. Just as their works of mercy were constantly evolving, the waxing and waning of the conferences was correlated with concurrent developments. The volunteers thus rose to meet the challenges of the Reforma, and after 1891 they were energized by the renewal of Catholic social activism inspired by Rerum Novarum. Finally, they were motivated by the great waves of rural migrants arriving in Mexican cities and the growing immiserization of the poor that accompanied the Porfirian economic boom.

In some respects the Vincentian sodalities presaged the progressive Social Catholic movements that emerged in the wake of the papal encyclical and—like them—can even be seen as foreshadowing some aspects of liberation theology. They shared a focus on the masses. They challenged the secularization of society through "an orthodox adherence to Catholic dogma and a progressive critique of liberal[ism]."[80] Although religious considerations were central to their work with the impoverished, they tended to people's material as well as spiritual needs. They did so by mobilizing the laity in collective associations and using them to shore up the faith, which Sánchez Santos extolled as "the Lay Apostolate." Their social activism formed part of a political agenda. In "going to the poor," the conferences thus anticipated some aspects of Social Catholicism long before it was officially adopted by the Vatican. Indeed, the rhetoric in Vincentian sources often sounded very modern, as when a *Boletín* in 1909 posited that their works of mercy were creating "a Church for the Poor."[81]

If the Vincentian approach prefigured the new approach to poverty, however, it was not the same as Social Catholicism. Although by the turn of the century some volunteers were simultaneously involved in the new initiatives, the conferences themselves did not modify their activities in response to Leo XIII's encyclical. In particular, they did not create Catholic trade unions—the hallmark of twentieth-century Social Catholicism. Neither did they organize people to fight for their rights as a matter of justice. Instead, the conferences mobilized a vanguard of devout upper- and middle-class activists—what nineteenth-century thinkers called the *clases dirigentes*—to lead the masses, or *clases inferiores*.[82] The Vincentian model was thus paternalistic, with hierarchy and clientelism prevailing. Indeed, since the poor were excluded from membership, the multiclass networks that included the conference clients were under elite control. The conferences may have resembled the base communities of liberation theology by regularly bringing committed Catholics together in small groups to deepen their faith and use it as inspiration to solve local problems. Yet, whereas those empowered individuals from the popular classes, the conferences mainly empowered the middle- and upper-class volunteers. Moreover, instead of conceiving of welfare as a right, the volunteers made it conditional on the recipients' willingness to accept their ideology. Finally, the Vincentian literature did not offer an analysis of the structural causes of poverty, which for Social Catholics resulted from the capitalists' exploitation of labor. Indeed, it never criticized the greed of the rich—a major theme in Rerum Novarum—as much as the moral failings of the poor, which the encyclical barely mentioned.[83]

Vincentian charity therefore occupied a transitional phase between traditional poor relief and full-fledged Social Catholicism, very much a product of its times rather than a simple continuation of earlier approaches to dealing with poverty. To some degree, it might be considered an early version of that movement. Indeed, some scholars consider Frédéric Ozanam and fellow society member Vicomte Armand de Melun to be among "the inventors of Social Catholicism" because of their attempts to address the Social Question through organized lay activism.[84] In addition, the conferences prepared the ground for the later initiatives by establishing the idea that the laity should take responsibility for helping the needy, by building a network of volunteers and institutions dedicated to serving the masses, and by expanding the base of support for the church. And it did not lose its relevance during the heyday of Social Catholicism. On the contrary, the delegates to the first National Catholic Congress in 1903 promoted the formation of new conferences—along with workers' associations—as part of a unified approach to dealing with Mexico's social problems.[85] Moreover, although the development of Social Catholicism has been portrayed as a masculine story, the prominence of the Ladies of Charity in the Vincentian lay movement meant that the women who participated in its conferences made important contributions to that process.

Pioneers of Modern Social Welfare

Vincentian charity likewise represented a transitional stage in the creation of a modern welfare system run by trained professionals. Although the predominant narrative of social welfare history privileges the role of the state, the conferences—along with other private organizations—made important contributions to developing Mexico's capacity to offer education, health care, and social assistance. Indeed, they pioneered certain approaches for which the government later took credit. And they did so independently of the state because, with the exception of the brief period under the Second Empire, the conferences appear to have operated without the public subventions that they enjoyed in some other Latin American countries.[86]

The volunteers constructed a national infrastructure of schools, hospitals, orphanages, soup kitchens, vocational workshops, discount pharmacies, lending libraries, mutual savings funds, employment agencies, and other establishments to help the poor. Their institutional presence expanded throughout the second half of the nineteenth century, as the conferences shifted from managing hospitals and funding the religious primer used to teach children the alphabet in the 1840s, for example, to establishing their own clinics and schools. So did their geographical presence, which extended throughout the Mexican republic. Their network might not have been as large as the government's—especially in the area of education, where public schools outnumbered Catholic ones—but it was nothing to scoff at, either.[87] While government services were concentrated in the capital and a few major cities, the conferences provided coverage in a much larger area that included provincial cities, small towns, and even some factories and haciendas. They consequently filled the many voids where public agencies or institutions had no presence.

In addition, the conferences serviced many needs that were not met by the

state. In the field of outdoor relief the Vincentian lay organizations were pioneers because the Mexican government had no organized system of home
relief and instead funneled its aid almost entirely through institutions such as
hospitals and asylums.[88] As public welfare became more selective by increasingly focusing on children, youths, the mentally ill, and the sick,[89] major seg-
ments of the impoverished population such as the working poor and
unemployed remained unserved. The conferences helped many of these people
through home-visiting programs as well as through soup kitchens, free
schooling, and occasional community celebrations. For example, one cocina
económica in Mexico City, created in 1895 specifically for "poor widows," fed
twenty-five women a day,[90] and the three such kitchens in Puebla provided
12,232 breakfasts and 27,487 dinners in the single year ending in June 1902.[91]
The Holy Week ceremonies sponsored by the conferences often treated hundreds of paupers to a special holiday dinner and distributed coins, blankets,
and clothes to those who attended. On the Feast Day of Saint Vincent at the
turn of the century, the Ladies of Charity in León reported feeding 1,608 paupers from the streets in addition to the girls in a local orphanage.[92] Another
distinctive Vincentian service was the proper burial of the dead, with a religious ceremony and simple coffins furnished by the volunteers.

The conferences also established some of the earliest popular libraries and
savings and loan cooperatives in Mexico, two initiatives that would be copied
by Catholic Action organizations in the early twentieth century. Indeed,
although some historians credit Miguel Palomar y Vizcarra with proposing
the *cajas Reiffeisen* at the first Catholic Congress in 1903, similar cooperative
savings funds were already promoted by the Vincentian conferences decades
earlier.[93] Later, when the Mexican government opened public libraries under
Minister of Culture José Vasconcelos in the 1920s, he followed the Vincentian precedent by insisting that the books in their collections should have
"redeeming moral value."[94]

The Vincentian schools and hospitals were every bit as modern as public
institutions. Their curricular offerings—with the exception of religious
instruction—were similar to those in the public schools.[95] Their Sunday
school classes for young women included lessons in first aid and hygiene.[96]
Already in 1863 the Ladies of Charity bylaws insisted that only modern medicines be offered rather than "superstitious" remedies.[97] The association's
hospitals incorporated the latest medical knowledge, medicines, and medical

instruments.[98] Just as in public institutions, the delivery of services was increasingly professionalized. Although the volunteers supervised their institutions and often attended the inmates personally, the daily management was usually in the hands of paid employees. For example, in 1878 the male society's eight primary schools in Mérida employed twenty-three full-time teachers.[99] Except for the period before the expulsion of the Sisters of Charity and, late in the Porfiriato, after the establishment of several new teaching and nursing orders, these employees were almost always lay people, often single or widowed women struggling to make ends meet. As their hospitals grew and became increasingly modernized, many conferences paid the salary of a full-time doctor as well. And over time their employees reflected the trend toward the professionalization of the medical, nursing, and teaching professions, for even when nuns again took over nursing duties in some of the hospitals during the early twentieth century, they usually received medical training to prepare them for the required tasks.[100]

Even the charitable visits, which had much in common with the centuries-old practice of the Dames de la Charité and of certain religious orders, anticipated some aspects of twentieth-century social work. For example, although the visits to paupers in their homes, hospitals, and prisons were in the hands of amateur volunteers, the conferences had formal programs to recruit, train, and deploy the visitors. These included instructing them through printed manuals, requiring probationary periods before inducting members (at least in the women's conferences), and preparing aspiring boys and girls to join the conferences through special *conferencias de niños*.[101] The visitors foreshadowed the role of social workers because they investigated potential client families before adopting them, evaluated the services they required to overcome the crisis of the moment, and then arranged for medical, nursing, or legal aid, or for placement in jobs, schools, or asylums as needed. Using techniques later associated with the new profession of social work, they classified clients as cases with code names, gathered information about them in written files, and reevaluated their situation periodically.[102]

The conferences also developed an efficient system for aiding a large number of paupers with a minimum overhead by using the Vincentian system of vouchers, known as vales or *bonos*. The visitors distributed these printed slips to their clients so they could obtain food, coal, clothes, and other necessities directly from central warehouses or from local shopkeepers. The coupons entitled the recipients to a standard ration—or to a half ration, in the case of children. Much like modern food stamps, this ingenious system permitted the conferences to maximize their impact with the help of participating businesses because each volunteer did not have to deliver these goods in person.[103]

Many of these Vincentian initiatives and techniques were later taken up, not only by other religious groups but also by public welfare organizations.[104] For example, the Ladies of Charity conferences served as a model for the secular Cruz Blanca established in 1911 under President Madero to heal the war wounded. Although primarily providing nursing care, the Cruz Blanca also created—or, because it was short-lived, planned to create—Sunday schools to educate workers, instructional projects in prisons, and campaigns against alcoholism.[105] In 1926, when the Mexico City Normal School established the specialty of *visitadora del hogar* (home visitor), these women followed in the footsteps of the Vincentian volunteers by "blurr[ing] the distinction between teacher, social worker, and nurse." Concerned with popular morality as well as health, they taught their charges everything from proper hygiene to how to solve family conflicts without violence.[106] So did the public school teachers sent on cultural missions into the countryside in the 1930s.[107]

In addition to providing precedents for twentieth-century public assistance, the conferences made more direct contributions when some of the buildings they had funded and outfitted for their schools, hospitals, and asylums were confiscated by revolutionary governments after 1913.[108] Consequently, the nascent welfare system not only incorporated many of the Vincentian concepts and strategies but also some of the infrastructure built by the volunteers. Moreover, some of the Vincentian foundations, such as four of the Ladies of Charity hospitals in the city of Guadalajara, survived the revolution and still continue to function today as private institutions.

The scale of assistance provided by the Vincentian conferences suggests that the history of Mexican welfare is in need of revision. The prevailing wisdom is that colonial traditions of religious and private charity disappeared after the Reforma when republican governments took over the responsibility for caring for the poor and the sick. The standard story is that in the colonial period, the church dominated the welfare system by operating hospitals, asylums, and soup kitchens. Members of religious confraternities and secular guilds took care of their own, including the widows and orphaned children of their members. A few individual philanthropists, usually from noble families, stood out for their generosity. But all this allegedly changed after independence. Beginning in 1821 and especially after 1861, hospitals, orphanages, and asylums were transferred from ecclesiastical to state jurisdiction. Religious orders were suppressed, including those that previously staffed establishments for the ailing poor. Artisan guilds and religious confraternities were abolished. And private giving was deterred when the government confiscated the assets of welfare institutions, many of which had originally been donated by charitable individuals.[109] These developments supposedly set the stage for the development of a modern and completely secular welfare system.

Yet the story is much more complicated. For starters, the end point of the narrative is inaccurate because public assistance was so limited in the twentieth century that Mexico cannot be said to have developed a modern welfare state. The beginning and middle of the story are inaccurate as well. The church never held a monopoly on poor relief in New Spain; instead the colonial system mixed public, private, and ecclesiastical welfare, and the mix continued throughout the nineteenth and into the twentieth century.[110] Church institutions were indeed diminished by the Reforma, but lay Catholics—as well as nonreligious voluntary groups—built a parallel welfare system that supplemented the federal and municipal offerings. The Vincentian volunteers not only took aid to the needy in their homes and in public hospitals and prisons, but they also founded and administered their own institutions. Thus, if private philanthropy largely abandoned the nationalized asylums it had once supported, it nonetheless flourished in new venues. Despite the state's rhetoric about taking over welfare functions, public assistance was in fact quite meager—a reality that was acknowledged when the Porfirian legislature decided to regulate private welfare establishments beginning in 1885 and culminating in the Law of Private Beneficence of 1904.[111] Nongovernmental organizations like the conferences of Saint Vincent de Paul therefore need to be reinserted in the history of social welfare in Mexico. And because they relied so much on the labor of female volunteers, the contributions of women need to be recognized as well.

Conclusion

We should beware of exaggerating the Vincentian accomplishments. Their aid was piecemeal, though not disorganized—two charges often leveled against private beneficence in general. They only reached a minority of the

Mexican poor, largely those living in or close to urban areas. The conferences nonetheless constructed an impressive system of health, education, and welfare that compared favorably with what the Mexican government offered at the time, reached many people and geographic areas that were not served by public assistance, and offered services that were not available from government agencies.

We should also beware of glorifying the volunteers. They wanted to help the needy but not to organize the poor so that they could demand their own rights or change the social structure. They did not envision a society of equals. Indeed, many middle- and upper-class volunteers undoubtedly considered themselves superior to their clients, and through their charitable activities they reinforced their class identity and social status. Their benevolent activities gave them community recognition and prestige. Their participation in the conferences over generations consolidated their families' power. Individuals also engaged in charity to gain their own salvation or to enjoy the sociability of gathering with friends and relatives who often participated in the same conference. Moreover, since it was part of a broad reform project, their assistance was far from disinterested.[112] Nonetheless, the complex motivations of the lay activists should not obscure their genuine humanitarian goals or their very real contributions toward meeting social needs. For, despite the influence of social Darwinism, many well-to-do Mexicans did not turn their backs on the poor. On the contrary, they continued to be motivated by the age-old Christian obligation to care for the less fortunate members of their communities.

It is difficult to know what the recipients of their largesse thought of this blend of material assistance and moral regulation. The conferences have been criticized for "exacting communions in exchange for a loaf of bread."[113] Yet there was no shortage of paupers willing to tolerate meddling visitors, even agreeing to pray with them and accompany them to church in return for assistance. The families that petitioned the conferences for help evidently incorporated the societies' services into their survival strategies. The conference publications included numerous stories of grateful clients to inspire the volunteers to continue performing good works. In truth, given the paucity of public relief in Mexico, the destitute had few other places to turn to in times of need—especially if rather than entering into demeaning public institutions, they preferred to stay at home and avoid the family breakup that so often accompanied crises among the Mexican poor.[114] By cooperating with the visitors, poor families received material aid and became part of the large Vincentian support network that could place them in jobs, schools, or hospitals.[115] In death, they avoided the dishonor of a pauper's funeral. It therefore appears that they willingly provided a large clientele to whom the volunteers could spread their critique of secularism and their vision of Catholic renewal.

Just as with Social Catholicism, it is difficult to pigeonhole Vincentian charity as "left" or "right."[116] Although Pope Pius IX condemned many aspects of modernity in his 1864 Syllabus of Errors, the church was far from monolithic, and it changed over time.[117] From the start the French conferences owed a great deal to the "liberal democratic" wing of the church represented by Lamennais, who argued that the institution should cooperate with the modern state and advocate for liberal freedoms so that it could function openly.[118] In Mexico, although the conferences never took official political positions, the volunteers often allied themselves with the Conservative party during the anticlerical Reforma. Yet during much of the Porfiriato they were part of the liberal Catholic wing that (unlike the earlier so-called *intransigentes*) collaborated with the government—even making President Díaz's wife the honorary president of the Ladies of Charity from 1895 to 1905.[119] Then, after Rerum Novarum, they joined the many Catholic social initiatives that offered a progressive alternative to socialism. The early twentieth-century Social Catholic congresses to which the male conferences sent delegates were quite radical in supporting the rights of workers, agricultural laborers, and indigenous peoples.[120] Vincentian volunteers like Victoriano Agüeros supported the striking workers at Cananea in 1906 and Río Blanco in 1907. Trinidad Sánchez Santos and others who formed the Partido Católico Nacional openly criticized the dictatorship and supported Madero's democratic revolution against Porfirio Diaz.[121] Although that movement later took an anticlerical turn and branded them as backward counterrevolutionaries, many Mexican Catholics shared the revolutionaries' ideals about democracy, civil rights, and social justice. What distinguished them from the ultimate victors in the struggle was their view of the place of Catholicism in Mexican life.[122]

After 1912 the Vincentian lay organizations entered a period of decline. Although this history has yet to be written, some broad outlines are beginning to come into focus. First, the conferences were weakened by the attacks of radical revolutionaries, which were particularly harsh in 1913 and 1914. At this point the struggling men's conferences disappeared from the archives for many years. The Ladies of Charity soon reappeared, reporting in 1921 that its conferences had never ceased to exist despite the "calamities that we have suffered for nearly ten years." Yet the association was much diminished: that year it only counted "some 15,000 active members" nationally, apparently an increase from a much lower point, though a considerable drop from the 21,187 of 1911.[123] Its conferences staged a brief recovery after 1920, despite facing competition from new Catholic Action organizations such as the Unión de Damas Católicas.[124] Then, like all Catholic associations, they suffered a devastating blow when the Cristeros lost their fight with the revolutionary government in 1929. Indeed, the defeat is often considered to mark the end of Catholic social movements in Mexico, as church leaders largely abandoned socioeconomic activities to focus on catechism.[125] Although historians are beginning to document the persistence of Catholic social ideals after that date,[126] the glory days of the conferences never returned.[127] The volunteers were apparently sidelined by the new lay organizations as well as by the professionalization of teaching, nursing, and social work that began in the late nineteenth century.[128] By the 1930s this process was in full swing.

As the revolutionary state expanded its role in providing education and health care, most volunteers retreated to their homes—or to more limited philanthropic roles, such as raising funds for the hospitals they had founded and decorating the hospital chapels.[129] In some countries, such as the United States and Argentina, many reformers lobbied for social welfare legislation and moved from their voluntary associations into new positions in government welfare agencies.[130] In Mexico few Catholic activists made this transition. On the one hand, they were excluded because the state did not extend its patronage to them for political reasons. On the other hand, especially in the case of the Ladies of Charity, many withdrew and left the paid positions in teaching, nursing, and social work to women of a lower social status.[131] For, with a few notable exceptions, women of the Mexican upper and upper-middle classes did not enter the labor force until much later in the twentieth century.

Although the Vincentian lay groups were thus eclipsed and then largely forgotten, they were important social and political actors in their heyday. Despite helping the Catholic Church recuperate after the attacks of the Reforma years, they cannot be dismissed as relics of an earlier age. They represented a new kind of lay activism that made the church relevant to the modern world. Dedicated to improving the lives of the masses long before this goal was proclaimed in Rerum Novarum, devout volunteers organized collectively to help solve pressing national problems. They provided essential educational, medical, and social services and built an extensive infrastructure for their delivery. They pioneered many features of the twentieth-century welfare system. They helped develop civil society and the public sphere. They disseminated capitalist values, democratic ideals, and new associational and administrative practices. They mobilized and empowered middle- and upper-class women.

By thus contributing to Mexican modernity, this movement of lay militants serves as a reminder that modernization does not require a shift from religious to secular world views, as Weberian theory posited. Nor was it just promoted by Liberals and opposed by the church, as the standard narrative of Mexican history would have us believe.[132] Moreover, Catholic women—often stereotyped as puppets of priests who represented an obstacle to progress—participated in modernizing trends and were effective agents of change. Although Vincentian charity retained many aspects of traditional Catholicism, these were combined with new ones and reconfigured to create something quite different from what came before. Instead of viewing the volunteers as reactionaries, it therefore makes more sense to see them as advocating "alternative modernities."[133] Volunteering for their cause, the idealistic ladies and gentlemen of the conferences of Saint Vincent de Paul were very much a part of—and at the same time helped to usher in—the modern world.

What My Grandmothers Taught Me

I NEVER MET my maternal grandmother, Zoraida Boscowitz Caminero, who died more than a decade before I was born. Yet what I learned about her as I grew up shaped this book in many ways. First, simply hearing about her charity work in Santiago de Cuba opened a window for me onto an unexplored aspect of Latin America's past. Her story inspired me to look for the proverbial needles in the haystacks of archives and libraries that would illuminate a lost history. Second, it helped answer the question that continued to perplex me, which is, why have the vibrant movements of Catholic volunteers been hidden for so long? By providing insights about historical memory and the production of knowledge, it offered clues about what we remember (and study) about the past, what we forget (or ignore), and why.

My personal experience suggests that this history was not only hidden from historians but even from most family lore. I was fortunate to have learned about my grandmother's activities due to a sad twist of fate. Like most daughters of benevolent ladies, my mother knew very little about her mother's volunteering, since the children remained in the care of loving maiden aunts and servants while she went out to tend the sick and ailing poor. It was only because my grandmother died prematurely, at the age of fifty-one in 1938, that my mother learned many details when hundreds of poor people came to the funeral and gratefully told her about how this Angel of Mercy had helped them in times of need. In the normal course of things, most volunteers would have outlived their clients and their funerals would not have provided an opportunity for these stories to be shared.

Still, I knew little about my grandmother's charity work until I sat down to help my mother write her memoirs when she was ninety-six years old. It was only then that I learned my grandmother was the president of the Damas Isabelinas in Santiago. Only then did I learn how she had a special knack for convincing doctors to provide their services free and for persuading shop-keepers to contribute food, clothes, and beds so that the stricken—and highly contagious—individuals could sleep apart from the other members of their families. Only then did I learn that the first thing she did when returning home was to take off her clothes, throw them in hot water, and bathe to remove any possible germs. This detail showed me how brave my severely asthmatic grandmother was because it was risky to enter the houses of peo-ple with tuberculosis, which plagued the Cuban poor in the 1920s and 1930s.

Other facts I learned serendipitously when a few years later a cousin sent a photograph of our grandmother in her Damas Isabelinas uniform, dating from approximately 1935 (fig. 7.1). As the only picture I have located of any Latin American volunteer, it proves the adage that an image is worth a thou-sand words.[1] Until then I had no idea that my grandmother wore a uniform while tending the poor—an indication that she took her volunteering seri-ously, perhaps considering herself closer to a professional than to an ama-teur. The uniform looks like a cross between that of a nun and a nurse. And, indeed, her benevolent activities represent a transition between the colonial era, when nuns and priests provided many social services, and the mid-twentieth century, when nursing became professionalized and public health systems were created. It is in that transitional period that female volunteers played an important role, with their unpaid labor providing a significant part of available welfare services.

The picture also showed me how much the president of this ladies' asso-ciation was appreciated by her contemporaries, indeed, how she was consid-ered one of the town dignitaries. Fortunately, my mother was still alive to identify the occasion—the inauguration of a new aqueduct—and to explain how her mother was invited as a leading member of the Santiago de Cuba community. Although my grandfather accompanied her with great pride, she was the guest of honor—and no one thought this transgressive in any way. So her charity organization was evidently well-known to the people who

Figure 7.1. Zoraida Boscowitz y Caminero (1886–1938), Cuban Dama Isabelina, ca. 1935, Santiago de Cuba. Personal collection of Silvia Arrom.

lived in Santiago at the time. Everyone who came to this public ceremony knew about it. So did the families and friends of the ladies involved. So did the people they helped. Nonetheless, these Cuban women have been just as invisible in the history books as the Mexican volunteers.

If my mother hadn't lived so long and agreed to dictate her memoirs, and if my cousin hadn't shared this picture, I might never have learned these details. It is interesting too that the impetus for my mother's memoirs was to tell her grandchildren about the famous men in her family, for the history that she thought they should know was about her great-grandfather Juan Nepomuceno Ravelo, hero of the Dominican independence revolution who reputedly designed the Dominican flag, and about her father, Angel Domingo Ravelo, one of the youngest veterans of the Cuban independence war who ran off at age fourteen to fight the Spaniards in 1896. If not for these illustrious male ancestors, the story of my grandmother might never have emerged.

I was given more clues about why the charitable ladies aren't part of our historical memory when I took down my father's memoirs. Although he told me wonderful anecdotes about life in small-town Cuba in the 1910s and 1920s, he barely mentioned his mother, Marina González Solís—saying mostly that she was very *simpática* and presided over wonderful family meals. Only when he finished and I asked for more information about my grandmother did the stories of her voluntary work and club memberships spill out, for she was the treasurer of Mayarí's Asociación de Damas Católicas as well as of the social Club Imperio. He hadn't thought to mention these before, partly because—since he didn't accompany her on visits to the poor— it wasn't part of the experience he had lived. Moreover, as a man, he was less interested in the highly feminized world of charity than in masculine activities, and he clearly identified more with his father, who occupied a central place in the memoir. If not for the questions from a pesky daughter who specializes in women's history, this information would have been lost.[2]

This personal history helped me understand why memoirs of the early twentieth century fail to mention the benevolent work of mothers. It was not that these women were totally devoted to domesticity, since they weren't. In part it was because they left us long ago and their children knew little about what they did. In part it may have been that the volunteers were so ubiquitous that they were considered unremarkable. In addition, sexism undoubtedly caused people to view what women did as less important than men's activities. A final reason was generational discontinuity. By the 1940s these volunteers were supplanted by trained nurses and social workers, and the care of the sick poor (to the extent that it existed) was increasingly the province of the state rather than of private individuals. Consequently, women in the next generation—my mother and aunts—were much more devoted to domesticity than in the previous one where ladies reached across the class divide to help the needy who lived in rude shacks on the outskirts of their cities, surrounded by mud and mosquitos. Although in the middle of the twentieth century many women entered the new professions of teaching, nursing, and social work, they were usually from a lower social class than that of most of the earlier volunteers. Thus my mother and her friends rarely participated in the workforce, and it was instead the next generation (mine) where the women chose to pursue paid careers.

My family's experience illustrates how women's history does not necessarily follow a linear progression from domesticity to professionalism, or from the home to civic engagement. But our stereotypes are often based on our mother's lives, not on the generation that came before. We have assumed that each previous generation was more limited and constricted, which it turns out was not always the case. This fallacy is another reason that the memory of these ladies' associations has been erased. Our preconceived notions have shaped the questions we ask about the past and prevented us from seeing what was before our very eyes, hiding in plain sight.

Unfortunately, the charitable volunteers are gone now, along with their children who might have answered more questions. I hope that this reconstruction of their activities does justice to their memory. Because of circumstances that in the 1930s and 1940s sent my parents out of Cuba—where this history has yet to be written—I have pursued it in Mexico, the country to whose history I have devoted my career. This little slice of family history opened my eyes to a lost world of voluntary associations that challenges much of the conventional wisdom about the Mexican past by revealing the importance of the private sector in providing welfare services, the persistence of religion in a supposedly secular time, the Catholic contributions to modernization, and, above all, the active participation of women in solving the urgent problems of their communities.

Society of Saint Vincent de Paul Superior Council Officers, 1845–1910

President

Bishop Joaquín Fernández de Madrid (1845–1848)
Luis Gonzaga Cuevas (January–November 1849; resigned)
Teófilo Marín (May 1850–d. November 1867)
Antonio de Vértiz (January–July 1868; resigned)
José María Rodríguez Villanueva (August 1868–d. September 1886)
Joaquín García Icazbalceta (October 1886–d. November 1894)
Agustín Rodríguez (1895–at least 1910)
Luis Torres y Ansorena (early 20th century)

Vice President

Manuel Andrade (1845–d. June 1848)
Pedro Rojas (July–December 1848)
Manuel Urquiaga (at least 1856, 1861)
Manuel Diez de Bonilla (1857–1861?)
Agustín Rodríguez (at least 1894)
Luis. G. Arnaldo (1895–at least 1910)

Treasurer

Manuel Canseco (1845–d. 1863)
Juan B. Alamán (1863–?)

Sánchez Barquera (at least 1894)
Francisco Urquiaga (at least 1899–1910)

Secretary

Joaquín Velázquez de la Cadena (1845–at least 1846)
Basilio José Arrillaga (at least 1848–1849)
Teófilo Marín (May 1849–?)
Ignacio González Cosío (1851?–1856)
José María López Monroy (at least 1857, 1871)
Juan B. Alamán (at least 1860–1861)
Jesús Urquiaga (at least 1868–1895)
José María Sánchez del Castillo (1896–at least 1902)
Carlos Vargas Galeana (at least 1910)

Sources: Sociedad, *Noticia* (1868–1870), *Memoria* (1871), *Boletín* (1882–1909), *Reseña*, 20, *Acta*, 8–9; "Asamblea general . . . 1857," ASSVP, CC113, Mexique; "Tableau Statistique," 1894, 1910, in ibid.

Ladies of Charity Superior Council Officers, 1863–1911[*]

Clerical Director

Pbro. Francisco Muñoz (1863–d. 1877)
Pbro. Félix Mariscal (1882–1890)
Pbro. Ildefonso Moral (1891–1907)
Pbro. Bruno Alvarez (1908–1911)

Clerical Secretary

Pbro. Clemente Vigo (at least 1892–1896)
Pbro. Cipriano Rojas (at least 1898–1900)
Pbro. Salvador Valgañón (at least 1903–1909)

Honorary President

Sra. Carmen Romero Rubio de Díaz (1895–at least 1905)

President

Sra. Ana Furlong de Guerra (1863–1867?)
Sra. Carmen del Vivar (at least 1892–d. 1896)

---

[*] The Superior Council had changed its name to General Council by 1892.

Srta. Ana Noguera (1896–d. 1904)
Sra. Dolores Araoz, Vda. de Villagrán, (1905–?)
Sra. Dolores Araoz de Vidal (at least 1909)
Sra. Elisa de Pindter, Vda. de Nájera (at least 1911)

Vice President

Srta. Ana Noriega de O'Gorman (1863–1865)
Srta. María Galinié (1866–?)
Srta. Ignacia Montes de Oca (at least 1892)
Srta. Ana Noguera (at least 1895)
Sra. Paz Elguero, Vda. de Campos (1896–1900?)*
Sra. Dolores Araoz de Vidal (at least 1903–1904)
Sra. Brígida Pérez Palacios de Alcorta (at least 1909–1911)

Treasurer

Josefa Quibrera (1863–?)
Srta. Guadalupe Bros (1864–at least 1866)
Sra. María Rejón de Arrache (at least 1892–1896)
Sra. Susana Elguero de García Pimentel (at least 1899–1900)
Sra. Manuela Escandón de Dosal (at least 1903–1909)
Srta. Isabel Fáges (at least 1911)

Secretary

Srta. Soledad Tijera (1864–1865)
Da. Agustina Castillo (at least 1866)
Srta. Concepción Arnaldo (at least 1878)
Srta. Marciala López (at least 1892)

Sources: Asociación, *Memoria* (1865–1911)

---

* She is listed as Sra. Paz Elguero de María y Campos in 1899 and 1900.

Guadalajara Society Central Council Officers, 1852–1909[*]

President

Manuel María Palomar (1852–?)
J. Valente de Quevedo (1864–1879)
Miguel Portillo (1879–1897)
Carlos Tapia (1897–at least 1907)

Secretary

Agustín F. Villa (1852–?)
Teófilo Loreto (at least 1894–at least 1912)

Acting Secretary

Francisco Loreto y Dieguez (May 1909)

Source: Sociedad Guadalajara, *Boletín* (1898–1912).

---

[*] Until the Central Council was created in 1889, the officers served on the Particular Council of Guadalajara.

Guadalajara Archdiocese Ladies of Charity Central Council Officers, 1864–1913

Clerical Director

Pbro. José María Gutiérrez Guevara (1864–?)
Pbro. Rafael S. Camacho (1869–1884)
Pbro. Atenógenes Silva (1884–1892)
Pbro. José Homobono Anaya (1892–1898)
Pbro. Luis Silva (1898–at least 1913)

Male Secretary

Don Julián Romero (1864–?)
Don J. Valente Quevedo (1869–d. 1879)
Lic. Pablo Reyes (1879–at least 1922)

Male Pro Secretary[*]

Lic. Dionisio Rodríguez (1864–?)
Don José Fructo Romero (at least 1887–1892)
Don Manuel Vásquez (1893–at least 1903)
Lic. Ignacio Enríquez (at least 1905–1908)

---

* No male pro secretary was listed after 1908.

President

Sra. Nicolasa Luna de Corcuera (1864–d. 1894)
Sra. Antonia Corcuera de Moreno (1895–d. 1910)
Sra. Concepción Corcuera de Palomar (1910–at least 1918)

Vice President

Sra. Guadalupe Villaseñor de Pérez Verdía (at least 1887–1892)[*]
Sra. Concepción Corcuera de Palomar (1893–1910)
Srta. Inés Rodríguez (1911–at least 1913)

Treasurer

Srta. Rosario Llamas (at least 1887–1889)
Sra. Catalina Palomar de Verea (at least 1896–at least 1913)[†]

Subtreasurer

Srta. Julia Clément (at least 1887–1895)[‡]
Srta. Margarita I. Matute (at least 1905–at least 1908)
Srta. Mercedes Aguilar (1908–?)

Pro Secretary

Srta. Mercedes Morfín Silva (at least 1909–1913)

Sources: Arquidiócesis de Guadalajara, *Memoria* (1887–1913) and "Caridad cristiana," 2–11, 104.

---

[*] Sra. Guadalupe Villaseñor was listed as "viuda de Pérez-Verdia" from 1889 on.
[†] Sra. Catalina Palomar was listed as "viuda de Verea" from 1912 on.
[‡] Srta. Julia Clément was listed as "Sra. Julia Clément de Tapia" in 1895.

NOTES

Introduction

1. The women's organization is now called the Voluntarias Vicentinas de México. According to their website, they had 2,500 members throughout the country in 2010. The website of the male Sociedad San Vicente de Paul de México advertised its 165-year presence in Mexico in 2010, but did not mention the size of its membership. In 1990 the Voluntarias counted some 4,000 members compared with the male society's 1,000 members. De Dios, *Historia de la familia vicentina*, 2:638, 666. See vicentinasmexico.org and www.paginasprodigy.com.mx/patriciaagrajeda, both accessed 2 December 2013.

2. Société de Saint-Vincent-de-Paul, *Livre du centenaire*; Foucault, *La Société de Saint-Vincent de Paul;* and Duroselle, *Les débuts du catholicisme social*, chap. 3. Recent scholars are giving the nineteenth-century conferences a second look, if only in article-length studies. For France, see Dumons, "L'oeuvre charitable," and Curtis, "Charitable Ladies." The society's founder has fared better, especially since his beatification in 1997. An example of a recent biography is Cholvy, *Frédéric Ozanam*. For the United States, see McColgan, *Century of Charity,* and Padberg and Hannefin, "St. Vincent's First Foundation."

3. See Adame Goddard, *El pensamiento político y social*; Ceballos Ramírez, *El catolicismo social* and "Las organizaciones"; Hanson, "Day of Ideals"; O'Dogherty Madrazo, *De urnas y sotanas*; Curley, "Slouching Towards Bethlehem"; Nesvig, *Religious Culture*; Overmyer-Velázquez, "New Political Religious Order" and *Visions of the Emerald City*; Wright-Rios, *Revolutions in Mexican Catholicism* and "Visions of Women"; and Moreno Chávez, *Devociones políticas*. Jean Meyer's early work, *Cristero Rebellion,* on the Cristero Revolt was seminal to the reevaluation of the Mexican church. For a review of the literature on the Mexican church, see Lida, "La Iglesia Católica."

4. See, for example, Rugeley, *Of Wonders and Wise Men*; Chowning, "La feminización de la piedad" and "Catholic Church and the Ladies"; Butler, *Popular Piety and Political Identity*; Nesvig, *Religious Culture*; Wright-Rios, *Revolutions in Mexican Catholicism* and "Visions of Women"; Voekel, "Liberal Religion"; and Connaughton, *Religión, política e identidad*.

5. See, for example, Miller, "Role of Women"; O'Dogherty, *"Restaurarlo todo en Cristo"*; Hanson, "Day of Ideals"; Schell, "Honorable Avocation" and "Of the Sublime Mission"; Fernández-Aceves, "Political Mobilization of Women"; Boylan, "Mexican Catholic Women's Activism" and "Gendering the Faith"; Vaca, *Los silencios de la historia*; Butler, *Popular Piety and Political Identity*; and Andes, "Catholic Alternative."

6. See Forment, *Democracy in Latin America*, and the review of this literature in Sábato, *Ciudadanía política y formación* and "On Political Citizenship."

7. Fowler and Morales Moreno, *El conservadurismo mexicano*; García Gutiérrez, "La experiencia cultural"; Pani, "Democracia y representación política," *Para mexicanizar el Segundo Imperio* and *Conservadurismo y derechas*; Torre, García Ugarte, and Ramírez Sáiz, *Los rostros del conservadurismo*; and Smith, *Roots of Conservatism*.

8. Moisés González Navarro led the way with his early studies: "Ejercicio caritativo" and *La pobreza en México*. Only recently have others followed. See Macías-González, "Mexican Aristocracy and Porfirio Díaz" and "Isabel Pesado y de la Llave"; Blum, "Conspicuous Benevolence"; articles in Villalobos Grzywobicz, *Filantropía y acción solidaria*; and Lorenzo Río, *"¿De quién son los pobres?"* For reviews of the literature on Mexican welfare, see Meyer, *Instituciones de seguridad social*; Valero Chávez, *De la caridad*; and Arrom, *Containing the Poor*, 8–9, 303nn28–33. On other areas of Latin America, see Matos Rodríguez, *Women and Urban Change*, chap. 5; Mead, "Beneficent Maternalism"; Verba, *Catholic Feminism*; Sanborn and Portocarrero, *Philanthropy and Social Change*; Ehrick, *Shield of the Weak*; Castro Carvajal, *Caridad y beneficencia*; Eraso, *Mujeres y asistencia social*; Guy, *Women Build the Welfare State;* and a special issue on "Philanthropy and Society" of the Colombian journal *Sociedad y Economía, 10 (April 2006)*.

9. Díaz Robles, "Medicina, religión y pobreza," *La práctica médica*, and "Señores y señoras." González Navarro included the Vincentian conferences in his discussion of private philanthropy but did not distinguish between the male and female organizations: "Ejercicio caritativo," 496, 502, 505–9, and *La pobreza en México*, 58 and 61. Forment briefly mentions them in his survey of private associations, *Democracy in Latin America*, 260, as do Plasencia, "Cien años de Acción Social," 27–28, 35–43; O'Dogherty Madrazo, *De urnas y sotanas*, 29–30, 43–47, 108, 112, 114, 249, 258, 279–80; Valero Chávez, *De la caridad*, 109; Oliver Sánchez, *Salud, desarrollo urbano y modernización*, 21–39; Alanís, "Algunas manifestaciones"; and Cárdenas Ayala, *El derrumbe*, 103–4, 412–14. For the Mixteca Baja, see Smith, *Roots of Conservatism*, 186, 198–99, 241, 277.

Research on the Vincentian conferences began earlier in other areas of Latin America. On Argentina, see Mead, "Gender, Welfare, and the Catholic Church"; Dalla Corte and Piacenza, "Cartas marcadas"; Bonaudo, "Cuando las tuteladas"; Eraso, "Maternalismo, religión y asistencia"; and Guy, *Women Build the Welfare State*, 51–53, 60–65. On Colombia, see Botero Herrera, "Los talleres"; Castro Carvajal, *Caridad y beneficencia*, chap. 4, and "Las visitas domiciliarias femeninas." On Chile see Serrano, *¿Qué hacer con Dios?*, 49–74; and Ponce de León Atria, *Gobernar la pobreza*, 233–308.

10. The archive of the male society is located at the Conseil Général International, Société de Saint-Vincent de Paul, 5 rue du Pré-aux-Clercs, 75007 Paris, France. A few reports of the international Ladies of Charity after 1892 are available in the Lazarist Convent that served as home base for the Vincentian priests who directed the organization: Congrégation de la Mission, 95, Rue de Sèvres/97, Paris 75006. The Dames de la Charité changed its name in 1971 to Association Internationale des Charités (AIC). Now headquartered in Brussels, it does not appear to have materials for the time period before 1913.

11. Most of these are in the Folletería section of the Archivo Histórico de la Arquidiócesis de Guadalajara (AHAG).

12. Although the author is listed as Vicente de Dios, he credits Father Juan José Muñoz with writing the chapters on the lay organizations, *Historia de la familia vicentina* 1:11.

13. Father Muñoz told me that he used the reports in the Consejo Nacional of the Sociedad San Vicente de Paul de México A. C. (Matías Romero 1412, Colonia Vértiz Navarte, Mexico D.F.), which was shuttered every time I visited Mexico City. Fortunately, I was able to find copies of most of the reports he cited in other repositories.

Chapter 1

1. For Mexico, see esp. Adame Goddard, *El pensamiento político y social*; Ceballos Ramírez, *El catolicismo social* and "Organizaciones laborales"; and Curley, "Slouching Towards Bethlehem." On Latin America, see Andes and Young, *Local Church*.

2. Cuevas, *Historia de la iglesia*, 5:chap. 6; Meyer, *Cristero Rebellion*, 8; Hanson, "Day of Ideals," 63–81; O'Dogherty Madrazo, *De urnas y sotanas*, 27–31; Overmyer-Velázquez, "New Political Religious Order," 132–35; Wright-Rios, *Revolutions in Mexican Catholicism*, 102; and Moreno Chávez, *Devociones políticas*.

3. Schmitt, "Catholic Adjustment," 193–96; Plasencia, "Cien años de Acción Social," 25–53; Olimón Nolasco, "Proyecto de Reforma"; and Smith, *Roots of Conservatism*.

4. Chowning, "From Colonial Cofradías"; and Gilbert, "Long Live the True Religion!," 39–43.

5. The Mexican society's fiftieth- and hundredth-anniversary chronicles were written by its lay officers: "Memoria del establecimiento de la Sociedad de San Vicente de Paul en la república Mexicana, y de su desarrollo en los primeros cincuenta años de su existencia," in Sociedad de San Vicente de Paul (hereafter Sociedad), *Reseña*, 6–89; Sociedad, *Acta*. See also the history written for the fiftieth anniversary of the aggregation of the society's Guadalajara branch: "Memoria general de la Sociedad de San Vicente de Paúl, en Guadalajara, durante 50 años," in Sociedad de San Vincent de Paúl, Consejo Central de Guadalajara (hereafter Sociedad Guadalajara), *Boletín* (September 1902), 72–85. Vincentian priests wrote two histories that placed the conferences within the broader story of the Vincentian family in Mexico: Camacho, *Los Padres Paúles*; and De Dios, *Historia de la familia vicentina*. See also Munguía, *Panegírico de San Vicente de Paul*.

6. See introduction to the bylaws, as in Sociedad, *Reglamento* (1860), 5; and Duroselle, *Les débuts du catholicisme social*, 154, 168–86, 705, 709.

7. According to Barbara Diefendorf, although Vincent de Paul himself credited his female collaborators with inspiring, funding, and helping establish his three foundations, these women have fared less well at the hands of his biographers. Diefendorf, *Penitence to Charity*, 203–10, 226–38, 245–51.

8. Sister Rosalie also directed the reconstituted Dames de la Charité and worked in the Paris slums until her death in 1856. Her biographer, the Vicomte Armand Marie Joachim de Melun, was himself an early member of the French men's society. The men worked hand in hand with the Filles de la Charité, who provided the volunteers with lists of needy paupers in their parishes. Foucault, *La Société de Saint-Vincent de Paul*, 82; Melun, *Life of Sister Rosalie*, 89; Padberg and Hannefin, "St. Vincent's First Foundation," 111; and Curtis, "Charitable Ladies,"147. On Sister Rosalie's role in creating the *patronages* of apprentices in 1834, see Duroselle, *Les débuts du catholicisme social*, 183, 212–13. On the 1856 controversy about her role in founding the conferences, see Cholvy, *Frédéric Ozanam*, 296.

9. Udovic, "'What About the Poor?'," 89; and Curtis, "Charitable Ladies," 144.

10. So do the Fagoaga sisters, Faustina and Julia, as well as General Cirilo Gómez Anaya, who also helped fund the foundation. The parish priest of Silao, José Guadalupe Romero, was also instrumental in establishing the order in Mexico, and Tadeo Ortiz, the Mexican consul in Bordeaux, had proposed it to the Mexican government in 1831. García Cubas, *El libro de mis recuerdos*, 41–42; and De Dios, *Historia de la familia vicentina*, 1:53–55. Laureana Wright de Kleinhans gave the ex-countess full credit (*Mujeres notables mexicanas*, 78–79).

11. Foucault, *La Société de Saint-Vincent de Paul*, 81–83, 90–97; and Sociedad, *Acta*, 13.

12. See aggregation letter of 19 September 1845, in Sociedad, *Acta*, 14. Foucault dates the Mexican branch to 1845 (when it was officially aggregated to the French society, rather than when the first conference was founded), the US branch to 1846, and the Canadian to 1847 (*La Société de Saint-Vincent de Paul*, 87–88). I found conflicting information on the foundation dates of these branches, however. The United States dates its organization to November 1845, when the first conference was founded in St. Louis. See Trotter, "St. Vincent de Paul, Society of."

13. Next came Chile (1854), Colombia (1857), Cuba and Uruguay (1858), and Argentina (1859). Foundations slowed in the next two decades, with only Ecuador (1866), Brazil (1872), and Haiti (1878). Most other Latin American foundations date to the 1880s or later. Foucault, *La Société de Saint-Vincent de Paul*; and Société de Saint-Vincent-de-Paul, *Livre du centenaire*, 281–303.

14. Sociedad, *Reseña*, 18, 25, 47, 50–51.

15. On France, see Foucault, *La Société de Saint-Vincent de Paul*, esp. 62.

16. See excellent discussions in Gilbert, "Long Live the True Religion!," 17–26; and Hanson, "Day of Ideals," 30–43, 67–72.

17. De Dios, *Historia de la familia vicentina*, 1:64–65.

18. See Hanson, "Day of Ideals," 41n23; and Gilbert, "Long Live the True Religion!," 40.

19. The presidential decree is cited in AHDF, Hospitales, vol. 2312, leg. 1, exp. 3, fol. 3v. De Dios refers to an order requiring the society to obtain government permission to hold its annual assemblies and to found new conferences; see *Historia de la familia vicentina*, 1:522. I have not located this document or discovered what date the requirement went into effect.

20. See discussion in Arrom, *Women of Mexico City*, 254, 263–68, and *Containing the Poor*, esp. 202.

21. Mora, *México y sus revoluciones*, 1:80–81, 469.

22. See Alvarez Amezquita, *Historia de la salubridad y asistencia*, 1:236–50; Muriel, *Hospitales de la Nueva España*, 283–90; and Arrom, "Popular Politics," 333–34n99, and *Containing the Poor*, 187, 193.

23. Vicente de Paul Andrade was born in February 1844, when his father was already deeply involved in the Vincentian movement. De Dios, *Historia de la familia vicentina*, 1:589–90; and Poole, "Eventful Life."

24. De Dios, *Historia de la familia vicentina*, 1:91–101; and Castro, "José María Andrade."

25. De Dios, *Historia de la familia vicentina*, 1:53–54, 65–68, 72, 521.

26. This statement appeared in all the editions of the 1835 bylaws. See, for example, Sociedad, *Reglamento* (1860), 7.

27. Sociedad, *Acta*, 8–11; Sociedad, *Reseña*, 18. The other two members of the drafting commission were Don Manuel Canseco and Dr. Domingo de la Fuente.

28. De Dios, *Historia de la familia vicentina*, 1:522; Sociedad, *Reseña*, 23. By 1877 Superior Council correspondence listed an address of Calle de los Medinas, núm. 7. Superior Council "Circular," 8 June 1877, ASSVP, Conseil Superior du Mexique, 1845–1930, CC113, Mexique.

29. Muriel, *Hospitales de la Nueva España*, 108–12.

30. AHDF, Hospitales, vol. 2312, leg. 1, exp. 3; García Icazbalceta, *Informe sobre los establecimientos*, 63; and Sociedad, *Reseña*, 23, 30.

31. Sociedad, *Reseña*, 23. It is unclear when the Sisters took over the asylum. Josefina Muriel says it was in 1847 (*Hospitales de la Nueva España*, 111). Manuel Rivera Cambas says it was in March 1845, although the first contract was signed in 1855, when the Vincentian priest Ramón Sanz and two board—and Superior Council—members, Col. Pedro Pablo Iturria and Don Domingo Pozo, signed a contract with the sisters (*México pintoresco*, 54).

32. Indeed a ladies' board, the Junta de Beneficencia del Hospital del Divino Salvador, had been running the asylum since 1842. In 1844 the organization reported on the conditions in the asylum as the committee prepared to turn it over to the society. At that time Da. Petra Barredo de Trigueros (possibly wife of Finance Minister Ignacio de Trigueros) was president. *Manifiesto*; Galí Boadella, *Historias del bello sexo*, 72; and Ballenger, "Modernizing Madness," 125–28.

33. De Dios, *Historia de la familia vicentina*, 1:65–77, 521, 541.

34. Note on letter of aggregation of 19 September 1845 reproduced in Sociedad, *Acta*, 15; and Sociedad, *Reseña*, 16.

35. Société de Saint-Vincent-de-Paul, *Livre du centenaire*, 274; and Sociedad, *Reseña*, 9, 15–16. The French society's centennial history claimed the original Mexican *reglamento* was "very long." It was in fact very short. See reproduction in Sociedad, *Acta*, 9–10.

36. Letter of aggregation reproduced in Sociedad, *Acta*, 13–15.

37. The importance of developing fraternity among the conference members is highlighted in the introduction to the bylaws: for example, Sociedad, *Reglamento* (1860), 9.

38. A signature on the front of the society's *Reglamento* on file in France dates it to 1846. See also letter of 29 January 1846 sent to the Conseil Général in Paris. Both in ASSVP, Conseil Superior du Mexique, 1845–1920, CC113, Mexique.

39. The Superior Council simultaneously served as a Particular Council to oversee the Mexico City conferences until 1848. It was called the Consejo Central until July 1849, then Consejo Particular until April 1850, when it became the Consejo Superior. The second Consejo Particular was founded in Toluca in 1851. Sociedad, *Reseña*, 20, 25, 50–51, 57; and Sociedad, *Acta*, 16.

40. Letter of 2 March 1846 to the Conseil Général in Paris, ASSVP, Conseil Superior du Mexique, 1845–1920, CC113, Mexique.

41. Quoted in Sociedad, *Reseña*, 28.

42. Letter of 6 February 1849 from the Conseil Général in Paris, ASSVP, Conseil Superior du Mexique, 1845–1920, CC113, Mexique.
43. Foucault, *La Société de Saint-Vincent de Paul*, 101.
44. Sociedad, *Reseña*, 28.
45. Ibid., 30.
46. The Spanish priest Jerónimo Martínez de Ripalda's 1618 *Catecismo y exposición breve de la doctrina Cristiana* was published in Mexico from at least 1758 until 1940. Although religious instruction was prohibited in public schools after 1875, Ripalda's *Catechism* continued to be used in many private—as well as some public—schools until the 1930s. Arredondo López, "Catecismo"; and González, *San José de Gracia*, 236.
47. On the collaboration of church and state in primary education, see Vaughan, "Primary Schooling."
48. Sociedad, *Reseña*, 23.
49. De Dios, *Historia de la familia vicentina*, 1:72, 448–49; and Sociedad, *Reseña*, 43.
50. Sociedad, *Reseña*, 17. De Dios says that Andrade died of cholera (*Historia de la familia vicentina*, 1:522–24), but according to Alvarez Amezquita, Mexico City suffered from a typhoid epidemic in 1848–1849 and the cholera outbreak came in 1850 (*Historia de la salubridad y asistencia*, 1:253–57).
51. Sociedad, *Reseña*, 31.
52. This trend contrasts with the United States, where the young Society of St. Vincent de Paul apparently followed the French model from the start and only shifted from parish-based to broader forms of assistance late in the century. McKeown, "Catholic Charities," 243.
53. For French naming customs, see Sociedad, *Reglamento* (1860), art. 4. The US conferences also followed the French practice (Trotter, "St. Vincent de Paul, Society of," 1249). The only Mexico City parish name used by a conference before 1854 was Señor San José, founded in 1848. Even after that date, the society's chapters rarely used the names of the capital's parishes, which were Sagrario Metropolitano, San Miguel, Santa Catarina Mártir, Santa Veracruz, San José, Santa Ana, Santa Cruz y Soledad, San Sebastián, Santa María la Redonda, San Pablo, Santa Cruz Acatlán, Salto del Agua, and Santo Tomás Palma. O'Hara, "El capital espiritual," 409. Compare conference names in Sociedad, *Reseña*, 50–60.
54. November 1848 letter to the Conseil Général in Paris, ASSVP, Conseil Superior du Mexique, 1845–1920, CC113, Mexique.
55. Sociedad, *Reglamento* [ca. 1848].
56. Letter of 4 October 1851 to Conseil Général in Paris, ASSVP, Conseil Superior du Mexique, 1845–1920, CC113, Mexique.
57. De Dios, *Historia de la familia vicentina*, 1:524; and Cárdenas de la Peña, *Tiempo y tarea*.

58. The other was interim president Vértiz, who according to the Sociedad's *Reseña* was prevented from continuing on because of his business responsibilities. Sociedad, *Reseña*, 20.

59. It was the Conferencia de la Anunciación de Nuestra Señora y Encarnación del Divino Verbo, founded in August 1849. Sociedad de San Vicente de Paul, "Asamblea general del dia 26 de Abril de 1857, verificada en el Palacio Arzobispal de la Ciudad de México," ASSVP, CC113, Mexique.

60. Letter of 2 March 1846, ASSVP, Conseil Superior du Mexique, 1845–1920, CC113, Mexique.

61. Sociedad, *Reseña*, 47.

62. See, for example, Foucault, *La Société de Saint-Vincent de Paul*, 70, 98–100.

63. The inauguration of this obra was mentioned in Sociedad, *Reseña* (30) but never appeared in the records of the early decades. In France the Société Saint-François Régis was founded as a separate organization in 1826 and flourished when it developed close ties with the Society of Saint Vincent de Paul, especially from 1844 to 1847, when Jules Gossin served as president for both charities. Ratcliffe, "Popular Classes," 325–26, 343–44.

64. On the early French patronages, see Duroselle, *Les débuts du catholicisme social*, 183–84.

65. Sociedad, "Asamblea general. . . 1857," ASSVP, CC113, Mexique.

66. "Tableau Statistique des Conferences de la Republique Mexicaine," 1856, ASSVP, CC113, Mexique.

67. Foucault, *La Société de Saint-Vincent de Paul*, 98.

68. These statistics may only describe the situation in 1863. García Icazbalceta, *Informe sobre los establecimientos*, 63.

69. The school apparently existed by 1851. See letters of 4 October 1851 and 3 January 1853 to Conseil Général in Paris, ASSVP, Conseil Superior du Mexique, 1845–1920, CC113, Mexique.

70. Belanger, "Cofradías"; Muriel, *Hospitales de la Nueva España*; and Alberro, *Apuntes para la historia*.

71. "Tableau Statistique," 1856, SSVP, CC113, Mexique.

72. Foucault, *La Société de Saint-Vincent de Paul*, esp. 71. This conclusion must remain tentative until the French organization receives a detailed historical treatment.

73. See notes to articles 1, 2, 17, and 20. These explanatory notes appeared in both of the undated early editions of the *Reglamento* that were probably those published in 1846 and 1848. Both versions are identical in content, although the formats differ. They appear to have predated the extensively annotated 1858 edition of the bylaws, whose title explains that it is a translation of the 1853 French edition (Sociedad, *Notas*). References in the footnotes to "nuestras conferencias"—in contrast to those "en Francia"—indicate that these clarifications were added to the Mexican editions rather than being translated from the French version.

74. In 1857 a few conferences also penned in "children prepared for first communion" under the "État du personnel et des oeuvres" section included as part of the "Tableau Statistique." ASSVP, CC114, Mexique. This category was probably hidden under "children taught" in other reports.

75. See Sociedad, *Noticia* (1868), "Cuadro Estadístico," n.p.; and Sociedad, *Instrucciones* [ca. 1865], "Estado de la Asociación," facing 16.

76. After the bishop of Tenagra's "effective" presidency, the following ecclesiastics became honorary presidents: the dean Manuel Moreno y Jove and the archbishops of Mexico, including Pelagio Antonio Labastida y Dávalos, Próspero María Alarcón y Sánchez Barquera, and Luis María Martínez. Sociedad, *Reseña*, 26; Sociedad, *Acta*, 61; and De Dios, *Historia de la familia vicentina*, 1, 523.

77. Sociedad, "Asamblea general. . . 1857," ASSVP, CC113, Mexique. In another sign of the society's close relationship with the church, this assembly was held in the Archiepiscopal Palace, and its retreats were held in the Misionero's convent.

78. See "Tableau Statistique des Conferences de la Republique Mexicaine," 1856, 1857, and 1858, ASSVP, CC113, Mexique.

79. Société de Saint-Vincent-de-Paul, *Livre du centenaire*, 11–12. As late as 1877 a priest, Presbítero Vicente Reyes, was still listed as the president of the Mexico City conference of Nuestra Señora de los Angeles y San Felipe de Jesús. "Lista de las conferencias que existen en esta capital," 1877, ASSVP, CC113, Mexique.

80. The society's 1860 manual insisted that the visitors should not send a servant in their place. Sociedad, *Guía*, 11.

81. In addition to working in hospitals, the Sisters ran several *escuelas gratuitas* in impoverished neighborhoods. De Dios, *Historia de la familia vicentina*, 1:97.

82. Gardida is listed as coeditor of an 1853 issue along with Francisco Pomar. He is identified as the member who established the society's lending library in 1858. Ibid., 1:102–4, 527.

83. Gilbert, "'Long Live the True Religion!,'" 83. Manuel Diez de Bonilla first appears in available records as vice president of the Superior Council in 1857.

84. Castro, "José María Andrade," esp. 392, 424; and Gilbert, "'Long Live the True Religion!,'" chap. 3.

85. The installments appeared in 1851, 1852, 1857, and 1859. Cárdenas de la Peña, *Tiempo y tarea*, esp. 259–60.

86. Pani, *Para mexicanizar el Segundo Imperio*, 390.

87. On this point, see Voekel, Moretón, and Jo, "Vaya con Dios," 1608–9; and Moreno Chávez, *Devociones políticas*.

88. Sociedad, *Reseña*, 28–29,

89. Ibid., 32. As late as 1909 the Mexican conferences sent 576 pesos to aid the earthquake victims in Messina and Reggio. Sociedad, *Boletín* (April 1909), 73, 77–78.

90. Sociedad, *Noticia* (1869), 11.

91. The periodic contributions to the church in Rome were quite substantial. The Mexican society donated 7,000 francs in 1871–1872, sent another 700 pesos to celebrate the elevation of Pope Pius IX to the Episcopado in 1877, contributed 700 pesos to celebrate the jubilee of Pope Leo XIII in 1887, and sent 1,000 francs to help build the Church of San Joaquín in honor of Leo XIII in 1893. Sociedad, *Reseña*, 31–32. In 1909 it sent 425.28 pesos for the Pope's jubilee. Sociedad, *Boletín* (April 1909), 73.

92. Sociedad Guadalajara, *Boletín* (July 1909), 153.

93. The quote refers to longtime Guadalajara society member Carlos Tapia, who visited Paris in 1888. He served as the Guadalajara's Central Council president from 1897 to at least 1909. Sociedad Guadalajara, *Boletín* (September 1902, 83; September 1909, 78).

94. Ponce de León Atria, *Gobernar la pobreza*, 244, 247–48, 257.

95. Société de Saint-Vincent-de-Paul, *Livre du centenaire*, 11–12.

96. De Dios, *Historia de la familia vicentina*, 1:524; Sociedad, *Reseña*, 18.

97. Forment, *Democracy in Latin America*, 99–103.

98. This pattern persisted: for example, Juan B. Alamán, who first appeared in the records as secretary of the Superior Council in 1860, was still listed forty-two years later as president of the conference of Nuestra Señora de la Luz in Mexico City. Sociedad, *Acta*, 8–9, 25; "Tableau Statistique des Conferences de la République," 1856–57; "État du personnel et des oeuvres des conferences et du Conseil Particulier, au 31 Décembre 1857," ASSVP, CC113, Méxique; Sociedad, *Reseña*, 20; Sociedad, *Boletín* (August 1902), "Cuadro de las Conferencias de esta Capital," n.p. A similar list is reproduced in fig. 6.2.

99. Juan Santelices is listed as a fifty-one-year-old clockmaker in the 1848 census of Mexico City. I am indebted to María Gayón for providing this information.

100. An exception is Londoño-Vega's study for Colombia, *Religion, Culture, and Society*, esp. chaps. 3 and 5.

101. This phrase is the title of Gabriel A. Almond and Sidney Verba's influential 1963 book, *The Civic Culture: Political Attitudes and Democracy in Five Nations*.

102. For a similar argument for the later Liga de Damas Chilenas, see Power, "Preface."

Chapter 2

1. On the conservative counternarrative that emphasizes the victimization of the church, see Gilbert, "'Long Live the True Religion!,'" 8–9.

2. Letter to Paris of 22 February 1858, ASSVP, Conseil Superior du Mexique, 1845–1920, CC113, Mexique.

3. The change was announced at the annual meeting in April 1857. Sociedad, "Asamblea general. . . 1857," ASSVP, CC113, Mexique.

4. See ASSVP, Conferences du Mexique, 1857–1920, CC114, Mexique.

5. The 1857 *Boletín* merely translated the February 1855 issue of the French bulletin. By February 1859 the *Boletín* included news about the Mexican conferences.

6. Sociedad, *Notas*.

7. On the different membership categories, see Sociedad, *Reglamento*, cap. v, arts. 53–56, and discussion in *Reglamento* (1898), 111–21.

8. Both of these men became corresponding members in 1856. "Tableau Statistique des Conferences de la Republique Mexicaine," 1856, ASSVP, CC113, Mexique.

9. See the "Etats du personnel et des oeuvres," in ASSVP, CC113 and CC114, Mexique. The February 1859 *Boletín* reported that the society was in the process of founding four conferences of artisans as well as several rural ones (204).

10. See Sociedad, "Asamblea general . . . 1857," ASSVP, CC113, Mexique Sociedad, *Boletín* (February 1859; February 1860); De Dios, *Historia de la familia vicentina*, 1:527–31; and "Cuadro Estadístico," 1860, ASSVP, Conseil Superior du Mexique, 1845–1920, CC113, Mexique.

11. In Mexico City the Sisters of Charity took control of the Hospitals of San Juan de Dios and Divino Salvador in 1845, San Pablo in 1847, and San Andrés in 1850. The order took over the Hospitals of Belén in Guanajuato in 1850, San Pedro in Puebla in 1852, Belén in Guadalajara in 1853, and a hospital in Toluca in 1858. Additional hospital contracts were awarded in the 1860s and early 1870s. De Dios, *Historia de la familia vicentina*, 1:506.

12. The visiting of "panaderos que . . . se encuentran reclusos" was first mentioned in Sociedad, *Boletín* (February 1860), 24.

13. The annual salary figures are from 1861. Arrom, *Containing the Poor*, 215.

14. Sociedad, *Boletín* (February 1859), 195–96. It is unclear whether these soup kitchens provided food to anyone who walked in or only to selected paupers. In Chile the *cocinas* were apparently open to the society's clients, who paid for the food with bonos. Ponce de León Atria, *Gobernar la pobreza*, 283.

15. Founded by society member Tomás Gardida, the library was located in the *tabaquería* at 2a Calle de Santo Domingo y Donceles. See De Dios, *Historia de la familia vicentina*, 1:527; and Sociedad, *Guía*, 43.

16. They were particularly concerned with the high levels of drunkenness on San Lunes. Sociedad, *Boletín* (February 1859), 204–5.

17. The commission that created this obra consisted of Father Andrés David Bradburn and society members José Urquiaga and Antonio Vértiz. See Sociedad, *Boletín* (February 1860), 26; De Dios, *Historia de la familia vicentina*, 1:526; and "Reglamento de los retiros espirituales para los socios de las conferencias de San Vicente de Paul," ASSVP, CC113, Mexique. Reproduced in fig, 2.1.

18. Sociedad, *Notas*, 36, 58, and passim.

19. De Dios, *Historia de la familia vicentina*, 1:284–85, 296–99.

20. Ibid., 1:535.
21. Ibid., 1:297–98.
22. Superior Council letters to Paris of 28 September and 28 October 1860, ASSVP, Conseil Superior du Mexique, 1845–1920, CC113, Mexique.
23. De Dios, *Historia de la familia vicentina*, 1:533–34.
24. Letters of 28 September and 28 October 1860, ASSVP, Conseil Superior du Mexique, 1845–1920, CC113, Mexique.
25. According to the society's August 1860 *Boletín* (cited in De Dios, *Historia de la familia vicentina*, 1:531), the supporters of Mexico City's twelve conferences consisted of 23 honorary and 348 subscribing members. In his "Dictamen," Marcelino Castañeda provides a higher number of active volunteers (315) and reports that there were three more chapters in Mexico City waiting to be aggregated, with a membership of 87 additional volunteers (*La Unidad Católica*, "Editorial: Las Conferencias"). The 1859 figures are from Sociedad, *Boletin* (February 1860), 28.
26. Letter of 28 September 1860, ASSVP, Conseil Superior du Mexique, 1845–1920, CC113, Mexique, 3–4. Note that the 1860 "Cuadro Estadístico" (ASSVP, Conseil Superior du Mexique, 1845–1920, CC113, Mexique) refers to fourteen conferences in Mexico City. It is unclear how many provincial conferences were included in its statistics.
27. The letter of 27 April 1861 that referred to "el huracán político" was signed by Secretary Juan B. Alamán and Vicepresident Manuel Urquiaga. ASSVP, Conseil Superior du Mexique, 1845–1920, CC113, Mexique.
28. Sociedad, *Guía*, 60.
29. Letter of 28 September 1860, ASSVP, Conseil Superior du Mexique, 1845–1920, CC113, Mexique.
30. The French General Council was prohibited from meeting from 1861 until 1870. Foucault, *La Société de Saint-Vincent de Paul*, 183–84, 204.
31. I have not located comprehensive lists of conference members, but I found these names among lists of Superior Council members or officers of individual conferences, ASSVP, CC113 and CC114, Mexique. Sociedad, *Reseña*, 5; and Castro, "José María Andrade," 389. On their political activities, see Pani, *Para mexicanizar el Segundo Imperio*, 367–74; De Dios, *Historia de la familia vicentina*, 1:500n9; *Diccionario Porrúa*, 881; and Bravo Ugarte, *Historia de México*, 3:201, 329–30.
32. Pani, "Dreaming of a Mexican Empire."
33. Letter of 27 April 1861, ASSVP, Conseil Superior du Mexique, 1845–1920, CC113, Mexique.
34. Ibid.; De Dios, *Historia de la familia vicentina*, 1:533–34.
35. Zarco's decree was based on a report by Marcelino Castañeda, director of the Fondos de Beneficencia Pública. *La Unidad Católica*, "Editorial: Las Conferencias" and "Editorial: Las Hermanas." See also Sociedad, *Reseña*, 27–28.

36. Letters to Paris of 27 April and 28 May 1861, ASSVP, Conseil Superior du Mexique, 1845–1920, CC113, Mexique. See also *La Unidad Católica*, "Editorial: La Sociedad."

37. Letter to Paris of 28 October 1861, ASSVP, Conseil Superior du Mexique, 1845–1920, CC113, Mexique.

38. Letters to Paris of 25 December 1861, 24 February 1862, and 21 April 1863, in ibid.

39. De Dios, *Historia de la familia vicentina*, 1:145, 179, 374, and passim.

40. Cited in González, "Los ceros sociales," 408.

41. See decrees of 18 February and 28 May 1861, in De Dios, *Historia de la familia vicentina*, 1:453–54, 496–97.

42. Ibid., 1:456, 465.

43. Cited in González, "Los ceros sociales," 408.

44. De Dios, *Historia de la familia vicentina*, 1:455, 495–98.

45. Ibid., 1:532–33; *Diccionario Porrúa*, 978.

46. Sociedad, *Reseña*, 31; and Sociedad, *Instrucciones* (ca. 1865). The last *Boletín* issue of August 1860 was no. 13; the November 1864 issue was no. 14. De Dios, *Historia de la familia vicentina*, 1:530–34.

47. An average of 9.6 conferences were founded each year from 1864 to 1866. The next highest rate was 8.5 per year from 1884 to 1887. For a chronological list of chapter foundations, see Sociedad, *Reseña,* 50–60.

48. De Dios, *Historia de la familia vicentina*, 1:534–36.

49. The schools were mentioned in the Sociedad's *Boletín* (November 1864); the 1865 *Boletín* (May 1865) reported that the school on the Hacienda de la Capellanía continued to thrive. Quoted in De Dios, *Historia de la familia vicentina*, 1:533, 536.

50. The twenty members consisted of one *comerciante* plus five *carpinteros*, two *zapateros*, two *plateros*, and one each *tornero, relojero, fabricante, dorador, latonero, pintor, herrero, hojalatero, tapicero*, and *sastre.* "Boletín de Agregación de la Conferencia del Santíssimo Sacramento," 7 March 1868, ASSVP, CC114, Mexique.

51. De Dios, *Historia de la familia vicentina*, 1:535–36.

52. Society member Dionisio Rodríguez was instrumental in its founding. See Díaz Robles, "Medicina, religión y pobreza" 44.

53. Cited in De Dios, *Historia de la familia vicentina*, 1:537.

54. Ibid., 536–37.

55. Both men had been members of the organization since at least 1857. "Etat du personnel et des ouevres, 1857," ASSVP, CC113, Mexique; García Icazbalceta, *Informe sobre los establecimientos;* Arrom, *Containing the Poor*, 229–35; and De Dios, *Historia de la familia vicentina*, 1:527.

56. *Diccionario Porrúa*, 881; Sociedad, *Reseña*, 20. José María Andrade also went into exile from 1867 to 1870, as he had from 1860 to 1862, and Juan B. Alamán

was placed under house arrest in July 1867 after a brief imprisonment. Case, "Resurgimiento de los conservadores," 230; Castro, "José María Andrade," 390; and Rivera, "Apéndice."

57. Sociedad, *Reseña*, 30; and De Dios, *Historia de la familia vicentina*, 1:538. On the good order in the asylum under Vincentian administration and its decline afterward, see Ballenger, "Modernizing Madness," chap. 3.

58. It is unclear whether the entire Guadalajara branch or only one Jalisco chapter changed its name. Sociedad, *Reseña*, 30; Sociedad Guadalajara, *Boletín* (October 1907), 183; and Sociedad, *Noticia* (1869), 12, 14.

59. Sociedad, *Reseña*, 53.

60. Sociedad, *Noticia* (1869), 11.

61. Sociedad, *Noticia* (1870, 15; 1869, 8, 10).

62. See Sociedad, *Noticia* (1869, 11–13; 1870, 9, 14, 18); and Sociedad, *Memoria* (1871), 8.

63. Sociedad, *Memoria* (1871), 12.

64. De Dios, *Historia de la familia vicentina*, 1:553; and Mecham, *Church and State*, 375.

65. Sociedad, *Reseña*, 34.

66. The first conference in Yucatán was established in Mérida in 1868. By the end of 1875 there were six conferences in Mérida, plus one in Izamal and one in Temax. Sociedad, *Reseña*, 53–54.

67. The chapter was founded in January 1874 and aggregated in 1878. ASSVP, Boletines de Agregación, 1878, CC113, Mexique.

68. These were the Hacienda de San Cristóbal and the Hacienda de los Ramírez, both in the state of Guanajuato. It is difficult to draw definitive conclusions because the available evidence is so fragmentary, but I only located one more conference on a hacienda, the Hacienda de San Gabriel in Morelos in 1884. Sociedad, *Reseña*, 54–55.

69. De Dios, *Historia de la familia vicentina*, 1:538–39.

70. Castro, "José María Andrade," 390. Of the 396 sisters, 46 chose to stay in Mexico to remain close to their families. De Dios, *Historia de la familia vicentina*, 1:504–7. On riots, see Meyer, *Cristero Rebellion*, 6.

71. See Cuevas, *Historia de la iglesia*, 5:chap. 6; Schmitt, "Conciliation Policy" and "Catholic Adjustment"; Meyer, *Cristero Rebellion*, 6–10; Ceballos Ramírez, *El catolicismo social*; Hanson, "Day of Ideals," 52–81; O'Dogherty Madrazo, *De urnas y sotanas*; Curley, "Slouching Towards Bethlehem"; Overmyer-Velázquez, "New Political Religious Order"; Wright-Rios, *Revolutions in Mexican Catholicism*; and Chowning, "La feminización de la piedad" and "Catholic Church and the Ladies."

72. See Galindo y Villa, *Reseña histórico-descriptiva*, 92–97; González Navarro, "Ejercicio caritativo" and *La pobreza en México*, 135–146; Blum, "Conspicuous Benevolence"; Ayala Flores, "Caridad y beneficencia"; Espejo López, "La

beneficencia privada"; Guadarrama Sánchez, "Filantropía y cohesión social"; and Lorenzo Río, "¿De quién son los pobres?"

73. "Circular," 8 June 1877, ASSVP, Conseil Superior du Mexique, 1845–1920, CC113, Mexique.

74. See, for example, De Dios, *Historia de la familia vicentina*, 2:629, 634–45; Sociedad, *Reseña*, 8, 21, 44, 47; Sociedad, *Boletín* (April 1896, esp. 100, 105, 109; March 1898, 71); and Montes de Oca y Obregón, "Breve elogio."

75. Volume and issue numbers indicate that the *tercera época* was published regularly since 1876, though I only located issues from 1882 onward. The July 1882 issue is vol. 7, no. 79. By 1902 the Sociedad's *Boletín* was in its *cuarta época*. Although issue numbers began at 1, the volume number of 27 again suggests that the monthly publication had appeared regularly since 1876.

76. De Dios, *Historia de la familia vicentina*, 1:539. In 1888 the Superior Council recommended that all conferences adopt the obra del aguinaldo, which was apparently pioneered by the Mérida council in 1884. The 1895 history notes that the cajas de ahorros—also known as *cajas de auxilio*—were a "recent" initiative. See Sociedad, *Reseña*, 11, 13, 33, 46. On the cajas de ahorros that García Icazbalceta established for the employees on his own estates, see García Pimentel, *Don Joaquín García Icazbalceta*, 15. On how they were supposed to work, see Sociedad, *Guía*, 38–39.

77. De Dios, *Historia de la familia vicentina*, 1:539. On how the patronatos were supposed to work, see the French regulations reprinted in Sociedad, *Boletín* (September 1899, 259–75; November 1899, 328–40).

78. García Icazbalceta, "Circular del Consejo Superior de México," 70, 74.

79. For example, in 1877 Mexico City's Conferencia de Nuestra Señora de los Angeles y San Felipe de Jesús listed Presbítero Don Vicente Reyes as its president. "Lista de las conferencias que existen en esta capital," 1877, ASSVP, CC113, Mexique. A biography of Father Silviano Carrillo credits him with founding several conferences in the Archdiocese of Guadalajara in the 1880s. Camacho, *Historia del Sr. Obispo D. Silviano Carrillo*, 74–77.

80. Carrillo y Ancona, *Orden circular*, 11.

81. *Quinto Concilio*, 110.

82. Twenty-two conferences were in Tabasco's capital and twenty in the countryside. De Dios, *Historia de la familia vicentina*, 2:630.

83. The Particular Council in Colima partly reflects a readjustment to the splitting off of that state from the Archdiocese of Guadalajara in 1881. Colima was also an area of growth, with thirteen conferences by 1908 compared with only three in 1895. Sociedad, *Boletín* (April 1909), 96.

84. Ibid. (November 1900), 317–18.

85. According to Guadalajara's Central Council, there had already been a notable drop in the number of volunteers in the archdiocese by 1901. Sociedad Guadalajara, *Boletín* (September 1902), 85.

86. De Dios, *Historia de la familia vicentina*, 1:515–16; and Chowning, "La feminización de la piedad," 498–508, and "Catholic Church and the Ladies."

87. Cuevas, *Historia de la iglesia*, 5:383–84; Adame Goddard, *El pensamiento político y social*, 19–27; and Sociedad Católica, *Estadística*.

88. "Exhortación Pastoral que los Ilmos. Sres. Arzobispos de México, Michoacán y Guadalajara dirigen a su Venerable Clero y a sus fieles con ocasión de la Ley Orgánica expedida por el Sob. Congreso Nacional en 10 de Diciembre del año próximo pasado y sancionada por el Supremo Gobierno en 14 del mismo mes," in Alcalá and Olimón, *Episcopado y gobierno en México*, 293–338.

89. The exclusion of the needy poor as members was apparently controversial but repeatedly reaffirmed by the French society. Sociedad, *Reglamento* (1898), 21.

90. Camacho, *Historia del Sr. Obispo D. Silviano Carrillo*, 75.

91. Sociedad, *Reseña*, 10, 12, 18. See also Sociedad, *Noticia* (1868), 8.

92. On the "bourgeois benevolence" that characterized Jalisco, see Oliver Sánchez, *Salud, desarrollo urbano y modernización*, 120–21, 135–37, 329.

93. On this point, see also Gilbert, "'Long Live the True Religion!,'" 9–14.

94. Ceballos Ramírez, *El catolicismo social*, esp. 16. See also O'Dogherty Madrazo, *De urnas y sotanas*, 19, 98, 112–13; and Meyer, *Cristero Rebellion*, 70, 75, 85.

95. Smith makes a similar point in his study of the Mixteca Baja, *Roots of Conservatism*, esp. 168, 298. On the Catholic revival in Oaxaca, see Overmyer-Velázquez, *Visions of the Emerald City*, chap. 3; and Wright-Rios, *Revolutions in Mexican Catholicism*.

96. Lorenzo Río, *El Estado como benefactor*, esp. 55–64.

97. On the recipients of public charity in 1879, see Peza, *La beneficencia*, 199. On the city's population, see Davies, "Tendencias demográficas urbanas," 501–5.

98. Rodríguez Kuri, *La experiencia olvidada*, 138–39.

99. Ibid., 144–45.

100. See Schmitt, "Catholic Adjustment," 193–96. In 1907 the provinces were still underserved. Although 57 percent of school-age children attended primary schools in Mexico City, the percentage was much lower in the provinces, for example, ranging from 37 percent in Jalisco to 27 percent in Puebla, and only 14 and 13 percent in Michoacán and Chiapas. Vaughan, *State, Education, and Social Class*, esp. 158.

101. Bastian, *Los disidentes* and "Protestants, Freemasons, and Spiritists"; Dorantes, "Protestantes de ayer y hoy"; Schraeder, "Spirits of the Times"; and Rugeley, *Of Wonders and Wise Men*, 194–201.

102. Quoted in Díaz Robles, "Señores y señoras," 71. See also Arquidiócesis de Guadalajara, *Memoria* (1911), 24; and Cárdenas Ayala, *El derrumbe*, 106–8, 115.

103. Sociedad Guadalajara, *Boletín* (September 1902), 85.

104. Sociedad Guadalajara, *Boletín* (March 1902), 26.

105. Sociedad Guadalajara, *Boletín* (September 1902).

106. Sociedad, *Boletín* (April 1896), 103.

107. See, e.g., Sociedad, *Boletín* (August 1902), 182; and Sociedad Guadalajara, *Boletín* (March 1902), 19.

Chapter 3

1. Because the earliest *Memoria* I had found at that point was from 1866, I assumed the association was founded in 1865. Arrom, *Containing the Poor*, 243–45.

2. Other contenders were also Catholic, namely the huge Sociedad Católica de Señoras y Señoritas and the Vela Perpetua devotional association. See chap. 2nn86–87.

3. On the Catholic restoration, see Cuevas, *Historia de la iglesia*, 5:409; Meyer, *Cristero Rebellion*, 6–10, 194–95; Ceballos Ramírez, *El catolicismo social*; Hanson, "Day of Ideals," 50–80; O'Dogherty Madrazo, *De urnas y sotanas*, 21–50; and Curley, "Slouching Towards Bethlehem," chaps. 2–4. Recent works noting the feminization of certain religious institutions and practices in the late nineteenth century include Rugeley, *Of Wonders and Wise Men*, 82–83; Chowning, "La feminización de la piedad" and "Catholic Church and the Ladies"; Wright-Rios, *Revolutions in Mexican Catholicism*, 111, 261–89; Voekel, "Liberal Religion"; and Smith, *Roots of Conservatism*, 107, 186–87.

4. On the original foundation in 1617, see Diefendorf, *From Penitence to Charity*. On its nineteenth-century refounding, see Curtis, "Charitable Ladies"; and Udovic, "'What About the Poor?,'" 82–91.

5. By 1892 the Superior Council of the Mexican Ladies of Charity had been renamed the Consejo General, or General Council. See Asociación de Señoras de la Caridad (hereafter Asociación), *Memoria* (1892), and subsequent *Memoria*s.

6. Foucault, *La Société de Saint-Vincent de Paul*, esp. 218; Société de Saint-Vincent-de-Paul, *Livre du centenaire*; Sociedad, *Reglamento* (1851), 6n2; and Asociación, *Reglamento* (1863), 16, 21–22. On the collaboration between the men and women, see also Sociedad, *Reglamento* (1898), 121.

7. On the early history see De Dios, *Historia de la familia vicentina*, 1:146, 541–42; and Asociación, *Memoria* (1902), 4. The first conference of the Ladies of Charity in Puebla was founded and directed by Paulist Father Juan Figuerola and, after his death in 1850, by Father José Recolons. The first Mexican publication of the association's bylaws was also in Puebla: Asociación, *Reglamento* (1848).

8. Note that the expanded published version of the 1901 history incorrectly listed the foundation date as 1862 because of a misreading of the draft manuscript. Compare Asociación, *Memoria* (1902), 5, with "Asociación de las Señoras de la Caridad, dirigida por los P. P. Paulinos, México," in AHAM, 110–35, c. 1901,

fol. 3. The canonical approval came on 8 April 1864; the date of the civil approval is unclear. De Dios, *Historia de la familia vicentina*, 1:541–43.

9. Asociación, *Memoria* (1902), 5–6.

10. Perhaps because they included the new Superior Council, both the manuscript and published version of the history claim there were twenty-two association chapters. See "Asociación de las Señoras de la Caridad, dirijida por los P. P. Paulinos, México," AHAM, 110–35, c. 1901, fol. 6; and Asociación, *Memoria* (1902), 10.

11. Asociación, *Memoria* (1902), 10.

12. Asociación, *Memoria* (1865, 4–6, and fold-out chart; 1866, 7); and De Dios, *Historia de la familia vicentina*, 1:544–49, 561. The 1896 *Rapport* explains that the girls' groups, the Enfants de Marie, were "puissantes auxiliaires des Dames et . . . les premieres dignitaires de l'Oeuvre." On the age requirement, see Asociación, *Reglamento* (1863), 7.

13. The conference in San José Tecualoya was only listed in the 1866 *Memoria* (38). The association's *Memorias* list another on the Hacienda de Treinta in Morelos in both 1865 (19) and 1878 (40). In 1878 there was also a chapter on the Hacienda de Pedernales in Michoacán (16).

14. Asociación, *Memoria* (1902, 8–9, and 1865).

15. See Arrom, *Containing the Poor*, 240–46.

16. The Sisters of Charity were also part of the Parisian municipal system, staffing Casas de Socorro, which provided medical care and medicines. Consejo General de Beneficencia, *Administración General, Estracto de los reglamentos, Obras de Caridad.*

17. Asociación, *Memoria* (1902, 9; 1865, 6; 1866, 9, and fold-out chart). Lottery funding continued as late as 29 February 1868, when the Liberal government suppressed all the lotteries. See Decree of 29 February 1868 in Dublán and Lozano, *Legislación mexicana*, 10:279, #6280; and Valero Chávez, *De la caridad*, 109–10.

18. Wright de Kleinhans, *Mujeres notables mexicanas*, 353.

19. The 1901 history names Antonio Vértiz as first secretary and Hilarión Romero y Gil as vice secretary. Romero, a well-known Catholic lawyer, was apparently based in Jalisco, where he indeed helped the Guadalajara Ladies of Charity Central Council. See Asociación, *Memoria* (1902), 8; Arquidiócesis de Guadalajara, "Caridad cristiana," 84; and *Diccionario Porrúa*, 1232.

20. Asociación, *Memoria* (1902, 8–10; 1866, 4); De Dios, *Historia de la familia vicentina*, 1:545; and Asociación, *Reglamento* (1863), 30. Male procuradores were occasionally still listed by name as late as 1911. See Arquidiócesis de Guadalajara, *Memoria* (1911), 27–34.

21. *Diccionario Porrúa*, 1212; and Asociación, *Memoria* (1902), 9.

22. De Dios (*Historia de la familia vicentina*, 1:550–51) states that in 1868 there were 12,274 members (counting active and honorary together), but this figure seems

suspiciously high. His figure of 20,212 for 1872 is also suspicious and is contradicted by Asociación, *Memoria* (1902), 10–11.

23. This point needs more research, especially for the Mexican provinces. In the
town of Atoyac (Jalisco), the city council provided land for the local conference
to build a hospital: Arquidiócesis de Guadalajara, *Memoria* (1911), 19. Díaz
Robles found examples of the Guadalajara municipal government giving certain conference foundations tax exemptions and letting them build on municipal land. Díaz Robles, "Medicina, religión y pobreza," 162.

24. Asociación, *Memoria* (1902), 10–11.

25. Muñoz, "Santa María de Jesús Sacramentado." The Superior of the Sisters of
Charity in Guadalajara apparently directed one of the conferences in the
working-class Analco barrio. Díaz Robles, "Medicina, religión y pobreza,"
100.

26. De Dios, *Historia de la familia vicentina*, 1:556, 639; and Asociación, *Memoria*
(1902), 12, 18–19.

27. Assuming that some of the nonreporting chapters still functioned, the number
of active conferences would have been higher than the hundred reported that
year. Asociación, *Memoria* (1878), 27, 37, 44, 48, 53.

28. De Dios, *Historia de la familia vicentina*, 1:556.

29. See Asociación, *Memoria* (1902), 12, 18–20; De Dios, *Historia de la familia
vicentina*, 1:11, 556, 631, 639; and ibid., 2:642, 645, 670.

30. Dames de la Charité, *Rapport* (1896), 83.

31. Reflecting an overly ambitious attempt to expand the conferences under Mariscal's
leadership, there were 35 Central Councils in 1888 and 38 in 1892. By 1895 only 23
Central Councils reported to the General Council in Mexico City. See Asociación,
Memoria (1902, 21; 1892, "Estado General," n.p; 1895, "Estado General," n.p.).

32. Asociación, *Reglamento* (1863).

33. Quoted in De Dios, *Historia de la familia vicentina*, 1:542–53.

34. Asociación, *Reglamento* (1864), 12.

35. Asociación, *Memoria* (1865), esp. 4.

36. De Dios, *Historia de la familia vicentina*, 1:546.

37. Asociación, *Reglamento* (1864), 5.

38. The Guadalajara Central Council included the phrase "para el socorro de los
pobres enfermos" in its 1887–1893 *Memoria*s as well, but substituted the general
description "obras de caridad" in later reports.

39. Asociación, *Memoria* (1865; 1866, 60); and De Dios, *Historia de la familia vicentina*, 1:545–46.

40. By June 1865 Mexico City's Central Council had taken the asylum under its
protection. Asociación, *Memoria* (1865, 7; 1866, 8, 10).

41. See Espejo López, "La beneficencia privada," 173.

42. Asociación, *Memoria* (1865, 1866); and De Dios, *Historia de la familia vicentina*,
1:547.

43. Asociación, *Memoria* (1902), 21.
44. Asociación, *Memoria* (1909), v–x, "Estado General," n.p.; and De Dios, *Historia de la familia vicentina*, 2:644–46.
45. Asociación, *Memoria* (1908, notation on "Estado" no. 4, n.p.; 1902, 55).
46. Asociación, *Reglamento* (1911), 47.
47. Asociación, *Memoria* (1865), 7.
48. Ibid. (1902), 17.
49. On the kind of religious observances they promoted, see esp. Gilbert, "'Long Live the True Religion!,'" 92; and Moreno Chávez, *Devociones políticas*, chap. 3.
50. See De Dios, *Historia de la familia vicentina*, 1:516. On the promotion of other pious organizations see Chowning, "La feminización de la piedad."
51. Asociación, *Memoria* (1865), 8.
52. Adame, *El pensamiento político y social*, 88. Even so, the 450 Mexican members of Sisters of Charity in 1875 (or perhaps 410, since Cuevas provides contradictory numbers) were far fewer than the thousands of laywomen who supposedly replaced them. Cuevas, *Historia de la iglesia*, 5:392, 409.
53. Quoted in Alcalá and Olimón, *Episcopado y gobierno en México*, 325, 328. See also the discussion in Adame, *El pensamiento político y social*, 90–91.
54. Dames de la Charité, *Rapport* (1894), 45. There is no good study of the conferences in France, only in Paris: Curtis, "Charitable Ladies."
55. Asociación, *Memoria* (1865), 11. The Tacubaya chapter was, however, described as practically directed by the president's husband, Joaquín M. de Ansorena, 13.
56. Asociación, *Memoria* (1866), 8.
57. Quoted in De Dios, *Historia de la familia vicentina*, 1:550–51.
58. Quoted in ibid., 1:551.
59. Arquidiócesis de Guadalajara, "Caridad," 26, 29, 42, 59, 97.
60. Chowning makes a similar argument about the role of women in founding the Vela Perpetua pious association in 1840. She wisely notes that it is impossible to determine who led whom, and that the point is that women were collaborators and not just followers of the parish priests. Chowning, "La feminización de la piedad," 498.
61. Asociación, *Reglamento* (1863), 4.
62. In contrast to Wright de Kleinhans, the association's *Memoria* (1895) listed her death as occurring in 1894. Asociación, *Memoria* (1895), notation on "Estado" no. 2, n.p.
63. Her husband was Manuel Loizaga y Corcuera; her donations "de su propio peculio" included the building for Analco's large hospital as well as its chapel in honor of the Virgen de Guadalupe. Wright de Kleinhans, *Mujeres notables mexicanas*, 352–56. Luna "cared for" the Guadalajara conferences after her death with a sizable bequest that still funded individual chapters in the Archdiocese of Guadalajara in 1924. See Asociación, *Memoria* (1902), 29; and

Arquidiócesis de Guadalajara, *Memoria* (1912, 2; 1924, 10). A charity association for the protection of orphans named after her, the Asociación Nicolasa Luna de Corcuera, functioned in the first decade of the twentieth century. Cárdenas Ayala, *El derrumbe*, 103–4; and Díaz Robles, "Medicina, religión y pobreza," 56. It is unclear whether or not it was related to the Ladies of Charity.

64. Asociación, *Memoria* (1865), 6–9, 15.

65. I thank Erika Pani for reviewing the membership lists with me and corroborating my own impressions.

66. Asociación, *Memoria* (1865), 4, 10.

67. The Campeche conferences were under the jurisdiction of the Central Council in Mérida, Yucatán. Asociación, *Memoria* (1900), 12, and "Estado" no. 1, n.p.

68. See Arrom, *Women of Mexico City*, 7–8.

69. See discussion in ibid., esp. chap. 1.

70. Adame, *El pensamiento político y social*, 105. This phenomenon requires further research.

71. See Arrom, *Women of Mexico City*, 47–49; and Rugeley, *Of Wonders and Wise Men*, 85.

72. Langlois, *Le catholicisme au féminin*. On Ireland see Magray, *Transforming Power of the Nuns*.

73. See Rugeley, *Of Wonders and Wise Men*, 82–84; Wright-Rios, *Revolutions in Mexican Catholicism*; and Chowning, "La feminización de la piedad" and "Catholic Church and the Ladies."

74. The Sociedad Católica de Señoras is in need of systematic study. Cuevas suggests that the organization declined after a few years (*Historia de la iglesia* 5:383–84). See also Adame, *El pensamiento político y social*, 19–27, 118; and Ceballos Ramírez, *El catolicismo social*, 100, 106. Yet a report I located for the Monterrey branch reported significant activity in 1896, and Edward Wright-Rios found it to be thriving in Oaxaca in 1899. Sociedad Católica de Señoras, *Informe*; and Wright-Rios, *Revolutions in Mexican Catholicism*, 105. On the persistence of the men's group and its collaboration with the Vincentian conferences, see Sociedad, *Boletín* (August 1895, 238–39; April 1896, 108).

75. There had already been a Ladies' Board in the Mexico City Poor House in 1828 and in the Hospital del Divino Salvador in 1842. The Poor House had a female board and female director from 1865 to at least 1871. See Arrom, *Containing the Poor*, 180, 228, 244–47, 260–61, 267–68, 296–97; *Manifiesto*; Galí Boadella, *Historias del bello sexo*, 170–74.

76. This term is from Magray, *Transforming Power of the Nuns*, viii.

77. For an analysis of a similar strategy in England, see Morgan, "'A sort of land debatable,'" 183–209.

78. Alcalá and Olimón, *Episcopado y gobierno en México*, 328.

79. Asociación, *Reglamento* (1863), 4.

80. Asociación, *Memoria* (1908), viii. For other examples of the rhetoric that portrayed charity as an extension of maternal roles, see Blum, "Conspicuous Benevolence," 56–57.

81. Asociación, *Reglamento* (1864), 8.

82. Asociación, *Memoria* (1865), 7.

83. Asociación, *Reglamento* (1864), 21.

84. The minutes describing the event notes that special guests included the Señoras Nicolasa Luna de Corcuera, Guadalupe Villaseñor de Pérez Verdia, Ignacia de la Peña de Moreno, and Srta. Guadalupe Palomar, along with the officers of the men's Particular Council as well as "the faithful of both sexes." Sociedad Guadalajara, *Boletín* (September 1902), 100.

85. Asociación, *Memoria* (1865, 6, 20; 1902, 5, 17); and Forment, *Democracy in Latin America*, 260.

86. See Arrom, *Women of Mexico City*, 34–35; Wright de Kleinhans, *Mujeres notables mexicanas*, 346–47; Couturier, "For the Greater Service of God," 133–34; Conway, "Sisters at War," 7–8; Zendejas, *La mujer en la intervención*, 59–60; and Calderón de la Barca, *Life in Mexico*, 285, 519–20, 531–33.

87. Asociación, *Reglamento* (1863), 4–5.

88. *Reseña de las Hermandades*, 7.

89. Asociación, *Reglamento* (1864), 4.

90. Asociación, *Memoria* (1902), 15, 43.

91. Asociación, *Reglamento* (1863), 7.

92. A few conferences had *roperas*, *celadoras*, and *calificadoras* as well. See Arquidiócesis de Guadalajara, *Memoria* (1896), 18–31.

93. The 1863 bylaws specify that volunteers were admitted after "*seis meses de ensayo*," while a 1909 report specifies a trial period of three months. Asociación, *Reglamento* (1863), 7; and Asociación, *Memoria* (1909), v.

94. Note that the publisher mistakenly printed 1865 on her report. Cf. Asociación, *Memoria* (1865, 5, 31; 1866, 4).

95. Arquidiócesis de Guadalajara, *Memoria* (1900), 17. Twentieth-century *Memorias* still listed Vincentian priests as director general of the association and as secretary of the Superior Council; individual conferences still listed the parish priest as their director, and occasionally listed a male *procurador* as well. It is possible, as Curtis posits for France, that the priest served more as a "spiritual director" than a supervisor ("Charitable Ladies," 135). By 1922 the Asociación's *Instrucciones* clarified that the *presidenta* of each conference could lead the prayers and read the religious text when the director was not present (4).

96. Chowning documents a similar trend of women taking increasingly prominent roles in managing Mexican pious associations and gradually requiring less male supervision as the nineteenth century progressed ("Catholic Church and the Ladies "). On the development of women's "social capital" in other religious and voluntary associations, see, for example, Scott, "Women's Voluntary

Associations"; Schell, "Honorable Avocation"; Levitt, *Transnational Villagers*, 161–62; Curtis, "Charitable Ladies"; Wright-Rios, *Revolutions in Mexican Catholicism*, 27, 34, 135–37; and Mettele, "City as a Field."

97. Asociación, *Memoria* (1902), 43.

98. See Arquidiócesis de Guadalajara, *Memoria* (1892), 8; Asociación, *Memoria* (1896), 5; and the eulogy that appeared in Arquidiócesis de Guadalajara, *Memoria* (1895), 5.

99. Valentín was the *proveedora* (purveyor) of the conference in Mexico City's Santa Catarina parish. Asociación, *Memoria* (1865), 15.

100. On the appeal of lay associations, see also Wright-Rios, *Revolutions in Mexican Catholicism*, 135–36; and Chowning, "Catholic Church and the Ladies," esp. 198.

101. Mead ("Gender, Welfare, and the Catholic Church") and Eraso ("Maternalismo, religión y asistencia") found similar trends in their study of the Argentine Ladies of Charity. So did scholars studying later Mexican Catholic voluntary organizations. See, for example, Schell, "Honorable Avocation"; Wright-Rios, *Revolutions in Mexican Catholicism*, 27, 34, 135–37; and Verba, *Catholic Feminism*. For a review of the extensive literature on how charity impacted women outside of Latin America, see McCarthy, "Parallel Power Structures."

102. In some cases the volunteers may have had to overcome initial male opposition. The biography of Father Pro, which credits his mother for fomenting his deep faith, claims that her husband at first opposed her work with the poor, including the foundation of a small hospital in Zacatecas in 1904. Ramírez Torres, *Miguel Agustín Pro*, 32–33.

103. For a discussion of this ideological shift in nineteenth-century Mexico, see Arrom, *Women of Mexico City*, 259–67.

104. Asociación, *Memoria* (1895), 11. The term "work of benevolence" is from Ginzberg, *Women and the Work of Benevolence*.

105. Asociación, *Memoria* (1902), 20.

106. On the contradictions in the church's messages to women, see Boylan, "Gendering the Faith," 201–2, 215–19; and Blasco, "Feminismo católico."

107. Landriot, *La mujer fuerte*; and "Acta del Consejo Central de Señoras de la Caridad, Culiacán," 6 August 1905, APCC, Sección Disciplinar, San Vicente de Paul, Caja 1, vol. 1, f. 0997. Landriot (1816–1874) wrote his book *La femme forte* in 1862, and a Mexican edition was apparently published the same year (referred to in Zavala, *Becoming Modern*, 60 and 287n157). As late as 1922 Guadalajara's archbishop recommended it as a text for reading in the Ladies of Charity conference sessions (Asociación, *Instrucciones*, 4.)

108. For a critique of these categories as they apply to the Mexican church, see Hanson, "Day of Ideals"; and Curley, "Slouching Towards Bethlehem," esp. 9, 21.

109. See esp. Pani, "'Ciudadana y muy ciudadana'"; and Chowning, "La feminización de la piedad," 495.

110. See esp. critique of Jürgen Habermas's 1989 work by Fraser, "Rethinking the Public Sphere."

111. Villanueva y Francesconi, *El libro de protestas*, index. Other examples of Mexican women's participation in the public sphere as conventionally defined include Arrom, *Women of Mexico City*, 32–46; Conway, "Sisters at War"; Pouwels, *Political Journalism*; and Alvarado, *Educación y superación*.

112. Baker, "Domestication of Politics," esp. 647. Amanda Vickery makes a similar critique of the notion of separate spheres ("Golden Age"), as does Mead ("Gender, Welfare, and the Catholic Church") for the Argentine Ladies of Charity.

113. The term "female dominion" is used by Robyn Muncy (*Creating a Female Dominion*) to refer to the institutions created by women reformers in the United States during the Progressive era, not to the earlier charity organizations comparable to the Ladies of Charity. Many scholars of the earlier organizations emphasize charitable women's focus on women and children. See, for example, McCarthy, "Parallel Power Structures," esp. 4; and Koven and Michel, *Mothers of a New World*, esp. their introduction, 2–5. On Latin America, see Verba, *Catholic Feminism*; and Guy, *Women Build the Welfare State*. Even Paula Baker posits that women's voluntary work, although political, was "directed at domestic concerns" ("Domestication of Politics," 647).

114. See esp. Koven and Michel, *Mothers of a New World*; and Mead, "Beneficent Maternalism."

115. On how women could use these stereotypes to bolster their power, see Wright-Rios, "Visions of Women," 181–2, 195–6; and Fraser, "Rethinking the Public Sphere," 115.

116. On this point, see Eraso, "Maternalismo, religión y asistencia."

Chapter 4

1. See Chowning, "Liberals, Women, and the Church" and "La feminización de la piedad"; Galí Boadella, *Historias del bello sexo*, 166–74; Beezley, "Porfirian Smart Set," 185–86; Rugeley, *Of Wonders and Wise Men*, 82–84; Blum, "Conspicuous Benevolence," 20–23; Porter, *Working Women*, 62–63; Peluffo, "Caridad y género"; and Guy, *Women Build the Welfare State*.

2. For recent overviews and critiques of the feminization theory, see Harrison, "Putting Faith"; Pasture, Art, and Buerman, *Beyond the Feminization Thesis*; Chowning, "Catholic Church and the Ladies"; and Butler, "Eucharistic Angels."

3. The number of female conferences, which looks suspiciously rounded, comes from the Dames de la Charité's *Rapport* (1896), 45. The number of members it reported for 1895 nonetheless matches the Asociación's *Memoria* (1895). The membership figures for the men are from 1894, while the number of conferences is from September 1895. Sociedad, *Reseña*, 47, 57.

4. Although the records do not list a Central Council in Tlaxcala after 1878, the Huamantla chapter still existed but was listed under the jurisdiction of Puebla's Central Council.

5. In addition, in 1908 the society only supported 43 orphans nationwide in its asylums. Sociedad Guadalajara, *Boletín* (July 1909), 152.

6. *Polémica*, 3–5, 7, 18, 20.

7. The first quote is from Voekel, "Liberal Religion," 87–90, the second from Wright-Rios, *Revolutions in Mexican Catholicism*, 136. See also Chowning, "Liberals, Women, and the Church," 3–4, 7, and "Catholic Church and the Ladies," 197–98; and Moreno Chávez, *Devociones políticas*, chap. 4.

8. Luis González's case study suggests that Catholicism was a central part of life for all residents of the region, and not just those of indigenous or mestizo descent. González, *San José de Gracia*.

9. See Adame, *El pensamiento político y social*; Ceballos Ramírez, *El catolicismo social* and "Las organizaciones"; De Dios, *Historia de la familia vicentina*, 2: 627–28; Hanson, "Day of Ideals," 83–130; Curley, "Slouching Towards Bethlehem"; Pani, "Democracia y representación política"; O'Dogherty Madrazo, *De urnas y sotanas*; Overmyer-Velázquez, *Visions of the Emerald City*, chap. 3; Wright-Rios, *Revolutions in Mexican Catholicism*; Smith, *Roots of Conservatism*; Moreno Chávez, *Devociones políticas*; and Butler, "Eucharistic Angels."

10. See, for example, Cuevas, *Historia de la iglesia*, 5: 415, and Overmyer-Velázquez, *Visions of the Emerald City*, 76–78.

11. In addition to the Cristero Rebellion of 1926–1929, there were several others including the "first Cristiada" in 1856, the revolt of the *religioneros* in 1874–1875, and the "last Cristiada" in the Mixteca Baja in 1962. See Meyer, *Cristero Rebellion*, 6–8; González, *San José de Gracia*, 52; and Smith, *Roots of Conservatism*, 95, 246–47.

12. Curley, "Slouching Towards Bethlehem," 2, 22–23, 83–84.

13. Asociación, *Reglamento* (1863), 11–13; Sociedad, *Reseña*, 26; De Dios, *Historia de la familia vicentina*, 1:521; and Sociedad, *Sumario*.

14. "Exhortación Pastoral," 19 March 1875, in Alcalá and Olimón, *Episcopado y gobierno en México*, 293–338; Pastoral Letters of 8 December 1907 and 5 June 1910, cited in González Navarro, *La pobreza en México*, 62–63, 75.

15. I found no evidence that, as Ralph Gibson suggested for France (*Social History*, 56–58), the Mexican Church favored clerically directed lay groups like the Ladies of Charity over more autonomous ones like the male society. On the contrary, see Camacho, *Historia del Sr. Obispo D. Silviano Carrillo*, 74–76; De Dios, *Historia de la familia vicentina*, 2:629–30; Ceballos Ramírez, *El catolicismo social* (1991), 121, 194; Munguía, *Panegírico de San Vicente de Paul*; and ecclesiastical directives in Asociación, *Memoria* (1900), 11; Carrillo y Ancona, *Orden Circular*, 9–17; Arquidiócesis de Guadalajara, *Memoria* (1896), 3; *Quinto*

Concilio, 110; and Sociedad Guadalajara, *Boletín* (August 1898, 20; September 1902, 76; March 1902, 18–20).

16. On the numerous nineteenth-century associations, see Forment, *Democracy in Latin America*. Nearly all of these civic associations—aside from the mutual associations of female workers—excluded women. There were some exceptions, however. For example, journalist Laureana Wright de Kleinhans was inducted as a member of three literary societies. *Diccionario Porrúa*, 1579. There was also one female Masonic Lodge in Jalisco. It was a very late development, however, and the only one I know of in Mexico. See Velasco López, "La mujer y masonería." I thank María Teresa Fernández Aceves for this reference.

17. Asociación, *Reglamento* (1863), 4.

18. See, for example, Alberro's study of the order of San Juan de Dios, *Apuntes para la historia*.

19. See ASSVP, Boletines de Agregación, CC114, Mexique.

20. Letter of 17 November 1887 to the General Council in Paris, Conseil Superior du Mexique, 1845–1920, ASSVP, C113, Mexique.

21. Sociedad Guadalajara, *Boletín* (May 1909), 13. On the Chilean volunteers' practice of handing out vales without visiting their clients, see Ponce de León Atria, *Gobernar la pobreza*, 248.

22. Asociación, *Memoria* (1878), 17. See also Arquidiócesis de Guadalajara, "Caridad," 66, 74–75, 77.

23. Asociación, *Memoria* (1902), 12, 14. On the Ladies of Charity's critical role in providing nursing services, see Díaz Robles, "Medicina, religión y pobreza," chap. 3 and 132–35.

24. Sociedad Guadalajara, *Boletín* (September 1902, 82; July 1912, 52).

25. Conferencia de la Villa de Coyoacán, AHAM, Libro de Actas (1912–1913), entry for July 1913, f. 86.

26. Sociedad, *Boletín* (November 1900), 318.

27. For example, Asociación, *Memoria* (1865, 15; 1909, viii); and Arquidiócesis de Guadalajara, *Memoria* (1909), 22–23.

28. For example, Sociedad, *Boletín* (May 1900), 143; and Sociedad, *Reseña*, 40–41.

29. Sociedad, *Boletín* (August 1895), 235.

30. Pedro, Arzobispo de Guadalajara, "Circular" of 7 September 1889, in Arquidiócesis de Guadalajara, *Memoria* (1892; 1902, 28).

31. Both organizations occasionally received donations from the church, as in 1898, when Father Moral contributed 2,000 pesos to the Ladies of Charity. Asociación, *Memoria* (1898), 11.

32. For a list of late nineteenth-century obras, see Sociedad, *Reseña*, 32–34, 45; Sociedad, *Boletín* (November 1900), 318; and Sociedad Guadalajara, *Boletín* (December 1911), 205.

33. The men's and women's conferences have not both been systematically studied in each country, however. The Colombian and Chilean research emphasizes the

men's while the Argentine emphasizes the women's. The Ladies of Charity was not established in Colombia until the 1920s. See Botero Herrera, "Los talleres"; Castro Carvajal, Caridad y beneficencia and "Las visitas domiciliarias," esp. 260; Serrano, ¿Qué hacer con Dios?; Ponce de León, Gobernar la pobreza; Mead, "Gender, Welfare, and the Catholic Church"; Bonaudo, "Cuando las tuteladas"; Dalla Corte and Piacenza, "Cartas marcadas"; Eraso, "Maternalismo, religión y asistencia"; and Guy, Women Build the Welfare State, 51–54.

34. Asociación, Memoria (1865, 4; 1866, "Estado General," n.p.).

35. Díaz Robles, "Medicina, religión y pobreza," 42–43, 123–24, 152. On Mariano Azuela (1873–1952), who continued providing free medical services to the poor after he left Jalisco, see Diccionario Porrúa, 147.

36. Asociación, Memoria (1902), esp. 8–10.

37. Asociación, Memoria (1908), 52.

38. Quoted in Wright de Kleinhans, Mujeres notables mexicanas, 352.

39. Castro, "José María Andrade," 392–93.

40. Montes de Oca, "Breve elogio"; Vigil, "Discurso," 36–38; Martínez, Don Joaquín García Icazbalceta, chap. 1; and Alessio Robles, La filantropía en México, 54–55.

41. It is possible that this view was more reflective of the 1930s and 1940s than of the earlier period. On this point Martínez (Don Joaquín García Icazbalceta, 12) follows Henry Wagner's 1935 study.

42. Macías-González," Mexican Aristocracy," chaps. 2–3. See also Urbina Martínez, "Prácticas cotidianas,"137; and Lorenzo Río, El Estado como benefactor, 63–64.

43. See esp. Alessio Robles, La filantropía en México, 43, 46–53; Gonzalez Navarro, La pobreza en México, 141; Blum, "Conspicuous Benevolence"; and Espejo López, "La beneficencia privada."

44. Founded in 1887, the institution cared for children ages three through nine while their mothers were at work. Galindo y Villa, Reseña histórico-descriptiva, 95.

45. The first lady was made honorary president in August 1895 (Asociación, Memoria, 1895, 13–14) and was listed in the Memorias I have located through 1905. She no longer appeared in the 1908 or 1909 reports.

46. On this point, see Arrom, Containing the Poor, 260, 267.

47. Alessio Robles, La filantropía en México; González Navarro, La pobreza en México, esp. 137–38; Alanís, "Algunas manifestaciones," 187; and Urbina Martínez, "Prácticas cotidianas," 131–40.

48. Galindo y Villa, Reseña histórico-descriptiva, 93; Alessio Robles, La filantropía en México, 38, 43–44; Ramírez Torres, Miguel Agustín Pro, 33; Blum, Domestic Economies, 23; and Urbina Martínez, Prácticas cotidianas, 123.

49. Alessio Robles, La filantropía en México, 44; and Peza, La beneficencia, 126.

50. On this point, see Arrom, Containing the Poor, 220–21; and Ayala Flores, "Caridad y beneficencia," 209–10.

51. Since the asylum was not connected with Díaz de León's conference, it was eligible for—and received—municipal funding. Indeed, by 1903 the city had taken it over. Lorenzo Río, "¿De quién son los pobres?," esp. 48–50. See also Sociedad, *Boletín* (August 1902), "Cuadro de las conferencias," n.p.; Peza, *La beneficencia*, 72–80, 125–28; Velasco Ceballos, *El niño mexicano*, 22; Galindo y Villa, *Reseña histórico-descriptiva*, 96–97; and Blum, "Conspicuous Benevolence," 15–16.

52. Urquiaga's school, entirely supported by his personal wealth, was already functioning by 1904 and still existed in 1944. García Pimentel, *Don Joaquín García Icazbalceta*, 83. On the school in 1904 and 1912, see Espejo López, "La beneficencia privada," 164, 166. Francisco Urquiaga was the vice president of Mexico City's conference of the Santo Niño de San Juan. Sociedad, *Boletín* (November 1900), "Cuadro de las conferencias," n.p.

53. See, for example, Ayala Flores, "Caridad y beneficencia," 215–18.

54. See, e.g., the Sociedad's *Boletín* (1859, 1902), *Notas* (1860), *Guía* (1860), and *Reglamento* (1860); the Asociación's *Reglamento* (1863); Consejo General de Beneficencia, *Administración*, *Estracto*, and *Obras*; and *Diccionario Porrúa*, 78, 470.

55. His publications include the popular *El Album en el Templo*, as well as biographies of Fray Gerónimo de Mendieta and Bishop Juan de Zumárraga. See García Pimentel, *Don Joaquín García Icazbalceta*, 16–17; and Martínez, *Don Joaquín García Icazbalceta*, 36 and chap. 3.

56. *Diccionario Porrúa*, 26; and De Dios, *Historia de la familia vicentina*, 2: 628. The *El Tiempo* publishing house also printed the 1909 editions of the society's *Boletín*.

57. *Diccionario Porrúa*, 1313. In their General Assembly of February 1896 the Superior Council Secretary reported that Trinidad Sánchez Santos was one of only four gentlemen to join the conferences that year. Sociedad, *Boletín* (April 1896), 100.

58. Lic. Rodríguez served as first president of Guadalajara's Conferencia de la Purísima Concepción and was instrumental in bringing the Sisters of Charity to Jalisco. In 1841 he established the Escuela de Artes y Oficios for impoverished boys, and in 1864 he served as president of Guadalajara's Junta de Caridad, which included several other conference members. *Diccionario Porrúa*, 1221; Sociedad Guadalajara, *Boletín* (October 1907), 182–83; Arquidiócesis de Guadalajara, "Caridad," 4; Oliver Sánchez, *Salud, desarrollo urbano y modernización*, 119–21; and Díaz Robles, "Medicina, religión y pobreza," 44–45, 92–93. His publications include Asociación, *Reglamento* (1864); *Pequeño examen*; and *Polémica*.

59. Cárdenas Ayala, *El derrumbe*, 104, 242–43.

60. Case, "Resurgimiento de los conservadores," 217–18.

61. See Islas García, *Trinidad Sánchez Santos*; Márquez, "Trinidad Sánchez Santos"; Ceballos Ramírez, *El catolicismo social*, esp. 188–98; Weiner, "Trinidad

Sánchez Santos"; and Overmyer-Velázquez, "New Political Religious Order," 148.

62. The *conferencias vicentinas* were represented by J. M. de Ovando. Trinidad Sánchez Santos was also in attendance, representing *El País*. Ceballos Ramírez, *El catolicismo social*, 183–216.

63. It is difficult to determine the extent of the overlap between the conferences and the PCN because complete membership lists are not available for either. Compare the list of the PCN Executive Committee in Curley ("Slouching Towards Bethlehem, 153) with the list of Mexico City conference presidents and vice presidents in 1902–1903: Sociedad, *Boletín* (December 1902; January 1903). See also O'Dogherty Madrazo, *De urnas y sotanas*, 108. Ceballos Ramírez suggests that Sánchez Santos was only temporarily affiliated with the party, *El catolicismo social*, 400n242.

Chapter 5

1. Ceballos Ramírez, *El catolicismo social*, esp. 16.

2. Guadalajara was designated as an archdiocese in 1863. For most of the second half of the nineteenth century the archdiocese was larger than the state of Jalisco and included the states of Colima, Aguascalientes, the territory of Tepic, and the southern part of Zacatecas. The smaller dioceses of Colima, Tepic, and Aguascalientes were carved out of Guadalajara's jurisdiction in 1881, 1891, and 1900. See O'Dogherty Madrazo, *De urnas y sotanas*, 27n12.

3. See esp. Hanson, "Day of Ideals," 63–81; O'Dogherty Madrazo, *De urnas y sotanas*, 27–31; Schmitt, "Catholic Adjustment," 193–96; and Plasencia, "Cien años de Acción Social," 25–53.

4. The Guadalajara branch of the Damas Católicas was founded in 1913, decimated during the civil war, and then reestablished in 1920. O'Dogherty, "Restaurarlo todo en Cristo."

5. See Boylan, "Mexican Catholic Women's Activism" and "Gendering the Faith"; Butler, *Popular Piety and Political Identity*, esp. 123, 127, 151, 168–69, 183–85, 192–93; Fernández-Aceves, "Political Mobilization of Women"; Hanson, "Day of Ideals"; Miller, "Role of Women"; Vaca, *Los silencios de la historia*; and Schell, "Honorable Avocation" and "Of the Sublime Mission."

6. O'Dogherty Madrazo, *De urnas y sotanas*, esp. 97–98, 107–114, 165–166, 249, 258–59. Elisa Cárdenas Ayala briefly notes the existence of the Ladies of Charity's conferences at the turn of the century, but only links the men's conferences to the PCN. Cárdenas Ayala, *El derrumbe*, 103–4, 412–14.

7. Recent works have begun providing a gendered history of the Catholic revival. Although they do not make connections to charity or to twentieth-century political movements, Edward Wright-Rios for Oaxaca (*Revolutions in Mexican*

Catholicism and "Visions of Women") and Margaret Chowning for one devotional association in Michoacán ("La feminización de la piedad" and "Catholic Church and the Ladies") have noted the prominence of women in late nineteenth-century lay organizations.

8. "Memoria general de la Sociedad de San Vicente de Paúl, en Guadalajara, durante 50 años," in Sociedad Guadalajara, *Boletín* (September 1902), 72–85; and "La Conferencia del Santísimo Sacramento de Guadalajara, fiesta del quincuagésimo aniversario de su agregación," in Sociedad Guadalajara, *Boletín* (October 1907), 181–84.

9. "Necrología" in Sociedad, *Noticia* (1869, 1870). See Sociedad Guadalajara, *Boletín* (October 1907), 181–84. On Dionisio Rodríguez, see Díaz Robles, "Medicina, religión y pobreza," 44–45, 92.

10. De Dios, *Historia de la familia vicentina*, 1:534.

11. Sociedad, *Reseña*, 29.

12. The 1865 *Memoria* is summarized in De Dios, *Historia de la familia vicentina*, 1:535–36.

13. The 1864 percentage is calculated by using the 1865 national total. De Dios, *Historia de la familia vicentina*, 1:535–36. Sociedad, *Reseña*, 52–53.

14. Figueroa noted that the Santísimo Sacramento conference was suspended from 1868 until the end of 1870. Sociedad Guadalajara, *Boletín* (October 1907), 183. See also Sociedad, *Reseña*, 30.

15. Arquidiócesis de Guadalajara, "Caridad cristiana," esp. 4–5.

16. Sociedad, *Noticia* (1869), 12.

17. Ibid., "Cuadro Sinóptico," n.p.; Sociedad, *Noticia* (1870), "Cuadro Sinóptico," n.p.; and Sociedad, *Memoria* (1871), "Cuadro Sinóptico," n.p.

18. Sociedad, *Noticia* (1869, 12; 1870, 19).

19. Ibid., 18, and "Cuadro Sinóptico," n.p. The conference in Tapalpa was no longer mentioned in the Sociedad's *Memoria* (1871).

20. "Instrucción pastoral," in Alcalá and Olimón, *Episcopado y gobierno en México*, 293, 334–35.

21. Sociedad, *Reseña*, 57–60.

22. Sociedad, *Boletín* (January 1883), 11–12.

23. See historical narratives in Sociedad Guadalajara, *Boletín* (March 1902, 19–21; September 1902, 76–80). Note that the former dates Father Silva's *retiros* to 1885 and the latter to 1886. Father Silva is also credited with promoting the Vincentian conferences in Zapotlán el Grande in the 1880s. Díaz Robles, "Medicina, religión y pobreza," 54. Parish priest Father Silviano Carrillo founded the male and female conferences in Cocula in 1889 and 1887 respectively. Camacho, *Historia del Sr. Obispo D. Silviano Carrillo*, 74–76.

24. For 1887 see Sociedad, *Boletín* (May 1887), 139. In 1898 the Guadalajara Central Council mentioned that, because another ten conferencias foráneas failed to send reports, they did not know whether those chapters still existed. Sociedad Guadalajara, *Boletín* (August 1898), 27.

25. Sociedad, *Reseña*, 47, 55–56.

26. Davies, "Tendencias demográficas urbanas," 493, 501.

27. Sociedad Guadalajara, *Boletín* (September 1902), 84.

28. According to the Guadalajara society's *Boletín* (August 1898, 28), the Conferencia del Seminario was created in 1893 "by men who would later become priests, in due time establishing conferences in the *poblaciones foráneas* of this archdiocese." The conference had folded by 1911. Sociedad Guadalajara, *Boletín* (December 1911), 200–203.

29. Sociedad, *Boletín* (November 1900), 318; and Sociedad Guadalajara, *Boletín* (September 1902, 79–82; March 1902, 22).

30. The Analco school and workshop were founded by the conference of Nuestra Señora de Guadalupe. In 1897 the workshop employed fifty workers a day. See Sociedad Guadalajara, *Boletín* (September 1902, 78–79; October 1907, 318); and Sociedad, *Boletín* (July 1897), 212–13.

31. Sociedad Guadalajara, *Boletín* (September 1902), 80, 84; and Sociedad, *Boletín* (July 1897), 212.

32. Sociedad Guadalajara, *Boletín* (September 1902), 79–81.

33. Ibid., esp. 80–85; and Sociedad Guadalajara, *Boletín* (March 1902), 18–19.

34. Letter from Carlos Vargas Galeana, Secretario del Consejo Superior de México de la Sociedad de San Vicente de Paul, to the Archbishop of Guadalajara, 20 February 1905, which includes proposals made in 4 April 1904, in AHAG, Sección Gobierno, Serie Asociaciones/San Vicente de Paul, 1888–1905.

35. A 1905 letter dated the merger to "some years ago." See letter of 15 November 1905 from Teofilo Loreto (por la Sociedad Católica) and Carlos Tapia (por la Sociedad de San Vicente de Paul) in AHAG, Gobierno, Asociaciones/San Vicente de Paul, 1888–1905, chap. 38, fol. 7.

36. Sociedad Guadalajara, *Boletín* (December 1911), 206.

37. Although the 1913 report listed a membership in the countryside of 439 active members (supposedly up from 287 in 1911), its own authors questioned the veracity of this statistic. In particular, they doubted that Teocuitatlán could have a hundred members when no more than fifty attended its conference sessions, and when their good works were limited to aiding one family, catechizing fifty children, preparing ten for the first communion, and visiting twenty prisoners and fifteen sick paupers. The decline in expenditures from 8,428 pesos in 1911 to 5,805 pesos throughout the archdiocese in 1913 also suggests a sharp drop in membership. Sociedad Guadalajara, *Informe*, 8–9.

38. Sociedad Guadalajara, *Boletín* (September 1902, 80–85; March 1902, 19–20).

39. For an excellent summary of these developments, see Plasencia, "Cien años de Acción Social," 25–53; O'Dogherty Madrazo, *De urnas y sotanas*; Curley, "Slouching Towards Bethlehem"; and Cárdenas Ayala, *El derrumbe*.

40. The national *Memoria* of 1865 dates the first Guadalajara conference, in the Sagrario parish, to 21 March 1864, 21; Arquidiócesis de Guadalajara, "Caridad cristiana" dates it to 24 May. The 1922 history dates the Tepatitlán and Tototlán

conferences to 1861, but this seems to be a typographical error. They do not appear in the association's *Memorias* of 1865 or 1866 or in the 1901 history that lists scattered conferences founded before the establishment of the national association in 1863. Asociación, *Memoria* (1902), 4.

41. Arquidiócesis de Guadalajara, "Caridad cristiana." See also Plasencia, "Cien años de Acción Social," 27–29, 35–36, 41–43.

42. Luna de Corcuera's obituary claims that the first conferences were founded to support field hospitals that cared for the war wounded during the "French invasion." Wright de Kleinhans, *Mujeres notables mexicanas*, 354. See also Arquidiócesis de Guadalajara, "Caridad cristiana," 3–4; and Plasencia, "Cien años de Acción Social," 27–28.

43. For example, the male society's president, J.Valente de Quevedo, served as the Ladies of Charity Central Council secretary, and Dionisio Rodríguez, president of the male conference of the Divina Providencia, served as its first pro secretary and *consejero*. See appendixes 3 and 4 and Sociedad Guadalajara, *Boletín* (October 1907), 183.

44. Arquidiócesis de Guadalajara, "Caridad cristiana," 29, 42, 47, 59, 97.

45. See ibid., 3–5; and Plasencia, "Cien años de Acción Social," 27–28.

46. Arquidiócesis de Guadalajara, "Caridad cristiana."

47. This description is of the Zapotlán conference founded in 1909. Arquidiócesis de Guadalajara, *Memoria* (1910), 13.

48. Ibid., 9–10; and Arquidiócesis de Guadalajara, *Memoria* (1911), 10.

49. Asociación, *Memoria* (1865), "Estado General," n.p.

50. Because information is not available for both places in 1887, the proportion of Jalisco volunteers is based on the 1886 national total.

51. Asociación, *Memoria* (1892), esp. 18 and "Estado General," n.p.

52. Asociación, *Memoria* (1895, "Estado General," n.p.; 1909, 7 and "Estado" no. 2, n.p.;1911, "Estado" no. 2, n.p.).

53. Note that, since the annual *Memorias* regularly complain that many conferences failed to report to the Central Council, it is possible that the number of conferences in the archdiocese did in fact continue growing.

54. Cárdenas Ayala, *El derrumbe*, 25.

55. Asociación, *Memoria* (1905), 30; Arquidiócesis de Guadalajara, *Memoria* (1913), 26; see also Arquidiócesis de Guadalajara, "Caridad cristiana," 47, 59.
Sra. Remus also experienced financial difficulties during that period. See Ulloa, "Los inconvenientes del progreso," 59.

56. Arquidiócesis de Guadalajara, *Memoria* (1910), 16.

57. Asociación, *Memoria* (1902), notation on "Estado General," n.p.

58. Note that statistics provided in the national *Memoria* contain a transcription error, for they reported 5,685 marriages, which was instead the number of *visitas al sacramento* (a category not included in the national tabulation). Compare with Arquidiócesis de Guadalajara, *Memoria* (1911, "Estado General," n.p.), reproduced in fig. 5.3.

59. Arquidiócesis de Guadalajara, "Caridad cristiana," 14.

60. Ibid., 76–79, 86–87; Díaz Robles, *La práctica médica*, 45–52; and Muñoz, "Santa María de Jesús Sacramentado." For more details on the Ladies of Charity hospitals, including a map of their geographical coverage, see Díaz Robles, "Medicina, religión y pobreza," chaps. 2–3.

61. See Asociación, *Memoria* (1902), 29–41; and Arquidiócesis de Guadalajara, "Caridad cristiana," esp. 77, 87. On the professionalization of nursing in the Ladies' hospitals, see Díaz Robles, *La práctica médica* and "Medicina, religión y pobreza."

62. Arquidiócesis de Guadalajara, *Memoria* (1909), 22–23.

63. Asociación, *Memoria* (1905), notation on "Estado" no. 2, n.p.

64. Asociación, *Memoria* (1904), notation on "Estado" no. 2.

65. See Arquidiócesis de Guadalajara, "Caridad cristiana," esp. 79, 86, 88.

66. Asociación, *Memoria* (1911), 12–13. The date of the accident is unclear; it could have been 1910.

67. Asociación, *Memoria* (1904), notation on "Estado" no. 2.

68. Asociación, *Memoria* (1921), 7.

69. Arquidiócesis de Guadalajara, *Memoria* (1909, 1; 1910, 25).

70. On the men's conferences, see Sociedad Guadalajara, *Boletín* (December 1911), 200–206; on the Ladies of Charity, see Asociación, *Memoria* (1911), "Estado" no. 2, n.p.

71. The report insisted that the parish priest and conference treasurer made sure that the families continued to receive their normal assistance. Sociedad Guadalajara, *Informe*, 5–9.

72. Arquidiócesis de Guadalajara, "Caridad cristiana," esp. 1–10, 38, 60–61, 77.

73. For 1915 and 1918, see ibid., 7 and 10. For 1920, see Arquidiócesis de Guadalajara, *Memoria* (1920), "Cuadro sinóptico," n.p.

74. In contrast, by 1918 the Ladies of Charity was spending more on good works than before the revolution: 65,966 pesos in 1918 and 105,117 in 1920. These total peso amounts may not have represented a real increase because of inflation, however.

75. The *Boletín* of the Guadalajara men's society lists 131 active members in five conferencias foráneas (February 1921, 3) and 143 in fifteen conferences in Guadalajara city in June (August 1921, 1–4). After that, figures are only available for Guadalajara city, where the membership fluctuated: in April 1922 there were 122 active members in fifteen conferences (May 1922, 3–5) and in December there were 170 in sixteen conferences (December 1922, 1–4).

76. See esp. Hanson, "Day of Ideals"; O'Dogherty Madrazo, *De urnas y sotanas*; Schell, "Honorable Avocation" and "Of the Sublime Mission"; and Curley, "Slouching Towards Bethlehem," chap. 7.

77. More research is needed on the conferences after the Cristero War. The situation may not have been entirely bleak, since the men's society resumed publication of its *Boletín* in 1932 and reported that there were sixteen conferences in

the city of Guadalajara (up from thirteen in 1922), though only eight in the countryside. Sociedad Guadalajara, *Boletín* (April 1932), 4–6. On the conferences in 1941, see Plasencia, "Cien años de Acción Social," 98.

78. Arquidiócesis de Guadalajara, *Memoria* (1909, 23; 1912, 25).

79. Asociación, *Memoria* (1911), notation on "Estado" no. 2, n.p.

80. Sociedad Guadalajara, *Memoria* (1911), 13.

81. Sociedad Guadalajara, *Boletín* (December 1911), 206.

82. Arquidiócesis de Guadalajara, *Memoria* (1909), 21.

83. For example, see news from the Juchitlán and Zapopán conferences. Arquidiócesis de Guadalajara, *Memoria* (1911), 22, 24.

84. The hospital opened in 1907. Arquidiócesis de Guadalajara, "Caridad cristiana," 90–92.

85. This inauguration ceremony took place in 1892. Ibid., 44.

86. The Archdiocese of Guadalajara had eighty-seven parishes in 1896. Although more parishes were added in the next decade, the total number remained constant because an equal number went to the Diocese of Aguascalientes when it was created in 1899. See O'Dogherty Madrazo, *De urnas y sotanas*, 27.

87. Asociación, *Memoria* (1905), 25; Arquidiócesis de Guadalajara, *Memoria* (1909, 18; 1910, 19); and Arquidiócesis de Guadalajara, "Caridad cristiana," 32–33.

88. Curley makes similar points about the Operarios Guadalupanos founded in 1909. Curley, "Slouching Towards Bethlehem," 167–70.

89. Cárdenas Ayala, *El derrumbe*, 35.

90. O'Dogherty Madrazo, *De urnas y sotanas*, 107–8, 112–14.

91. Ibid., 107n93.

92. Ibid., 108.

93. Cárdenas Ayala, *El derrumbe*, 32, 412–14.

94. Similar links can be seen in the 1917 petition drive, where many towns with female conferences sent letters requesting the revocation of the anticlerical Decree 1913. Fernández-Aceves, "Political Mobilization of Women," 83n110.

95. O'Dogherty Madrazo, *De urnas y sotanas*, esp. 109. Miguel de la Mora addressed the assemblies of the men's conferences on several occasions and collected—and signed his name on the front of—several copies of the bulletins housed in the archive of Guadalajara's archdiocese (AHAG, Sección Folletería). See, for example, Sociedad Guadalajara, *Boletín* (August 1907, 169; July 1908, 56).

96. See, for example, O'Dogherty Madrazo, *De urnas y sotanas*, 97; "El celo de la Iglesia en la aplicación de la doctrina sobre el derecho político," in Sociedad Guadalajara, *Boletín* (July 1912), 29–50; and Adame Goddard, *El pensamiento político y social*.

97. Arquidiócesis de Guadalajara, *Memoria* (1910), 31–33. This conference was known by the name of Purísimo Corazón de María until 1886.

98. On Palomar de Verea as well as connections between members of the Unión de

Damas Católicas and Catholic militants, see Boylan, "Mexican Catholic Women's Activism," esp. 224. On the Palomar family see Fregoso Centeno, "Dolores Palomar Arias," 41–65.

99. See lists of officers in Arquidiócesis de Guadalajara, "Caridad cristiana," and in the annual *Memorias* of the Guadalajara association. Identification of Luna de Corcuera's daughter in Arquidiócesis de Guadalajara, *Memoria* (1895), 5; and of Catalina Palomar de Verea's mother in Díaz Robles, "Medicina, religión y pobreza," 56.

100. See, for example, Arquidiócesis de Guadalajara, *Memoria* (1896, 24–25; 1911, 27–28).

101. Arquidiócesis de Guadalajara, *Memoria* (1934), 22.

102. I have not located a full run of Guadalajara *Memorias* for the period after 1913, only those for 1920–1925, 1930–1932, and 1934. The information for 1937 comes from Asociación, *Memoria* (1937).

103. In France the Louise de Marillac conferences were the "Junior Ladies of Charity." Padberg and Hannefin, "St. Vincent's First Foundation," 111.

104. In 1923 Catalina Palomar de Verea signed the ten-year report of that organization as its outgoing president: Unión de Damas Católicas (1923). On her role in the Catholic movement, see Boylan, "Mexican Catholic Women's Activism," 223–24.

105. Sociedad Católica, *Estadística*, 24.

106. See Sociedad Guadalajara, *Boletín* (September 1902), 77–78, 83.

107. Cárdenas Ayala, *El derrumbe*, 269; and Curley, "Slouching Towards Bethlehem," esp. 170.

108. O'Dogherty Madrazo, *De urnas y sotanas*, 108.

109. Sociedad Guadalajara, *Boletín* (October 1907), 182–83; and O'Dogherty Madrazo, *De urnas y sotanas*, 44.

110. The Ladies of Charity's conference at the Fábrica de Atemajac functioned until 1904, when the factory's new owners suppressed it. See O'Dogherty Madrazo, *De urnas y sotanas*, 44n64; and Arquidiócesis de Guadalajara, "Caridad cristiana," 47–48. On the factory, see also Curley, "Slouching Towards Bethlehem," 172.

111. On the importance of extended familial and lay sodality networks to religious resistance in the 1930s, see Smith, *Roots of Conservatism*, 235–37.

112. O'Dogherty Madrazo, *De urnas y sotanas*, 19.

Chapter 6

1. Such was the conclusion drawn by Hubert J. Miller in his review of Ivereigh's book in the *Hispanic American Historical Review*.

2. The founding dates of many of the Ladies of Charity chapters are unclear. The

US branch of the Ladies of Charity, established in St. Louis in 1857, was apparently the first in the hemisphere (Gay, "Relevance of the Ladies of Charity USA"). The Mexican women's association may have been created around the same time as Peru's, which was already referred to in the association's *Memoria* of 1865, along with an association in Bahia (Brazil) that did not send a report to the central office in Paris (39). Ponce de León Atria found a Chilean chapter in 1864 (*Gobernar la pobreza*, 291). By 1893 the *Rapport* of the international Dames de la Charité listed branches in Costa Rica, Ecuador, Guatemala, Martinique, Peru, and Brazil. Karen Mead analyzes another association, founded in Argentina in 1889, that was not apparently affiliated with the international body ("Gender, Welfare, and the Catholic Church," 100).

3. On the complicated relationship between tradition and modernity, see O'Hara, "El capital espiritual"; Overmyer-Velázquez, *Visions of the Emerald City*, esp. 1–15; and Wright-Rios, *Revolutions in Mexican Catholicism*, 24–28.

4. Serrano, "Estudio preliminar," 71.

5. See Guerra, *México*, vol. 1; Guerra and Lempérière, *Los espacios públicos*; Sábato, *Ciudadanía política y formación* and "On Political Citizenship"; and Forment, *Democracy in Latin America*.

6. Curtis, "Charitable Ladies," 123, 154.

7. Duroselle, *Les débuts du catholicisme social*, 46, 199, 216.

8. In some cases the new may have grown directly out of the old, as in one conference in Acatlán whose members were former members of the old confraternity of the Good Death. In any case, despite the 1859 law abolishing confraternities, many continued to exist, especially in the rural areas. See Smith, *Roots of Conservatism*, esp. 186.

9. Lavrin, "La Congregación," 568; and De Dios, *Historia de la familia*, 1:512–14.

10. Guardino, *Time of Liberty*, 33.

11. Sociedad, *Reseña*, 26.

12. Sociedad, *Notas*, 4.

13. Asociación, *Reglamento* (1863), chap. iv.

14. Sociedad, *Notas*, 124. This note also appeared in the two undated Mexican editions of the Sociedad's *Reglamento* that were probably published in the late 1840s.

15. De Dios, *Historia de la familia vicentina*, 1:3n2.

16. Conferencia de la Villa de Coyoacán, Libro de Actas (16 June 1912–5 August 1913), AHAM, Lib. Actas, L4C/2, 1912.

17. See the insightful analysis of Catholic lay associations by Juan José Muñoz in De Dios, *Historia de la familia vicentina* (1993), 1:512–19; also Sociedad, *Reglamento* (1898), 21; and Serrano, "La escuela chilena," 143–44.

18. There was considerable diversity among confraternities, however, with some occasionally aiding the poor by rescuing foundlings, burying executed criminals, or providing dowries for single women to marry. See, e.g., Lavrin, "La

Congregación"; Bazarte Martínez, *Las cofradías de españoles*, esp. 71–73, 89–92; Pescador, *De bautizados a fieles difuntos*, 297–337; Belanger, "Cofradías"; Valero Chávez, *De la caridad*, 90–91; and Von Germeten, *Black Blood Brothers*, esp. 38.

19. *La Unidad Católica*, "Editorial: Las Conferencias."

20. See Overmyer-Velázquez, *Visions of the Emerald City*, 8.

21. Sociedad, *Notas*, 64–65, 89; Sociedad, *Guía*, 52–53.

22. Guerra, *México*, 1: esp. 158–59. On the construction of a counterhegemonic Catholic identity, see Curley, "Slouching Towards Bethlehem," esp. 22–23 and chap. 3; and Wright-Rios, *Revolutions in Mexican Catholicism*, esp. 47, 104, 109.

23. Sábato, "On Political Citizenship," 1308.

24. Indeed the women's association was more democratic than the men's society. Although the Ladies of Charity Central Council president was chosen by the clerical director from a list of three candidates selected by the members, the local conferences voted for their officers by secret ballot. The men's society was more hierarchical since, in order to maintain unity, local conferences elected only their president, who then appointed the rest of the officers. Where there was a Particular Council, it appointed the president and vice president of each conference. The women elected their officers annually, while the men's served for an indefinite term. See Asociación, *Reglamento* (all dates), chap. 1, arts. 8–9; Sociedad, *Reglamento* (all dates), chap. 1, art. 9, and chap. 3, art. 40. When honorary members attended conference sessions, they did not have the *voto deliberativo* granted to each active member. Sociedad, *Notas*, 115.

25. Forment, *Democracy in Latin America*, xi, xiii. In his half page on the Vincentian conferences, Forment excludes them from this trend by arguing that, because they had a centralized structure, they were authoritarian (260). I have found no support for this statement.

26. Arquidiócesis de Guadalajara, *Memoria* (1896), 5.

27. The composition of the ration standardized in 1890 was still in use two decades later. See notations on "Estado General," n.p., in Arquidiócesis Guadalajara, *Memoria* (1896, 1909).

28. The bylaws recognized that in the poorest rural areas, the ration might only consist of corn, beans, and salt. Asociación, *Reglamento* (1911), 27.

29. Sociedad, *Notas*, 48–49, 55; and *Pequeño examen*, 8.

30. In later years they sometimes included the total number of sick assisted and the number who died, the names of women who wanted to become members, and the names of those who were absent from the meeting. But they provided no details about the council's deliberations or the conference clients. Consejo Central de Culiacán de Señoras de la Caridad, Libro de Actas, 10 April 1894–2 December 1912, APCC, Sección Disciplinar, San Vicente de Paul, caja 1, vol. 1.

31. Conferencia de San Vicente de Paul, Actas 10 January 1897–24 January 1898, APCC, Sección Disciplinar, San Vicente de Paul, caja 1, vol. 1.

32. Conferencia de la Villa de Coyoacán, AHAM, Lib. Actas, L4C/2, 1912. This conference had so few members that it only attended a handful of families at any given time.

33. Asociación, *Reglamento* (1911), 26, 56.

34. Minutes of July 1913, Conferencia de la Villa de Coyoacán, AHAM, Lib. Actas, L4C/2, 1912, fols. 83v–85.

35. De Dios, *Historia de la familia vicentina*, 1:535; and Sociedad, *Boletín* (November 1900), 330–32.

36. Letter of 17 November 1887 to General Council in Paris, ASSVP, Conseil Superior du Mexique, C113, Mexique.

37. Sociedad Guadalajara, *Boletín* (1898), 25, 28.

38. Although the preface is dated 8 January 1900, the Asociación's *Reglamento* was not published until 1911. Most of the differences were minor, such as whether only two members of each conference attended the monthly Central Council meetings or whether all conference officers attended; the length of the probationary period for each new member, etc.

39. See Silva, "Prácticas de lectura"; and Desramé, "Comunidad de lectores."

40. Minutes of 6 September 1896, Consejo Central de Culiacán de Señoras de la Caridad, Libro de Actas, 10 April 1894–2 December 1912, APCC, Sección Disciplinar, San Vicente de Paul, caja 1, vol. 1, fol. 7v.

41. For example, the Sociedad Guadalajara, *Informe* (7) notes that the men's conference in Encarnación, Jalisco, had twelve volumes. The society's national statistics listed 247 volumes in conference libraries in 1908. Sociedad Guadalajara, *Boletín* (July 1909), 152.

42. Schell, *Church and State Education*, 137. Although Schell is referring to the catechism courses of the 1920s, her statement also applies to earlier ones.

43. On the *emancipación legítima de la mujer*, see Arquidiócesis de Guadalajara, "Caridad cristiana," 18, 78.

44. For a discussion of shifting notions of poor relief in Mexico, see Arrom, *Containing the Poor*, esp. 32–39, 59–62, 72–74.

45. Sociedad, *Boletín* (February 1859), 200.

46. Sociedad, *Reseña* (1895), 11; and Minutes of 17 December 1912, Conferencia de la Villa de Coyoacán, AHAM, Lib. Actas, L4C/2, 1912, fol. 38.

47. *La Unidad Católica*, "Editorial: Las Conferencias."

48. In the early years, some of the conferences may have received the names of needy paupers from the Sisters of Charity, as specified by its bylaws. Asociación, *Reglamento* (1863). 16. Yet given how few sisters operated in Mexico even before their expulsion in 1875, this cannot have been the method most conferences used to find client families.

49. See Conferencia de la Villa de Coyoacán, AHAM, Lib. Actas, L4C/2, 1912; Sociedad, *Notas*, esp. 56.

50. Sociedad, *Boletín* (February 1859), 214.

51. Sociedad Guadalajara, *Boletín* (November 1907), 187.

52. Asociación, *Reglamento* (1911), 28; and Arquidiócesis de Guadalajara, *Memoria* (1896), 21–31.

53. The Ladies of Charity mandated the three-month check-in; previous bylaws of the women's association did not specify how often to conduct these investigations. Asociación, *Reglamento* (1911), 21. For the men's conferences, see Sociedad, *Notas*, 56, 60.

54. See discussion in García Icazbalceta, *Informe sobre los establecimientos*, 142; and Conferencia de la Villa de Coyoacán, AHAM, Lib. Actas, L4C/2, 1912, esp. fols. 62, 82.

55. García Icazbalceta, *Informe sobre los establecimientos*, 136–44, 154–55, 165.

56. Sociedad, *Reseña*, 12.

57. On the traditional favoring of *pobres vergonzantes*, the elderly, sick and disabled, women, and children, see Arrom, *Containing the Poor*, 90–92.

58. Sociedad, *Boletín* (1859), 197.

59. Minutes of 25 September 1910, Consejo Central de Culiacán de Señoras de la Caridad, Libro de Actas, 10 April 1894–2 December 1912, APCC, Sección Disciplinar, San Vicente de Paul, caja 1, vol. 1. See also Asociación, *Memoria* (1902), 35.

60. Sociedad, *Boletín* (April 1893), 101. See also Sociedad, *Guía*, 14–15.

61. See discussion in Sociedad, *Notas*, 56–58; Asociación, *Reglamento* (1911), 21, 28; and Minutes of 20 May 1913, Conferencia de la Villa de Coyoacán, AHAM, Lib. Actas, L4C/2, 1912, fol. 74v.

62. Sociedad, *Reseña*, 76.

63. Asociación, *Memoria* (1892), 9. On the broader civilizing goals, see esp. Sociedad, *Guía*.

64. Sociedad, *Reseña*, 76.

65. Ibid., 13.

66. Arquidiócesis de Guadalajara, *Memoria* (1910), 10.

67. Overmyer-Velázquez makes a similar point for the Catholic workers' circles (*Visions of the Emerald City*, chap. 3).

68. Sociedad, *Reseña*, 71. In 1864 García Icazbalceta also proclaimed the superiority of Vincentian charity over public welfare. García Icazbalceta, *Informe sobre los establecimientos*, 199.

69. Asociación, *Memoria* (1892), 8–9; and Sociedad Guadalajara, *Memoria* (July 1909), 156.

70. García Icazbalceta, *Informe sobre los establecimientos*, 124, 129–30.

71. De Dios, *Historia de la familia vicentina*, 1:539.

72. See esp. Agustín Rodríguez, address to the society's annual assembly, in Sociedad, *Reseña*, 65–81; and Arquidiócesis de Guadalajara, "Caridad cristiana," 8.

73. Sociedad, *Boletín* (1892), 3.

74. Gonzaga Cuevas, *Porvenir de México*, esp. iv–viii.

75. Sánchez Santos, *Obras selectas*, esp. 51, 89; and Weiner, "Trinidad Sánchez Santos."

76. Quoted in Alcalá and Olimón, *Episcopado y gobierno en México*, 330; see also ibid., 303, 306, 331.

77. Sociedad, *Boletín* (April 1893), back page.

78. On this point, see Gilbert, "'Long Live the True Religion!,'" 10–11. On their use of the discourse of liberalism, see esp. the protests against the Organic Law (Villanueva y Francesconi, *El libro de protestas*). On the similar Catholic defense of civil liberties in Chile, see Serrano, "La escuela chilena," esp. 361–62. We must be careful not to overstate the point, however: one conference in Orizaba reported "collecting a large number of prohibited works, which it turned over to its parish priest." This is the only reference to censorship I encountered. Sociedad, *Reseña*, 45.

79. See Lida, "La Iglesia Católica," esp. 1400–5, 1413–14; and Hanson, "Day of Ideals," 100–104.

80. Curley, "Social Catholicism," 1347. See also *New Catholic Encyclopedia* articles: "Catholic Social Movements," 13:321; "Social Action," 13:310–312; and "Rerum Novarum," 12:387.

81. On Vincentian charity creating "la Iglesia para los pobres," see Sociedad, *Boletín* (July 1909), 138.

82. On this view, which was widespread in Catholic circles, see Schell, *Church and State Education*, 10; and Wright-Rios, *Revolutions in Mexican Catholicism*, 109.

83. See esp. articles 3, 22, 42, and 60 in Pope Leo XIII, "Rerum Novarum."

84. The quote is from Curtis, "Charitable Ladies," 127. Duroselle considers Lamennais to be the inventor of Social Catholicism. Although crediting Ozanam with contributing to its development, Duroselle does not consider the early société to be part of the Social Catholic movement. Yet he posits that Melun had "converted" to Social Catholicism by 1838, while still a leading member of the conferences, and he noted that some conference activities, such as the *patronages* of apprentices, were evolving in the direction of Social Catholicism. Duroselle, *Les débuts du catholicisme social*, 16–17, 28, 36, 46, 56, 80–81, 175, 183–86, 709. De Dios also considers Ozanam to be an early participant in the Social Catholic movements (*Historia de la familia vicentina*, 1:43).

85. As late as 17 April 1910 a Pastoral Instruction still promoted the conferences as well as workers' circles. González Navarro, *La pobreza en México*, 75, 77.

86. On Argentina, see Mead, "Gender, Welfare, and the Catholic Church," 102, 104; and Guy, *Women Build the Welfare State*, 51–54, 133. On Colombia, see Castro Carvajal, *Caridad y beneficencia*, 185, 193.

87. Schmitt, "Catholic Adjustment," 193–96; and Vaughan, *State, Education, and Social Class*, chaps. 2 and 153.

88. On the lack of outdoor relief in Mexico, see González Navarro, *La pobreza en México*, 87–146; and Peza, *La beneficencia*, esp. 75. In 1876 the private Sociedad

de Beneficencia Española began providing cash handouts as a form of home relief, but only to needy Spaniards. Laguarta, *Historia de la beneficencia*, 148.

89. Lorenzo Río, *El Estado como benefactor*, chap. 4.

90. Asociación, *Memoria* (1895), 14.

91. Asociación, *Memoria* (1902), 54.

92. Ibid., 45.

93. It is unclear when the first savings funds were established in Mexico. They were promoted in France by 1860 and mentioned in Mexican documents by the 1890s. See Sociedad, *Guía*, 39, 43; and Sociedad, *Reseña*, 11, 13, 33. On Palomar y Vizcarra, see Plasencia, "Cien años de Acción Social,"47–48; and Curley, "Slouching Towards Bethlehem," esp. 152, 180–81.

94. Schell, *Church and State Education*, 149.

95. Schell similarly argues that in the 1920s the curriculum of Catholic schools was just as modern as that of public schools. Ibid., esp. 10–11, 137.

96. Arquidiócesis de Guadalajara, "Caridad cristiana," 77.

97. Asociación, *Reglamento* (1863), 24. This instruction was dropped from later, less chatty, editions.

98. On their contributions to modernizing medical practices in Jalisco, see Oliver Sánchez, *Salud, desarrollo urbano y modernización*, 139, 329; and Díaz Robles, "Medicina, religión y pobreza."

99. Sociedad, *Reseña*, 33.

100. On the professionalization of nursing and medicine in the Ladies of Charity hospitals, see Díaz Robles, *La práctica médica* and "Medicina, religión y pobreza"; and on the hiring of a *preceptora titulada* in the society's schools, see Díaz Robles, "Señores y señoras," 73. On the medical training of the Sisters of Charity and the modern medical practices in its hospitals, see Ballenger, "Modernizing Madness," 133, 138, 152–53.

101. Where there were too few aspiring youths to form their own conferences, they could participate in the work of the local conference as assistants under the mentorship of a regular member. Sociedad, *Notas*, 109.

102. On the professionalization of home visits in Colombia, see Castro Carvajal, "Las visitas domiciliarias."

103. The Yucatán conferences reported raising the ration for each person to eight bonos a week in 1902. Asociación, *Memoria* (1902), 42. On how vouchers were apportioned, see also Conferencia de la Villa de Coyoacán, AHAM, Lib. Actas, L4C/2, 1912.

104. The Vincentian organizational structure as well as many of its activities served as a model for the Sociedad Católica as well as for the Catholic Action groups of the 1920s. See esp. Sociedad Católica de Señoras, *Estadística*; and O'Dogherty, "Restaurarlo todo en Cristo," 139–41. In the early twentieth century spiritist women's groups followed a similar outreach model that included visits to hospitals and women's prisons, lectures on morality and alcohol

temperance, free weekend classes for children, and night classes for adults. Schraeder, "Spirits of the Times," 112.

105. Cano, *Se llamaba Elena Arizmendi*, 105–8.

106. Schell, *Church and State Education*, 75, 61. See also Sanders, *Gender and Welfare*, 131–33, 136–37.

107. Vaughan, "Nationalizing the Countryside," esp. 158–61.

108. The 1922 history of the Guadalajara Ladies of Charity conferences was partly written to prove their ownership of certain institutions in the face of the confiscation of these properties. Arquidiócesis de Guadalajara, "Caridad cristiana." Further research is required to determine what happened to the property and capital that the conferences had accumulated.

109. For versions of the standard story line, see, for example, Macedo, "La asistencia pública"; Velasco Ceballos, *El niño mexicano*, 103–4; Centro Mexicano para la Filantropía, "Understanding Mexican Philanthropy," 185–87; and, most recently, López-Alonso, *Measuring Up*, esp. 3, 17–18, 56.

110. For critiques of the standard narrative, see esp. Arrom, *Containing the Poor*; Alanís, "Algunas manifestaciones"; Ayala Flores, "Caridad y beneficencia"; Guadarrama Sánchez, "Filantropía y cohesión social"; and Urbina Martínez, "Prácticas cotidianas." On the growing scholarly recognition of the "mixed economy of welfare" in Europe, see Harris and Bridgen, "Introduction."

111. Espejo López, "La beneficencia privada"; Blum, "Conspicuous Benevolence," 34–38, and *Domestic Economies*, 9–10; and Porter, *Working Women*, 162. Religious groups did not apparently come under this regulatory apparatus.

112. On these points see Macías-González, "Mexican Aristocracy," chaps. 2–3; Serrano, "Estudio preliminar," 70–72; Curtis, "Charitable Ladies," esp. 139; Bejar, "Voluntariado"; Guy, *Women Build the Welfare State*, esp. 8, 57; and Díaz Robles, "Medicina, religión y pobreza," esp. 48.

113. Quoted in González Navarro, "Ejercicio caritativo," 496.

114. On this point see Blum, *Domestic Economies*, part 1.

115. On this point see also Castro Carvajal, *Caridad y beneficencia*, 199.

116. On the problems with these binary categories, including "liberal" and "conservative," see Pani, "'Las fuerzas oscuras'"; and, for other countries, the articles in Ivereigh, *Politics of Religion*.

117. Pope Pius IX, "Quanta Cura" and "Syllabus of Errors."

118. Although Lamennais directly influenced Ozanam, they parted ways when Lamennais left the church in 1833. See Degert, "Lamennais"; Udovic, "'What About the Poor?'," 78–79; and Duroselle, *Les débuts du catholicisme social*, 36–46.

119. Ceballos Ramírez, *El catolicismo social*, esp. chap. 1, and "Conservadores e instransigentes"; and Case, "Resurgimiento de los conservadores."

120. Adame Goddard, *El pensamiento político y social*, 189–220; Ceballos Ramírez, *El catolicismo social*, 175–252; Curley, "Social Catholicism," 1348; and Cárdenas, "Conservadurismos para salir."

121. Márquez, "Trinidad Sánchez Santos," 18; and Ceballos Ramírez, *El catolicismo social*, 223, 412–14.

122. See Hanson, "Day of Ideals"; Curley, "Slouching Towards Bethlehem"; and Knight, "Mentality and Modus Operandi."

123. Asociación, *Memoria* (1921), 5–6; and De Dios, *Historia de la familia vicentina*, 2:635–36, 646–51.

124. The Unión de Damas Católicas was the largest of the four lay organizations founded by the energetic Jesuit Alfredo Méndez Medina. Although founded in 1912 nationally and 1913 in Jalisco, most chapters were decimated during the civil war and reestablished in 1920. See O'Dogherty, "Restaurarlo todo en Cristo"; Hanson, "Day of Ideals"; and Schell, "Honorable Avocation" and "Of the Sublime Mission." On the Señoras de la Caridad, see De Dios, *Historia de la familia vicentina*, 2:657–59.

125. Hanson, "Day of Ideals," 11. De Dios dates the Ladies of Charity's second decline to 1925 in *Historia de la Familia vicentina*, 2:657.

126. In the 1930s and 1940s female activists apparently continued to outnumber male, as the Unión Femenina Católica Mexicana was the largest of the new Catholic lay organizations. Boylan, "Mexican Catholic Women's Activism" and "Gendering the Faith"; and Andes, "Catholic Alternative."

127. On the continued, if diminished, existence of the conferences in the 1930s and 1940s, see De Dios, *Historia de la familia vicentina*, 2:636–39, 658–67; and Smith, *Roots of Conservatism*, 241, 277.

128. Mexico City's normal school for men was founded in 1887, the one for women in 1890 (Schell, "Honorable Avocation," 5–6). The Escuela Normal Católica para Señoritas was founded in Jalisco in 1902 and lasted until 1914 (Plasencia, "Cien años de Acción Social," 40). Mexico's first nursing school was founded in Mexico City's Hospital General in 1907 (Cano, *Se llamaba Elena Arizmendi*, 53). The first courses in social work date to the 1920s (Sanders, *Gender and Welfare*, 119, 125).

129. See esp. Fregoso Centeno, "Dolores Palomar Arias," 58–60; and Muñoz, "Santa María de Jesús Sacramentado." Many women with the same last names as former conference members also volunteered with the new Cruz Roja (Alessio Robles, *La filantropía en México*, 61–67). The new revolutionary state still collaborated with secular charity women, at least in the early years. Sanders, *Gender and Welfare*, 54, 75–77, 115–16.

130. See Muncy, *Creating a Female Dominion*; Koven and Michel, *Mothers of a New World*; Skocpol, *Protecting Soldiers*, esp. chap. 6; and Guy, *Women Build the Welfare State*.

131. See Sanders, *Gender and Welfare*, esp. chap. 5.

132. On Catholic modernity, see Silva, "Prácticas de lectura," esp. 81; Hanson, "Day of Ideals"; Anderson, "Divisions of the Pope"; Ivereigh, "Introduction."; Londoño, "Politics of Religion"; Valenzuela and Maza Valenzuela, "Politics of Religion"; Hernández, "El efecto de la guerra"; Pani, "'El tiro por la culata'"; and

Overmyer-Velázquez, "New Political Religious Order," 130–31, 135. On the contribution of religious groups to the progress of Mexican science and medicine, see also Díaz Robles, "Medicina, religión y pobreza," xxiv–xxv, 51–52, 175.

133. The term is from Holston, "Alternative Modernities." See also O'Hara, "Supple Whip"; Overmyer-Velázquez, *Visions of the Emerald City*, esp. 1–15; and Wright-Rios, *Revolutions in Mexican Catholicism*, 24–28.

Epilogue

1. Laura Díaz Robles includes an undated picture of Catalina Palomar de Verea, a leading Lady of Charity in twentieth-century Jalisco, in her dissertation, "Medicina, religión y pobreza," facing 3.

2. Arrom, "Recuerdos de un niño de Mayarí."

BIBLIOGRAPHY

Archives and Special Collections

AHAG   Archivo Histórico de la Arquidiócesis de Guadalajara, Guadalajara

AHAM   Archivo Histórico de la Arquidiócesis de México, Mexico City

AHDF   Archivo Histórico del Distrito Federal, Mexico City

AL   Archives Lazaristes, Paris

APCC   Archivo Parroquial de la Catedral de Culiacán, Culiacán

ASSVP   Archives de la Société de Saint-Vincent de Paul, Paris

BFXC   Biblioteca Francisco Xavier Clavigero, Universidad Iberoamericana, Mexico City

BNM   Biblioteca Nacional de México, Mexico City (Colección Lafragua)

BPEJ   Biblioteca Pública del Estado de Jalisco "Juan José Arreola," Guadalajara (Fondos Especiales)

HL   Houghton Library, Harvard University, Cambridge, MA

INAH   Biblioteca Nacional de Antropología e Historia, Instituto Nacional de Antropología e Historia, Mexico City (Fondo Reservado)

Vincentian Conference Publications

ARQUIDIÓCESIS DE GUADALAJARA

"Caridad cristiana: Conferencias de Señoras de San Vicente de Paul, en la Arquidiócesis de Guadalajara, reseña de las obras de caridad, practicadas por dichas Conferencias, desde su establecimiento por los Padres Paulinos, en 24 de Mayo de 1864, hasta 1 de Junio de 1920." In *Obras católicas de caridad en la arquidiócesis de Guadalajara, de 1864–1920,* 1–104. Guadalajara: Tip. C. M. Sainz, 1922.

Informe que el Consejo Central de Guadalajara rinde al Consejo Superior de México
    de las obras de caridad realizadas por las Conferencias de Señoras de S. Vicente
    de Paul de esta Arquidiócesis . . . desde 1 de Junio de 1893 hasta fin de Mayo de
    1894. Guadalajara: Ant. Tip. de N. Parga, 1894.
Memoria de las Obras de las Asociaciones de Señoras de la Arquidiócesis de Guadala-
    jara, destinadas principalmente para el Socorro de enfermos pobres. . . .
    1887–1893.
Memoria de las Obras de caridad realizadas por las conferencias de Señoras de
    S. Vicente de Paul, que han sido agregadas al Consejo General de la Arquidióce-
    sis de Guadalajara. . . . 1895–1896.
Memoria de las Obras de Caridad de las Conferencias de Señoras de San Vicente de
    Paul, agregadas al Consejo Central de Guadalajara. . . . 1898–1902.
Memoria de las Obras de Caridad de las Conferencias de Señoras de San Vicente de
    Paul de la Arquidiócesis de Guadalajara. . . . 1903–1916.
Memoria detallada de las Obras de Caridad de las Conferencias de S. Vicente de Paul,
    de Señoras, de la Arquidiócesis de Guadalajara. . . . 1920, 1922–1924.
Memoria de las obras practicadas por las Señoras de la Caridad de San Vicente de
    Paul en la Arquidiócesis de Guadalajara. . . . 1925, 1934.
Memoria de las obras de caridad practicadas por las Cofradías de San Vicente de Paul
    de señoras, en la Arquidiócesis de Guadalajara. . . . 1930–1932.

ASOCIACIÓN DE SEÑORAS DE LA CARIDAD

Instrucciones del Consejo Diocesano a las Mesas Directivas de las Conferencias de
    S. Vicente de Paul, de Señoras; aprobadas por el . . . Arzobispo de Guadalajara.
    Guadalajara: Tip. Litografía y Encuadernación J. M. Yguiniz, 1922.

Memorias
(listed in chronological order)

Memoria que el Consejo Superior de las Asociaciones de Señoras de la Caridad del
    Imperio Mexicano dirige al General de Paris, de las obras que ha practicado y
    cantidades colectadas e invertidas en el socorro de los pobres enfermos, desde
    1 de julio de 1864 á 30 de junio de 1865. Mexico City: Comercio, 1865.
Memoria que el consejo superior de las asociaciones de Señoras de la Caridad de
    México, dirije al general de Paris . . . 1866. Mexico City: Imp. de Mariano Vil-
    lanueva, 1867.
Memoria que el Consejo superior de las Señoras de la Caridad de Méjico leyó en la Asam-
    blea general . . . 1878. Mexico City: Tip. Religiosa de Miguel Torner y Cía, 1879.

*Decimoctava memoria del Consejo General de las Señoras de la Caridad de México . . .
de las Obras de la Caridad de los años de 1889 á 1892.* Mexico City: Imp. del
Sagrado Corazón de Jesús, 1892.

*Vigésimasegunda memoria del Consejo General de las Señoras de la Caridad de
México . . . de las Obras de Caridad del año de 1894 á 1895.* Mexico City: Imp. y
Lit. de F. Diaz de León Sucesores, 1895.

*Vigésimatercera memoria del Consejo General de las Señoras de la Caridad de México
. . . de las Obras de Caridad del año de 1895 á 1896.* Mexico City: Imp. y Lit. de
F. Díaz de León Sucesores, 1896.

*Vigésimaquinta memoria del Consejo General de las Señoras de la Caridad de México
. . . de las Obras de Caridad del año de 1897 á 1898.* Mexico City: Tip. y Lit. "La
Europea" de J. Aguilar Vera y Ca., 1899.

*Vigésima séptima memoria del Consejo General de las Señoras de la Caridad de
México . . . de las Obras de Caridad del año de 1899 á 1900.* Mexico City: Imp.
J. de Elizalde, 1901.

*Vigésima novena memoria del Consejo General de las Señoras de la Caridad de Méjico
. . . de las Obras de Caridad del año de 1901 á 1902.* Mexico City: Talleres
Tipográficos "J. de Elizalde," 1902.

*Trigésima memoria del Consejo General de las Señoras de la Caridad de Méjico . . . de
las Obras de la Caridad del año de 1902 á 1903.* Mexico City: Talleres Tipográficos "J. de Elizalde," 1904.

*Trigésima primera memoria del Consejo General de las Señoras de la Caridad de
Méjico . . . de las Obras de Caridad del año de 1903 á 1904.* Mexico City: Talleres
Tipográficos "J. de Elizalde," 1905.

*Trigésima segunda memoria del Consejo General de las Señoras de la Caridad de
México . . . de las Obras de Caridad del año de 1904 á 1905.* Mexico City:
Imprenta, Encuadernación y Rayados, Puerta Falsa de Sto. Domingo, 1906.

*Trigésima quinta memoria del Consejo General de las Señoras de la Caridad de
México . . . de las Obras de Caridad del año de 1907 á 1908.* Mexico City: Guerrero Hnos., 1908.

*Trigésima sexta memoria del Consejo General de las Señoras de la Caridad de México
. . . de las Obras de Caridad del año de 1908 á 1909.* Mexico City: Guerrero
Hnos., 1909.

*Trigésima octava memoria del Consejo General de las Señoras de la Caridad de
México . . . de las Obras de Caridad del año de 1910 á 1911.* Mexico City: Guerrero Hnos., 1911.

*Memoria sobre la obra de las Señoras de la Caridad de San Vicente de Paul en México,
Año de 1921.* Mexico City: Imp. "La Moderna," 1922.

*Memoria de las obras practicadas por las Señoras de la Caridad de San Vicente de
Paul en la República Mexicana, correspondiente al año de 1936–1937.* Mexico
City, n.p., 1937.

Reglamentos

Reglamento de la Asociación de las Señoras de la Caridad . . . establecida en varios
    lugares por los padres de la Congregación de la Misión. . . . Puebla: Imp. del Ora-
    torio de San Felipe Neri, 1848.
Reglamento de la Asociación de las Señoras de la Caridad instituida por San Vicente
    de Paul en beneficio de los pobres enfermos, y establecida en varios lugares por
    los Padres de la Congregación de la Misión con licencia de los ordinarios. Mexico
    City: Imp. de Andrade y Escalante, 1863.
Reglamento de la Asociación de Caridad de San Vicente de Paul, en que se hallan
    refundidos los reglamentos de Paris y Méjico. Guadalajara: Tip. de Rodríguez,
    1864.
Reglamento de la Asociación de las Señoras de la Caridad . . . formado según el origi-
    nal de Paris y mandado observar por el Director General de la República. Mex-
    ico City: Iglesia de la Inmaculada Concepción, 1911.

DAMES DE LA CHARITÉ

Rapport sur les oeuvres des Dames de la Charité pendant l'année . . . lu a l'Assemblée
    Générale. Paris: 95 Rue de Sèvres, 1892–1897.

SOCIEDAD DE SAN VICENTE DE PAUL

Acta de la Asamblea General Extraordinaria celebrada el día quince de septiembre de
    1945, en ocasión del Centenario de la agregación de esta sociedad a la de Paris.
    Mexico City: n.p., 1945.
Boletín de la Sociedad de San Vicente de Paul. 1855–96.
Boletín de la Sociedad de San Vicente de Paúl en México. 1897–1909.
Guía práctica de las Conferencias de San Vicente de Paul, traducción del francés
    para las Conferencias Mexicanas. Mexico City: Imp. de Andrade y Escalante,
    1860.
Instrucciones acerca de las reglas que deberán seguirse para la formación de las con-
    ferencias de San Vicente de Paul. N.p., n.d. [ca. 1865]. In BPEJ, Miscelánea 576,
    no. 12.
Instrucciones acerca de las reglas que deberán seguirse para la formación de las confer-
    encias de San Vicente de Paul. 3d Mexican ed. Mexico City: Tip. de Aguilar é
    Hijos, 1894.
Memoria de las Obras de las Conferencias de la Sociedad de San Vicente de Paul,
    dependientes del Consejo Superior de la República Mexicana durante el año de
    1871. Mexico City: Imp. de la V. e Hijos de Murguía, 1872.

*Notas explicativas sobre los artículos del Reglamento General de la Sociedad de
S. Vicente de Paul, traducidas para las Conferencias de la República Mejicana.*
Mexico City: Imp. de Andrade y Escalante, 1858.

*Noticia sobre las Conferencias de la Sociedad de San Vicente de Paul, dependientes del
Consejo Superior de México, durante el año de . . . 1868–1870.*

Reglamento de la Sociedad de San Vicente de Paul, 1835. Translated by Sociedad de
San Vicente de Paul. Mexico City, n.p., n.d. [ca. 1846 in ASSVP Conseil Supe-
rior du Mexique, 1845–1920, CC113, Mexique; and ca. 1848 in BPEJ, Fondos
Especiales, Miscelánea 191, no. 5].

Reglamento General de la Sociedad de San Vicente de Paul (Diciembre de 1835). Rev.
ed. Mexico City: Imp. de Andrade y Escalante, 1860.

*Reglamento General de la Sociedad de San Vicente de Paul con notas explicativas
(Diciembre de 1835).* Mexico City: Imp. del Sagrado Corazón de Jesús, 1898.

Reseña del Quincuagenario de la Sociedad. Mexico City: Imp. y Lit. de Francisco Díaz
de León, 1895.

Sumario de las Indulgencias y Gracias concedidas a la Sociedad de S. Vicente de Paul.
Guadalajara: Tip. de Atilano Zavala, 1885.

SOCIEDAD DE SAN VICENTE DE PAUL, CONSEJO CENTRAL DE GUADALAJARA

Boletín del Consejo Central de Guadalajara, 1898–1912.

Boletín del Consejo Central de la Sociedad de S. Vicente de Paul, de Señores,
1920–1923.

Boletín del Consejo Central de Guadalajara. Nueva Época, 1932–1934.

*Informe sobre el estado y obras de las conferencias de San Vicente de Paul, de la
Arquidiócesis de Guadalajara, de Noviembre de 1912 á Octubre de 1913. . . .*
Guadalajara: Lit. y Tip. Loreto y Ancira y Cía, 1913.

Other Published Works Cited

Abadiano, Juan. *Establecimientos de beneficencia: Apuntes sobre su orígen y relación
de los actos de su junta directiva.* Mexico City: Imp. de la Escuela de Artes y
Oficios, 1878.

Adame Goddard, Jorge. *El pensamiento político y social de los católicos mexicanos,
1867–1914.* Mexico City: Universidad Nacional Autónoma de México, Instituto
de Investigaciones Históricas, 1981.

Alanís, Mercedes. "Algunas manifestaciones de la filantropía en las últimas décadas
del siglo XIX y principios del XX." In Villalobos Grzywobicz, *Filantropía y
acción solidaria* (2010), 177–204.

Alberro, Solange. *Apuntes para la historia de la Orden Hospitalaria de San Juan de Dios en la Nueva España: México, 1604–2004.* Mexico City: Colegio de México, 2005.

Alcalá, Alfonso, and Manuel Olimón, eds. *Episcopado y gobierno en México: Cartas pastorales colectivas del Episcopado Mexicano, 1859–1875.* Mexico City: Ediciones Paulinas, 1989.

Alessio Robles, Miguel. *La filantropía en México.* Mexico City: Ediciones Botas, 1944.

Almond, Gabriel, and Sidney Verba. *The Civic Culture: Political Attitudes and Democracy in Five Nations.* Princeton, NJ: Princeton University Press, 1963.

Alvarado, Lourdes, ed. *Educación y superación femenina en el siglo XIX: Dos ensayos de Laureana Wright.* Mexico City: Universidad Nacional Autónoma de México, Centro de Estudios Sobre la Universidad, 2005.

Alvarez Amezquita, José, et. al. *Historia de la salubridad y de la asistencia en México.* 4 vols. Mexico City: Secretaría de Salubridad y Asistencia, 1960.

Anderson, Margaret Lavinia. "The Divisions of the Pope: The Catholic Revival and Europe's Transition to Democracy." In Ivereigh, *Politics of Religion* (2000), 22–42.

Andes, Stephen. "A Catholic Alternative to Revolution: The Survival of Social Catholicism in Postrevolutionary Mexico." *The Americas* 68, no. 4 (2012): 529–62.

Andes, Stephen J., and Julia G. Young, eds. *Local Church, Global Church: Catholic Activism in Latin America from Rerum Novarum to Vatican II.* Washington, DC: Catholic University Press, forthcoming.

Arredondo López, María Adelina. "El catecismo de Ripalda." Accessed 18 December 2014. http://biblioweb.tic.unam.mx/diccionario/htm/articulos/sec_1.htm.

Arrom, José Juan. "Recuerdos de un niño de Mayarí que viajó a la región de las nieves." In *De donde crecen las palmas,* edited by José Juan Arrom, Silvia Marina Arrom, and Judith A. Weiss, 383–448. Havana: Centro de Investigación y Desarrollo de la Cultura Cubana Juan Marinello, 2005.

Arrom, Silvia Marina. *Containing the Poor: The Mexico City Poor House, 1774–1871.* Durham, NC: Duke University Press, 2000.

———. "Popular Politics in Mexico City: The Parián Riot, 1828." *Hispanic American Historical Review* 68, no. 2 (1988): 245–68.

———. *The Women of Mexico City, 1790–1857.* Stanford, CA: Stanford University Press, 1985.

Ayala Flores, Hubonor. "Caridad y beneficencia privada en el porfiriato: El caso del estado de Veracruz." In Villalobos Grzywobicz, *Filantropía y acción solidaria* (2010), 205–28.

Baker, Paula. "The Domestication of Politics: Women and American Political Society, 1780–1920." *American Historical Review* 89, no. 3 (1984): 620–47.

Ballenger, Stephanie Sharon. "Modernizing Madness: Doctors, Patients and Asylums in Nineteenth-Century Mexico City." PhD diss., University of California, Berkeley, 2009.

Bastian, Jean-Pierre. *Los disidentes: Sociedades protestantes y revolución en México, 1872–1910*. Mexico City: Colegio de México, 1989.

———. "Protestants, Freemasons, and Spiritists: Non-Catholic Religious Sociabilities and Mexico's Revolutionary Movement, 1910–20." In Butler, *Faith and Impiety* (2007), 75–92.

Bazarte Martínez, Alicia. *Las cofradías de españoles en la ciudad de México (1526–1860)*. Mexico City: Universidad Autónoma Metropolitana-Azcapotzalco, 1989.

Beezley, William H. "The Porfirian Smart Set Anticipates Thorstein Veblen in Guadalajara." In *Rituals of Rule, Rituals of Resistance: Public Celebrations and Popular Culture in Mexico*, edited by William H. Beezley, Cheryl English Martin, and William E. French, 73–90. Wilmington, DE: Scholarly Resources, 1994.

Bejar, Helena. "¿Voluntariado, compasión o autorealización?" *Sociedad y Economía* (Cali) 10 (April 2006): 99–119.

Belanger, Brian C. "Cofradías." In Werner, *Encyclopedia of Mexico* (1997). Vol. 1: 276–79.

Blasco, Inmaculada. "Feminismo católico." In *Historia de las mujeres en España y América Latina*, edited by Isabel Morant, 4:55–75. Madrid: Cátedra, 2006.

Blum, Ann S. "Conspicuous Benevolence: Liberalism, Public Welfare, and Private Charity in Porfirian Mexico City, 1877–1910." *The Americas* 58, no. 4 (2001): 7–38.

———. *Domestic Economies: Family, Work, and Welfare in Mexico City, 1884–1943*. Lincoln: University of Nebraska Press, 2009.

Bonaudo, Marta. "Cuando las tuteladas tutelan y participan: La Sociedad Damas de la Caridad (1869–1894)." *Signos Históricos*, no. 15 (2006): 70–97.

Botero Herrera, Fernando. "Los talleres de la Sociedad San Vicente de Paúl de Medellín: 1889–1910." *Boletín Cultural y Bibliográfico* (Bogotá) 33, no. 42 (1996): 3–21.

Boylan, Kristina. "Gendering the Faith and Altering the Nation: Mexican Catholic Women's Activism, 1917–1940." In *Sex in Revolution: Gender, Politics, and Power in Modern Mexico*, edited by Jocelyn Olcott, Mary Kay Vaughan, and Gabriela Cano, 199–222. Durham, NC: Duke University Press, 2006.

———. "Mexican Catholic Women's Activism, 1929–1949." PhD diss., University of Oxford, 2000.

Bravo Ugarte, José. *Historia de México*. 3 vols. Rev. ed. Mexico City: Jus, 1962.

Butler, Matthew. "Eucharistic Angels: Mexico's Nocturnal Adoration and the Masculinization of Postrevolutionary Catholicism, 1910–1930." In Andes and Young, *Local Church, Global Church* (forthcoming).

———, ed. *Faith and Impiety in Revolutionary Mexico*. New York: Palgrave Macmillan, 2007.

———. *Popular Piety and Political Identity in Mexico's Cristero Rebellion: Michoacán, 1927–29*. Oxford: Oxford University Press, 2004.

Calderón de la Barca, Fanny. *Life in Mexico: The Letters of Fanny Calderón de la Barca with New Material from the Author's Private Journals*, edited by Howard T. Fisher and Marion Hall Fisher. Garden City, NY: Doubleday, 1966.

Camacho, Ramiro. *Historia del Sr. Obispo D. Silviano Carrillo Fundador de las Siervas de Jesús Sacramentado.* Guadalajara: Editorial "El Estudiante," 1946.

———. *Los Padres Paúles en la República Mexicana, 1845–1945.* Guadalajara: Editorial "El Estudiante," 1945.

Cano, Gabriela. *Se llamaba Elena Arizmendi.* Mexico City: Tusquets Editores, 2010.

Cárdenas, Elisa. "Conservadurismos para salir de la dictadura: El Partido Católico y la Revolución Mexicana." In Torre, García Ugarte, and Ramírez Sáiz, *Los rostros del conservadurismo* (2005), 139–50.

Cárdenas Ayala, Elisa. *El derrumbe: Jalisco, microcosmos de la revolución mexicana.* Mexico City: Tusquets Editores, 2010.

Cárdenas de la Peña, Enrique. *Tiempo y tarea de Luis Gonzaga Cuevas.* Mexico City: Contabilidad Ruf Mexicana, 1982.

Carrillo y Ancona, Crescencio. *Orden Circular del Illmo. Sr. Dr. D. Crescencio Carrillo y Ancona . . . sobre la Tercera Orden de San Francisco de Asis y las Conferencias de San Vicente de Paul.* Mérida: Imp. a cargo de José Gamboa Guzmán, 1886.

Case, Robert. "Resurgimiento de los conservadores en México, 1876–1877." *Historia Mexicana* 25, no. 2 (1975): 204–31.

Castro, Miguel Angel. "José María Andrade, del amor al libro." In *Constructores de un cambio cultural: Impresores-editores y libreros en la ciudad de México, 1830–1855,* edited by Laura Suárez de la Torre, 381–435. Mexico City: Instituto Mora, 2003.

Castro Carvajal, Beatriz. *Caridad y beneficencia: El tratamiento de la pobreza en Colombia, 1870–1930.* Bogotá: Universidad Externado de Colombia, 2007.

———. "Las visitas domiciliarias femeninas en Colombia: Del trabajo voluntario a su profesionalización." In Eraso, *Mujeres y asistencia social* (2009), 241–74.

Ceballos Ramírez, Manuel. "Conservadores e intransigentes en la época de Porfirio Díaz." In Torre, García Ugarte, and Ramírez Sáiz, *Los rostros del conservadurismo* (2005), 123–38.

———. *El catolicismo social: Un tercero en discordia, Rerum Novarum, la "cuestión social" y la movilización de los católicos mexicanos (1891–1911).* Mexico City: Colegio de México, 1991.

———. "Las organizaciones laborales católicas a finales del siglo XIX." In Matute, Trejo, and Connaughton, *Estado, Iglesia y sociedad* (1995), 367–98.

———. "Siglo XIX y Guadalupanismo: De la polémica a la coronación y de la devoción a la política." In *Memoria del I Coloquio Historia de la Iglesia en el Siglo XIX,* edited by Manuel Ramos Medina, 317–32. Mexico City: Colegio de México, 1998.

Centro Mexicano para la Filantropía. "Understanding Mexican Philanthropy." In *Changing Structure of Mexico: Political, Social, and Economic Prospects,* edited by Laura Randall, 183–91. London: M. E. Sharpe, 1996.

Cholvy, Gérard. *Frédéric Ozanam (1813–1853): L'engagement d'un intellectual catholique au XIXe siècle.* Paris: Librairie Arthème Fayard, 2003.

Chowning, Margaret. "The Catholic Church and the Ladies of the Vela Perpetua: Gender and Devotional Change in Nineteenth-Century Mexico." *Past and Present*, no. 221 (2013): 197–237.

———. "From Colonial Cofradías to Porfirian Pious Associations: A Case Study in the Feminization of Public Piety in Mexico." Unpublished paper presented at the meeting of the Latin American Studies Association, Washington, DC, September 2001.

———. "La feminización de la piedad en México: Género y piedad en las cofradías de españoles. Tendencias coloniales y poscoloniales en los arzobispados de Michoacán y Guadalajara." In Connaughton, *Religión, política e identidad* (2010), 475–514.

———. "'Liberals, Women, and the Church in Mexico: Politics and the Feminization of Piety, 1700–1930." Unpublished paper presented at the Boston Area Workshop on Latin American History, Harvard University, September 2000.

Connaughton, Brian, ed. *Religión, política e identidad en la Independencia de México*. Mexico City: Universidad Autónoma Metropolitana/Benemérita Universidad Autónoma de Puebla, 2010.

Consejo General de Beneficencia, trans. *Administración General de la Asistencia Pública en Paris: Reglamento de los socorros á domicilio en la ciudad de Paris*. Mexico City: Andrade y Escalante, 1865.

. *Estracto de los reglamentos generales de la asistencia pública y de los acuerdos de la Junta para el uso de las Hermanas, Comisarios y Señoras de la Caridad*. Mexico City: Andrade y Escalante, 1865.

———. *Obras de Caridad que se practican en varios establecimientos de beneficencia: Apuntes escritos para el Consejo de Beneficencia*. Mexico City: Andrade y Escalante, 1865.

Conway, Christopher. "Sisters at War: Mexican Women's Poetry and the U.S.-Mexican War." *Latin American Research Review* 47, no. 1 (2012): 3–15.

Couturier, Edith. "'For the Greater Service of God': Opulent Foundations and Women's Philanthropy in Colonial Mexico." In McCarthy, *Lady Bountiful Revisited* (1990), 119–41.

———. "The Philanthropic Activities of Pedro Romero de Terreros: First Count of Regla." *The Americas* 32, no. 1 (1975): 13–30.

Cuevas, Mariano. *Historia de la iglesia en México*. 5 vols. El Paso, TX: Ed. "Revista Católica," 1928.

Curley, Robert E. "'The First Encounter': Catholic Politics in Revolutionary Jalisco, 1917–19." In Butler, *Faith and Impiety* (2007), 131–48.

———. "Slouching Towards Bethlehem: Catholics and the Political Sphere in Revolutionary Mexico." PhD diss., University of Chicago, 2001.

———. "Social Catholicism." In Werner, *Encyclopedia of Mexico* (1997). Vol. 2:1347–50.

Curtis, Sarah A. "Charitable Ladies: Gender, Class and Religion in Mid-Nineteenth-Century Paris." *Past and Present*, no. 177 (2002): 121–56.

Dalla Corte, Gabriela and Paola Piacenza. "Cartas marcadas: mujeres, identidad e inmigración en la Argentina, 1880–1920." *Signos Históricos*, no. 13 (2005): 70–93.

Davies, Keith A. "Tendencias demográficas urbanas durante el siglo XIX en México." *Historia Mexicana* 21, no. 3 (1972): 81–524.

De Dios, Vicente. *Historia de la familia vicentina en México (1844–1994)*. 2 vols. Salamanca: Editorial CEME, 1993.

Degert, Antoine. "Felicité Robert de Lamennais." *Catholic Encyclopedia* online. Accessed 4 January 2015. http://oce.catholic.com/index.php?title=Felicite_ Robert_de_Lamennais.

Desramé, Celine. "La comunidad de lectores y la formación del espacio público en el Chile revolucionario: De la cultura del manuscrito al reino de la prensa (1808– 1833)." In Guerra and Lampérière, *Los espacios públicos* (1998), 273–99.

Díaz Robles, Laura C. *La práctica médica en 3 hospitales de Guadalajara (1930–1965)*. Guadalajara: Universidad de Guadalajara, 2005.

———. "Medicina, religión y pobreza: Las señoras de la caridad de San Vicente de Paul, enfermeras religiosas en Jalisco (1864–1913)." PhD diss., Colegio de Michoacán, 2010.

———. "Señores y señoras de las conferencias de san Vicente de Paul, educadores católicos e informales ¿Por tanto invisibles?" *Revista de Educación y Desarrollo*, no. 10 (2012): 69–76.

Diccionario Porrúa de Historia, Biografía y Geografía de México. Mexico City: Porrúa, 1964.

Diefendorf, Barbara B. *From Penitence to Charity: Pious Women and the Catholic Reformation in Paris*. New York: Oxford University Press, 2004.

Dorantes, Alma. "Protestantes de ayer y hoy en una sociedad Católica: El caso Jalisciense." PhD diss., Centro de Investigaciones y Estudios Superiores de Antropología Social, 2004.

Dublán, Manuel, and José María Lozano, eds. *Legislación mexicana o colección completa de las disposiciones legislativas expedidas desde la independencia de la República*. 34 vols. Mexico City, 1876–1904.

Dumons, Bruno. "De l'oeuvre charitable á l'institution d'assistance: la Société de Saint-Vincent de Paul en France sous la Troisième République." *Revue d'Histoire Ecclésiastique*, nos. 1–2 (1998): 46–65.

Duroselle, Jean-Baptiste. *Les débuts du catholicisme social en France (1822–1870)*. Paris: Presses Universitaires de France, 1951.

Ehrick, Christine. *The Shield of the Weak: Feminism and the State in Uruguay, 1903– 1933*. Albuquerque: University of New Mexico Press, 2005.

Eraso, Yolanda, ed. "Maternalismo, religión y asistencia: La Sociedad de Señoras de San Vicente de Paul en Córdoba, Argentina." In Eraso, *Mujeres y asistencia social* (2009), 199–239.

————. *Mujeres y asistencia social en Latinoamérica, siglos XIX y XX: Argentina, Colombia, México, Perú y Uruguay*. Córdoba, Argentina: Alción Editora, 2009.

Espejo López, Edith. "La beneficencia privada en el D.F.: Un breve panorama de su legislación (1861–1910)." In Villalobos Grzywobicz, *Filantropía y acción solidaria* (2010), 145–75.

Fernández-Aceves, María Teresa. "The Political Mobilization of Women in Revolutionary Guadalajara, 1910–1940." PhD diss., University of Illinois–Chicago, 2000.

Forment, Carlos A. *Democracy in Latin America, 1760–1900*. Vol. 1: *Civic Selfhood and Public Life in Mexico and Peru*. Chicago: University of Chicago Press, 2003.

Foucault, Albert. *La Société de Saint-Vincent de Paul: Histoire de cent ans*. Paris: Editions SPES, 1933.

Fowler, Will, and Humberto Morales Moreno, eds. *El conservadurismo mexicano en el siglo XIX*. Puebla: Benemérita Universidad Autónoma de Puebla, 1999.

Fraser, Nancy, "Rethinking the Public Sphere: A Contribution to the Critique of Actually Existing Democracy." In *Habermas and the Public Sphere*, edited by Craig Calhoun, 109–42. Cambridge, MA: MIT Press, 1992.

Fregoso Centeno, Anayanci. "Dolores Palomar Arias: 1898–1972, la familia y la religión en la construcción del sujeto." In *Siete historias de vida: mujeres jaliscienses del siglo XX*, edited by Anayanci Fregoso Centeno, 41–65. Guadalajara: Editorial Universitaria, Universidad de Guadalajara, 2006.

Galí Boadella, Montserrat. *Historias del bello sexo: La introducción del Romanticismo en México*. Mexico City: Universidad Nacional Autónoma de México, Instituto de Investigaciones Estéticas, 2002.

Galindo y Villa, Jesús. *Reseña histórico-descriptiva de la Ciudad de México*. Mexico City: Imp. de Francisco Díaz de León, 1901.

García Cubas, Antonio. *El libro de mis recuerdos: Narraciones históricas, anecdóticas y de costumbres mexicanas anteriores al actual orden social*. Mexico City: Imp. de Arturo García Cubas, 1904.

García Gutiérrez, Blanca. "La experiencia cultural de los conservadores durante el México independiente: Un ensayo interpretativo." *Signos Históricos*, no. 1 (1999): 128–49.

García Icazbalceta, Joaquín. "Circular del Consejo Superior de México" (15 August 1891). In García Pimentel, *Don Joaquín García Icazbalceta*, 66–77.

————. *Informe sobre los establecimientos de beneficencia y corrección de esta capital: Su estado actual, noticia de sus fondos, reformas que desde luego necesitan y plan general de su arreglo*. Mexico City: Moderna Librería Religiosa, 1907.

García Pimentel y Elguero, Luis. *Don Joaquín García Icazbalceta como católico: Algunos testimonios publicados por su nieto*. Mexico City: Editorial "Clásica" Hoyos y Cía, 1944.

Gay, Gregory G. "Relevance of the Ladies of Charity USA after 150 Years." *Vincentian Family News*, 17 September 2007. http://famvin.org/en/2012/09/02/ the-ladies-of-charity-as-a-foundation-in-the-united-states.

Gibson, Ralph. *A Social History of French Catholicism, 1789–1914*. London: Routledge, 1989.

Gilbert, David A. "'Long Live the True Religion!' Contesting the Meaning of Catholicism in the Mexican Reforma (1855–1860)." PhD diss., University of Iowa, 2003.

Ginzberg, Lori D. *Women and the Work of Benevolence: Morality, Politics, and Class in the Nineteenth-century United States*. New Haven, CT: Yale University Press, 1990.

Glazier, Michael, and Thomas Shelley, eds. *The Encyclopedia of American Catholic History*. Collegeville, MN: The Liturgical Press, 1997.

Gonzaga Cuevas, Luis. *Porvenir de México, o juicio sobre su estado político en 1821 y 1851*. Mexico City: Imp. de Ignacio Cumplido, 1851.

González, Armida de. "Los ceros sociales." In *Historia Moderna de México: La República Restaurada, la vida social*, edited by Daniel Cosío Villegas, 369–450. 2d. ed. Mexico City: Editorial Hermes, 1974.

González, Luis. *San José de Gracia: Mexican Village in Transition*. Translated by John Upton. Austin: University of Texas Press, 1972.

González Navarro, Moisés. "Ejercicio caritativo." In *Historia Moderna de México, el Porfiriato: vida social*, edited by Daniel Cosío Villegas and Moisés González Navarro, 495–526. 3d ed. Mexico City: Editorial Hermes, 1973.

———. *La pobreza en México*. Mexico City: Colegio de México, 1985.

Guadarrama Sánchez, Gloria. "Filantropía y cohesión social: Las instituciones asistenciales en el estado de México." In Villalobos Grzywobicz, *Filantropía y acción solidaria* (2010), 229–64.

Guardino, Peter. *The Time of Liberty: Popular Political Culture in Oaxaca, 1750–1850*. Durham, NC: Duke University Press, 2005.

Guerra, François-Xavier. *México: Del Antiguo Régimen a la Revolución*. 1971. Translated by Sergio Fernández Bravo. 2 vols. Mexico City: Fondo de Cultura Económica, 1988.

Guerra, François-Xavier, and Annick Lempérière. *Los espacios públicos en Iberoamérica: Ambiguedades y problemas, siglos XVIII–XIX*. Mexico City: Centro Francés de Estudios Mexicanos y Centroamericanos/Fondo de Cultura Económica, 1998.

Guy, Donna J. *Women Build the Welfare State: Performing Charity and Creating Rights in Argentina, 1880–1955*. Durham, NC: Duke University Press, 2009.

Hanson, Randall S. "The Day of Ideals: Catholic Social Action in the Age of the Mexican Revolution, 1867–1929." PhD diss., Indiana University, 1994.

Harris, Bernard, and Paul Bridgen. "Introduction: The 'Mixed Economy of Welfare' and the Historiography of Welfare Provision." In *Charity and Mutual Aid in*

Europe and North America Since 1800, edited by Bernard Harris and Paul Bridgen, 1–18. New York: Routledge, 2007.

Harrison, Carol E. "Putting Faith in the Middle Class: The Bourgeoisie, Catholicism, and Postrevolutionary France." In López and Weinstein, *Making of the Middle Class* (2012), 315–34.

Hernández, Conrado. "El efecto de la guerra en el conservadurismo mexicano (1856–1867)." In Torre, García Ugarte, and Ramírez Sáiz, *Los rostros del conservadurismo* (2005), 71–98.

Holston, James. "Alternative Modernities: Statecraft and Religious Imagination in the Valley of the Dawn." *American Ethnologist* 26, no. 3 (1999): 605–31.

Islas García, Luis. *Trinidad Sánchez Santos: Biografía, selección y notas de Luis Islas García*. Mexico City: Editorial "Jus," 1945.

Ivereigh, Austen, ed. *The Politics of Religion in an Age of Revival: Studies in Nineteenth-Century Europe and Latin America*. London: Institute of Latin American Studies, 2000.

Knight, Alan. "The Mentality and Modus Operandi of Revolutionary Anticlericalism." In Butler, *Faith and Impiety* (2007), 21–56.

Koven, Seth, and Sonya Michel, eds. *Mothers of a New World: Maternalist Politics and the Origins of Welfare States*. New York: Routledge, 1993.

Laguarta, Pablo Lorenzo. *Historia de la beneficencia española en México (síntesis)*. Mexico City: Editorial España en América, 1955.

Landriot, Jean François Anne Thomas. *La mujer fuerte: Conferencias dictadas a las señoras de la Congregación del Sagrado Corazón de Jesús. 1862*. Translated by Bartolomé Rojas. Mexico City: Librería Religiosa Herrero Hnos, 1895.

Langlois, Claude. *Le catholicisme au féminin: Les congrégations françaises à supérieure générale au XIXe siècle*. Paris: Editions du Cerf, 1984.

La Unidad Católica. "Editorial: Las Conferencias de San Vicente de Paul, dictamen del Sr. Castañeda." 15 June 1861.

———. "Editorial: Las Hermanas de la Caridad y los Padres Paulinos." 13 June 1861.

———. "Editorial: La Sociedad de San Vicente de Paul y el 'Monitor.'" 14 June 1861.

Lavrin, Asunción. "La Congregación de San Pedro: Una cofradía urbana del México colonial, 1604–1730." *Historia Mexicana* 29, no. 4 (1980): 562–601.

Levitt, Peggy. *The Transnational Villagers*. Berkeley: University of California Press, 2001.

Lida, Miranda. "La Iglesia Católica en las más recientes historiografías de México y Argentina: Religión, modernidad y secularización." *Historia Mexicana* 56, no. 4 (2007): 1393–1426.

Londoño, Patricia. "The Politics of Religion in a Modernising Society: Antioquia (Colombia), 1850–1910." In Ivereigh, *Politics of Religion* (2000), 143–65.

Londoño-Vega, Patricia. *Religion, Culture, and Society in Colombia: Medellín and Antioquia, 1850–1930*. Oxford: Clarendon Press, 2002.

López, Ricardo A., and Barbara Weinstein, eds. *The Making of the Middle Class: Toward a Transnational History*. Durham, NC: Duke University Press, 2012.

López-Alonso, Moramay. *Measuring Up: A History of Living Standards in Mexico, 1850–1950*. Stanford, CA: Stanford University Press, 2012.

Lorenzo Río, María Dolores. "¿De quién son los pobres? La experiencia del Asilo Particular de Mendigos." In *"Instantáneas" de la ciudad de México: Un álbum de 1883–1884*, edited by Alicia Salmerón Castro and Fernando Aguayo. Vol. 2:43–59. Mexico City: Instituto Mora/Universidad Autónoma Metropolitana–Unidad Cuajimalpa, 2013.

———. *El Estado como benefactor: Los pobres y la asistencia pública en la ciudad de México, 1877–1905*. Mexico City: Colegio de México/Colegio Mexiquense, 2011.

Macedo, Miguel. "La asistencia pública en México, hasta 1900." In *México: Su evolución social*, edited by Justo Sierra et al. Vol. 2:706–24. Mexico City: J. Ballescá, 1900.

Macías-González, Victor Manuel. "Isabel Pesado y de la Llave, duquesa pontificia de Mier, 1832–1913." In *Mujeres en Veracruz: Fragmentos de una historia*, edited by Rosa María Spinoso Arcocha and Fernanda Núñez Becerra. Vol. 2:193–207. Xalapa, Mexico: Editora del Gobierno del Estado de Veracruz, 2010.

———. "The Mexican Aristocracy and Porfirio Díaz, 1876–1911." PhD diss., Texas Christian University, 1999.

Magray, Mary P. *The Transforming Power of the Nuns: Women, Religion, and Cultural Change in Ireland, 1750–1900*. Oxford: Oxford University Press, 1998.

Manifiesto que la junta de beneficencia del Hospital del Divino Salvador da al público sobre el estado en que encontró dicho hospital, y en el que lo deja. Mexico City: Imp. de Tomás Uribe y Alcalde, 1844.

Márquez, Octaviano. "Trinidad Sánchez Santos: Semblanza biográfica." In Trinidad Sánchez Santos, *Obras selectas* (1962).

Martínez, Manuel Guillermo. *Don Joaquín García Icazbalceta: His Place in Mexican Historiography*. Washington, DC: Catholic University of America, 1947.

Matos Rodríguez, Félix V. *Women and Urban Change in San Juan, Puerto Rico, 1820–1868*. Gainesville: University Press of Florida, 1999.

Matute, Alvaro, Evilia Trejo, and Brian Connaughton, eds. *Estado, Iglesia y sociedad en México: Siglo XIX*. Mexico City: Universidad Nacional Autónoma de México/Porrúa, 1995.

McCarthy, Kathleen D., ed. *Lady Bountiful Revisited: Women, Philanthropy, and Power*. New Brunswick, NJ: Rutgers University Press, 1990.

———. "Parallel Power Structures: Women and the Voluntary Sphere." In McCarthy, *Lady Bountiful Revisited* (1990), 1–31.

McColgan, Daniel T. *A Century of Charity: The First One Hundred Years of the Society of St. Vincent de Paul in the United States*. 2 vols. Milwaukee, WI: Bruce, 1951.

McKeown, Elizabeth. "Catholic Charities," In Glazier and Shelley, *Encyclopedia of American Catholic History* (1997), 242–45.

Mead, Karen. "Beneficent Maternalism: Argentine Motherhood in Comparative Perspective, 1880–1920." *Journal of Women's History* 12, no. 3 (2000): 120–45.

———. "Gender, Welfare and the Catholic Church in Argentina: Conferencias de Señoras de San Vicente de Paul, 1890–1916." *The Americas* 58, no. 1 (2001): 91–119.

Mecham, J. Lloyd. *Church and State in Latin America: A History of Politico-Ecclesiastical Relations*. Rev. ed. Chapel Hill: University of North Carolina Press, 1966.

Melun, Armand Marie Joachim. *Life of Sister Rosalie: A Sister of Charity*. Translated by Joseph D. Fallon. Norwood, MA: Plimpton Press, 1915.

Mettele, Gisela. "The City as a Field of Female Civic Action: Women and Middle-Class Formation in Nineteenth-Century Germany." In López and Weinstein, *Making of the Middle Class* (2012), 299–314.

Meyer, Jean A. *The Cristero Rebellion: The Mexican People Between Church and State, 1926–1929*. Cambridge: Cambridge University Press, 1976.

Meyer, Rosa María. *Instituciones de seguridad social (proceso historiográfico)*. Mexico City: Instituto Nacional de Antropología e Historia, Departamento de Investigaciones Históricas, Cuadernos de Trabajo no. 10, 1975.

Miller, Barbara Ann. "The Role of Women in the Mexican Cristero Rebellion: Las Señoras y las Religiosas." *The Americas* 40, no. 1 (1984): 303–23.

Miller, Hubert J. Review of Ivereigh, *Politics of Religion*. *Hispanic American Historical Review* 82, no. 2 (2002): 438.

Montes de Oca y Obregón, Ignacio. "Breve elogio" (23 December 1894). In García Pimentel, *Don Joaquín García Icazbalceta* (1944), 13–19.

Mora, José María Luis. *México y sus revoluciones*. 3 vols. 1836. Reprint. Mexico City: Porrúa, 1950.

Moreno Chávez, José Alberto. *Devociones políticas: Cultura católica y politización en la Arquidiócesis de México, 1880–1920*. Mexico City: Colegio de México, 2013.

Morgan, Simon. "'A sort of land debatable': Female Influence, Civic Virtue and Middle-Class Identity, c. 1830–1860." *Women's History Review* 13, no. 2 (2004): 183–209.

Muncy, Robyn. *Creating a Female Dominion in American Reform, 1890–1935*. New York: Oxford University Press, 1991.

Munguía, Clemente de Jesús. *Panegírico de San Vicente de Paul predicado en México el día 19 de julio de 1860 en la Iglesia del Espíritu Santo*. Mexico City: Imp. de Andrade y Escalante, 1860.

Muñoz, Juan José. "Santa María de Jesús Sacramentado." Accessed 5 January 2013. http://somos.vicencianos.org/blog/2011/07/30/santa-maria-de-jesus-sacramentado.

Muriel, Josefina. *Hospitales de la Nueva España*. Vol. 2: *Fundaciones de los Siglos XVII y XVIII*. Mexico City: Editorial "Jus," 1960.

Nesvig, Martin Austin, ed. *Religious Culture in Modern Mexico.* Lanham, MD: Rowman and Littlefield, 2007.

New Catholic Encyclopedia. 15 vols. New York: McGraw-Hill, 1967.

O'Dogherty, Laura. "Restaurarlo todo en Cristo: Unión de Damas Católicas Mejicanas, 1920–1926." *Estudios de Historia Moderna y Contemporánea de México* 14 (1991): 129–58.

O'Dogherty Madrazo, Laura. *De urnas y sotanas: El Partido Católico Nacional en Jalisco.* Mexico City: Consejo Nacional para la Cultura y las Artes, 2001.

O'Hara, Matthew D. "El capital espiritual y la política local: La ciudad de México y los curatos rurales en el México central." In Connaughton, *Religión, política e identidad* (2010), 388–424.

———. "The Supple Whip: Innovation and Tradition in Mexican Catholicism." *American Historical Review* 117, no. 5 (2012): 1373–1401.

Olimón Nolasco, Manuel. "Proyecto de reforma de la Iglesia en México (1867 y 1875). In Matute, Trejo, and Connaughton, *Estado, Iglesia y sociedad* (1995), 267–92.

Oliver Sánchez, Lilia V. *Salud, desarrollo urbano y modernización en Guadalajara (1798–1808).* Guadalajara: Universidad de Guadalajara, 2003.

Overmyer-Velázquez, Mark. "'A New Political Religious Order': Church, State, and Workers in Porfirian Mexico." In Nesvig, *Religious Culture* (2007), 129–56.

———. *Visions of the Emerald City: Modernity, Tradition, and the Formation of Porfirian Oaxaca, Mexico.* Durham, NC: Duke University Press, 2006.

Padberg, Colette, and Daniel Hannefin, "St. Vincent's First Foundation: The Ladies of Charity." *Vincentian Heritage* 3, no. 1 (1982): 105–30.

Pani, Erika. "'Ciudadana y muy ciudadana'? Women and the State in Independent Mexico, 1810–30." Translated by James Scorer. *Gender & History* 118, no. 1 (April 2006): 5–19.

———."Democracia y representación política: La visión de dos periódicos católicos de fin de siglo, 1880–1910." In *Modernidad, tradición y alteridad: la ciudad de México en el cambio de siglo (XIX–XX),* edited by Claudia Agostoni and Elisa Speckman, 143–60. Mexico City: Universidad Nacional Autónoma de México, Instituto de Investigaciones Históricas, 2001.

———. "Dreaming of a Mexican Empire: The Political Projects of the 'Imperialistas.'" *Hispanic American Historical Review* 82, no. 1 (2002): 1–31.

———. "'El tiro por la culata': Los conservadores y el imperio de Maximiliano." In Torre, García Ugarte, and Ramírez Sáiz, *Los rostros del conservadurismo* (2005), 99–122.

———. *Para mexicanizar el Segundo Imperio: El imaginario político de los imperialistas.* Mexico City: Colegio de México/Instituto Mora, 2001.

———, coord. *Conservadurismo y derechas en la historia de México.* 2 vols. Mexico City: Fondo de Cultura Económica/Consejo Nacional para la Cultura y las Artes, 2009.

———. "'Las fuerzas oscuras': El problema del conservadurismo en la historia de México." In Pani, *Conservadurismo y derechas* (2009), 11–42.

Pasture, Patrick, Jan Art, and Thomas Buerman, eds. *Beyond the Feminization Thesis: Gender and Christianity in Modern Europe.* Leuven, Belgium: Leuven University Press, 2012.

Peluffo, Ana. "Caridad y género: El imperio de la solidaridad femenina en el Perú del siglo XIX." In Eraso, *Mujeres y asistencia social* (2009), 33–56.

Pequeño examen de conciencia de un miembro de la Sociedad de S. Vicente de Paul. Guadalajara: Tip. de Dionisio Rodríguez, 1867.

Pescador, Juan Javier. *De bautizados a fieles difuntos.* Mexico City: Colegio de México, 1992.

Peza, Juan de Dios. *La beneficencia en México.* Mexico City: Imp. de Francisco Díaz de León, 1881.

Plasencia, Manuel. "Cien años de Acción Social de la Arquidiócesis de Guadalajara: El poder social de seis arzobispos tapatíos, 1863–1963. Monografía sociológica histórico-doctrinal." In *Anuario de la Comisión Diocesana de Historia del Arzobispado de Guadalajara*, 11–153. Mexico City: Editorial "Jus," 1968.

Polémica entre J. M. Plancarte y el Sr. Canónigo D. I. Aguilar, con motivo del artículo intitulado: "Las Conferencias de caridad," publicado en el núm. 2 de "El Torrente." Guadalajara: Tip. de Dionisio Rodríguez, 1870.

Ponce de León Atria, Macarena. *Gobernar la pobreza: Prácticas de caridad y beneficencia en la ciudad de Santiago, 1830–1890.* Santiago, Chile: Editorial Universitaria/ Dibam/Centro de Investigaciones Diego Barros Arana, 2011.

Poole, Stafford. "The Eventful Life of Vicente de Paúl Andrade." *Vincentian Heritage* 22, no. 1 (2001): 11–33.

Pope Leo XIII. "Rerum Novarum: On Capital and Labor." Encyclical of 15 May 1891. Accessed 14 November 2014. http://www.papalencyclicals.net/Leo13/l13rerum.htm.

Pope Pius IX. "Quanta Cura" and "Syllabus of Errors." Encyclical of 8 December 1864. Accessed 14 November 2014. http://papalencyclicals.net/Pius9/p9syll.htm.

Porter, Susie S. *Working Women in Mexico City: Public Discourses and Material Conditions, 1879–1931.* Tucson: University of Arizona Press, 2003.

Pouwels, Joel Bollinger. *Political Journalism by Mexican Women During the Age of Revolution, 1876–1940.* Lewiston, NY: Edwin Mellen Press, 2006.

Power, Margaret. "Preface." In Verba, *Catholic Feminism* (2003), n.p.

Quinto Concilio Provincial Mexicano celebrado en 1896, presidido por el Illmo. Sr. Doctor D. Próspero María Alarcón y Sánchez de la Barquera, Metropolitano de México. Mexico City: Imp. de "El Catecismo," 1900.

Ramírez Torres, Rafael. *Miguel Agustín Pro: Memorias biográficas.* Mexico City: Editorial Tradición, 1976.

Ratcliffe, Barrie M. "Popular Classes and Cohabitation in Mid-Nineteenth-Century Paris." *Journal of Family History* 21, no. 3 (1996): 316–50.

Reseña de las Hermandades de Caridad compuestas de Señoras y reglamento para las mismas sacado todo de la vida y escritos de San Vicente de Paul. Barcelona: Imp. y Lib. de Pablo Riera, 1856.

Rivera, Agustín. "Apéndice: Hechos posteriores al Segundo Imperio relativos a 1867." In *Anales mexicanos de la Reforma y del Segundo Imperio* (1897), n.p. Accessed 5 January 2014. www.antorcha.net/biblioteca_virtual/historia/anales/3_1.html.

Rivera Cambas, Manuel. *México pintoresco, artístico y monumental: Vistas, descripción, anécdotas y episodios de los lugares mas notables de la capital y de los estados.* . . . 3 vols. Mexico City: Imp. de la Reforma, 1880–1883.

Rodríguez Kuri, Ariel. *La experiencia olvidada, el Ayuntamiento de México: Política y gobierno, 1876–1912.* Mexico City: Universidad Autónoma Metropolitana-Azcapotzalco/Colegio de México, 1996.

Rugeley, Terry. *Of Wonders and Wise Men: Religion and Popular Cultures in Southeast Mexico, 1800–1876.* Austin: University of Texas Press, 2001.

Sábato, Hilda, ed. *Ciudadanía política y formación de las naciones: Perspectivas históricas de América Latina.* Mexico City: Colegio de México/Fondo de Cultura Económica, 1999.

———. "On Political Citizenship in Nineteenth-Century Latin America." *American Historical Review* 106, no. 4 (2001): 1290–1315.

Sanborn, Cynthia, and Felipe Portocarrero, eds. *Philanthropy and Social Change in Latin America.* Cambridge, MA: Harvard University, David Rockefeller Center for Latin American Studies, 2005.

Sánchez Santos, Trinidad. *Obras Selectas de Don Trinidad Sánchez Santos.* 2d ed. 2 vols. Mexico City: Editorial "Jus," 1962.

Sanders, Nichole. *Gender and Welfare in Mexico: The Consolidation of a Postrevolutionary State.* University Park: Pennsylvania State University Press, 2011.

Schell, Patience A. *Church and State Education in Revolutionary Mexico City.* Tucson: University of Arizona Press, 2003.

———. "An Honorable Avocation for Ladies: The Work of the Mexico City Unión de Damas Católicas Mexicanas, 1912–1926." *Journal of Women's History* 10, no. 4 (1999): 78–103.

———. "Of the Sublime Mission of Mothers of Families: The Union of Mexican Catholic Ladies in Revolutionary Mexico." In *The Women's Revolution in Mexico, 1910–1953*, edited by Stephanie Mitchell and Patience A. Schell, 99–123. Lanham, MD: Rowman and Littlefield, 2007.

Schmitt, Karl M. "Catholic Adjustment to the Secular State: The Case of Mexico, 1867–1911." *Catholic Historical Review* 48, no. 2 (1962): 182–204.

———. "The Díaz Conciliation Policy on State and Local Levels, 1876–1911." *Hispanic American Historical Review* 40, no. 4 (1960): 513–32.

Schraeder, Lia. "The Spirits of the Times: The Mexican Spiritist Movement from Reform to Revolution." PhD diss., University of California, Davis, 2009.

Scott, Anne Firor. "Women's Voluntary Associations: From Charity to Reform." In McCarthy, *Lady Bountiful Revisited* (1990), 35–54.

Serrano, Sol. "Estudio preliminar." In *Vírgenes viajeras: Diarios de religiosas francesas en su ruta a Chile, 1837–1874,* edited by Sol Serrano, 13–114. Santiago, Chile: Ediciones Universidad Católica de Chile, 2000.

———. "La escuela chilena y la definición de lo público." In Guerra and Lampérière, *Los espacios públicos* (1998), 340–62.

———. *¿Qué hacer con Dios en la República? Política y secularización en Chile (1845–1885).* Santiago, Chile: Fondo de Cultura Económica, 2008.

Silva, Renán. "Prácticas de lectura, ámbitos privados y formación de un espacio público moderno: Nueva Granada a finales del Antiguo Régimen." In Guerra and Lempérière, *Los espacios públicos* (1998), 80–108.

Skocpol, Theda. *Protecting Soldiers and Mothers: The Political Origins of Social Policy in the United States.* Cambridge, MA: Belknap Press of Harvard University Press, 1992.

Smith, Benjamin T. *The Roots of Conservatism in Mexico: Catholicism, Society, and Politics in the Mixteca Baja, 1750–1962.* Albuquerque: University of New Mexico Press, 2012.

Sociedad Católica de Señoras. *Estadística de la Sociedad Católica de Señoras, hasta el día 2 de febrero de 1872.* Mexico City: Imp. de J. M. Lara, 1872.

———. *Informe de la Sociedad Católica de Señoras de Monterrey, leido en la Asamblea General que celebró en la Santa Iglesia Catedral el día 29 de Abril de 1896.* Monterrey, Mexico: Tip. de Ramón Diaz y Cia, 1896.

Société de Saint-Vincent-de-Paul. *Livre du centenaire: L'oeuvre d'Ozanam à travers le monde, 1833–1933.* Paris: Gabriel Beauchesne et ses fils, 1933.

Torre, Renée de la, Marta Eugenia García Ugarte, and Juan Manuel Ramírez Sáiz, eds. *Los rostros del conservadurismo mexicano.* Mexico City: Centro de Investigaciones y Estudios de Antropología Social, 2005.

Trotter, Robert. "St. Vincent de Paul, Society of." In Glazier and Shelley, *Encyclopedia of American Catholic History* (1997), 1249–50.

Udovic, Edward R. "'What About the Poor?' Nineteenth-Century Paris and the Revival of Vincentian Charity." *Vincentian Heritage* 14, no. 1 (1993): 69–94.

Ulloa, Sergio Valerio. "Los inconvenientes del progreso: La Hacienda de Bellavista contra el Ferrocarril Central Mexicano." *Takwá,* no. 13 (2008): 35–60.

Unión de Damas Católicas. *Informe general de las labores desarrolladas por la Unión de Damas Católicas Mexicanas, Centro Regional de Jalisco, durante diez años comprendidos desde su fundación, 26 de abril de 1913 a enero de 1923. . . .* Guadalajara: Talleres Lino-Tipográficos de Gallardo y Alvarez del Castillo, 1923.

Urbina Martínez, Gilberto. "Prácticas cotidianas de ayuda a finales del siglo XIX y principios del XX." In Villalobos Grzywobicz, *Filantropía y acción solidaria* (2010), 119–44.

Vaca, Agustín. *Los silencios de la historia: Las cristeras*. Zapopan, Mexico: Colegio de Jalisco, 1998.

Valenzuela, J. Samuel, and Erika Maza Valenzuela. "The Politics of Religion in a Catholic Country: Republican Democracy, *Cristianismo Social* and the Conservative Party in Chile, 1850–1925." In Ivereigh, *Politics of Religion* (2000), 188–223.

Valero Chávez, Aída. *De la caridad a la beneficencia pública en la ciudad de México (1521–1910)*. Mexico City: Universidad Nacional Autónoma de México, 2002.

Vaughan, Mary Kay. "Nationalizing the Countryside: Schools and Rural Communities in the 1930s." In *The Eagle and the Virgin: National and Cultural Revolution in Mexico, 1920–1940*, edited by Mary Kay Vaughan and Stephen E. Lewis, 157–75. Durham, NC: Duke University Press, 2006.

———. "Primary Schooling in the City of Puebla, 1821–60." *Hispanic American Historical Review* 67, no. 1 (1987): 39–62.

———. *The State, Education, and Social Class in Mexico, 1880–1928*. De Kalb: Northern Illinois University Press, 1982.

Velasco Ceballos, Rómulo. *El niño mexicano ante la caridad y el estado: Apuntes históricos que comprenden desde la época precortesiana hasta nuestros días*. Mexico City: Editorial Cultura, 1935.

Velasco López, Octavio. "La mujer y la masonería en el Jalisco del siglo XIX: Catalina Álvarez Rivera." In *Mujeres jaliscienses del siglo XIX: Cultura, religion y vida privada*, edited by Octavio Vázquez Parada, Lourdes Celina, and Darío Armando Flores Soria, 110–31. Guadalajara: Editorial Universitaria, Universidad de Guadalajara, 2008.

Verba, Ericka Kim. *Catholic Feminism and the Social Question in Chile, 1910–1917: The Liga de Damas Chilenas*. Lewiston, ME: Edwin Mellen Press, 2003.

Vickery, Amanda. "Golden Age to Separate Spheres? A Review of the Categories and Chronology of English Women's History." *Historical Journal* 36, no. 2 (1993): 383–414.

Vigil, José María. "Discurso." In *Sesión Pública que celebró la Academia Mexicana de la Lengua correspondiente de la Real Española, el sábado 19 de Enero de 1895, para honrar la memoria de su insigne Director Don Joaquín García Icazbalceta, muerto el dia 16 de noviembre de 1894*, 15–39. Mexico City: Oficina Tip. de la Secretaría de Fomento, 1895.

Villalobos Grzywobicz, Jorge, ed. *Filantropía y acción solidaria en la historia de México*. Mexico City: Centro Mexicano para la Filantropía, 2010.

Villanueva y Francesconi, Mariano, comp. *El libro de las protestas: Recopilación de las manifestaciones y protestas de los mexicanos católicos, contra la ley anticonstitucional orgánica de la Reforma, que ataca la libertad del culto y las inmunidades de la Iglesia de Jesucristo*. Mexico City: Imp. del Cinco de Mayo, 1875.

Voekel, Pamela. "Liberal Religion: The Schism of 1861." In Nesvig, *Religious Culture* (2007), 78–105.

Voekel, Pamela, Bethany Moretón, and Michael Jo. "Vaya con Dios: Religion and the Transnational History of the Americas." *History Compass* 5, no. 5 (2007): 1604–39. doi: 10.1111/j.1478–0542.2007.00466.x

Von Germeten, Nicole. *Black Blood Brothers: Confraternities and Social Mobility for Afro-Mexicans*. Gainesville: University Press of Florida, 2006.

Weiner, Richard. "Trinidad Sánchez Santos: Voice of the Catholic Opposition in Porfirian Mexico." *Mexican Studies* 17, no. 2 (2001): 321–49.

Werner, Michael, ed. *Encyclopedia of Mexico: History, Society, and Culture.* 2 vols. Chicago: Fitzroy Dearborn, 1997.

Wright de Kleinhans, Laureana. *Mujeres notables mexicanas.* Mexico City: Tip. Económica, 1910.

Wright-Rios, Edward. *Revolutions in Mexican Catholicism: Reform and Revelation in Oaxaca, 1887–1934.* Durham, NC: Duke University Press, 2009.

———. "Visions of Women: Revelation, Gender, and Catholic Resurgence." In Nesvig, *Religious Culture* (2007), 178–202.

Zavala, Adriana. *Becoming Modern, Becoming Tradition: Women, Gender, and Representation in Mexican Art.* University Park: Pennsylvania State University Press, 2010.

Zendejas, Adelina. *La mujer en la intervención francesa.* Mexico City: Sociedad Mexicana de Geografía y Estadística, 1962.

INDEX

Page numbers in italic text indicate illustrations.